CURRENT TREATMENTS OF OBSESSIVE-COMPULSIVE DISORDER

Clinical Practice

Number 18
Judith H. Gold, M.D., F.R.C.P.(C)
Series Editor

CURRENT TREATMENTS OF OBSESSIVE-COMPULSIVE DISORDER

Edited by

Michele Tortora Pato, M.D.

Department of Psychiatry and Behavioral Sciences
State University of New York at Stony Brook
Stony Brook, New York

Joseph Zohar, M.D.

Beer Sheva Mental Health Centre
Ben Gurion University
Beer Sheva, Israel

Washington, DC
London, England

Note: The authors have worked to ensure that all information in this book concerning drug dosages, schedules, and routes of administration is accurate as of the time of publication and consistent with standards set by the U.S. Food and Drug Administration and the general medical community. As medical research and practice advance, however, therapeutic standards may change. For this reason and because human and mechanical errors sometimes occur, we recommend that readers follow the advice of a physician who is directly involved in their care or the care of a member of their family.

Books published by the American Psychiatric Press, Inc., represent the views and opinions of the individual authors and do not necessarily represent the policies and opinions of the Press or the American Psychiatric Association.

Copyright © 1991 American Psychiatric Press, Inc.
ALL RIGHTS RESERVED
Manufactured in the United States of America on acid-free paper
First Edition
94 93 92 91   4 3 2 1

American Psychiatric Press, Inc.
1400 K Street, N.W., Washington, DC 20005

Library of Congress Cataloging-in-Publication Data

Current treatments of obsessive-compulsive disorder / edited by
  Michele Tortora Pato, Joseph Zohar.
      p.   cm.—(Clinical practice ; no. 18)
    Includes index.
    ISBN 0-88048-351-2 (alk. paper)
    1. Obsessive-compulsive disorder—Treatment. I. Pato, Michele
  Tortora, 1956-   . II. Zohar, Joseph. III. Series.
    [DNLM: 1. Obsessive-Compulsive Disorder—therapy. W1
  CL767J no. 18 / WM 176 C976]
  RC533.C87 1991
  616.85′22706—dc20
  DNLM/DLC
  for Library of Congress   90-14497
                                                                  CIP

British Library Cataloguing in Publication Data

A CIP record is available from the British Library.

The difference between body dysmorphic disorder and delusional disorder, somatic type, depends on whether the thoughts of a defect in appearance represent an overvalued idea (with uncertainty), as in the case of dysmorphophobia (Thomas 1984), or reach delusional intensity (with certainty), as in the case of monosymptomatic hypochondriacal psychosis (Munro and Chmara 1982). However, it has been unclear whether this difference reflects two different disorders (American Psychiatric Association 1987; Thomas 1985) or rather two variants of the same disorder (Brotman and Jenike 1985).

DSM-III-R defines OCD as the presence of either obsessions or compulsions that cause marked distress, are time consuming, and/or significantly interfere with functioning. Obsessions are defined as persistent ideas, thoughts, impulses, or images that are experienced, at least initially, as intrusive or senseless. This definition could conceivably include patients with body dysmorphic disorder. However, some body dysmorphic patients experience their overvalued beliefs as ego-syntonic rather than ego-dystonic. This is somewhat problematic, since OCD typically, but not always, is characterized by ego-dystonic obsessions.

A review and phenomenological analysis of OCD (Insel and Akiskal 1986) suggest that delusions can arise in the course of this illness. These delusions do not signify a schizophrenic diagnosis, but represent generally transient reactive affective or paranoid psychoses. The authors argue that OCD represents a psychopathological spectrum varying along a continuum of insight, with patients at the extreme end having an "obsessive compulsive psychosis" (Insel and Akiskal 1986). In body dysmorphic disorder patients lie along a continuum of insight or certainty. Patients at the extreme end who are currently classified as having delusional disorder, somatic type, or hypochondriacal psychosis, may be considered as having body dysmorphic disorder psychosis. Phenomenologically there may be a spectrum, but additional biological mechanisms may occur when patients reach the delusional end and when concerns become fixed beliefs. This characteristic may explain the partial efficacy of pimozide (Munro and Chmara 1982), a dopamine-receptor blocker, in changing certainty to uncertainty.

Patients with OCD manifest abnormality of central serotonergic function based on pharmacological response (Insel et al. 1983; Thorén et al. 1980b), cerebrospinal fluid (Thorén et al. 1980a), and peripheral platelet (Flament et al. 1985) findings. Furthermore, oral administration of m-chlorophenylpiperazine (m-CPP), a selective 5-HT agonist, has been shown to exacerbate OCD symptoms transiently (Hollander et al. 1988a; Zohar et al. 1987). Body dysmorphic disorder patients may also respond preferentially to 5-HT reuptake inhibitors, which is consistent with possible serotonergic dysregulation. There is a report of one patient who manifested exacerbation of body dysmorphic symptoms of delusional intensity while smoking marijuana (Hollander et al. 1989c), which has central serotonergic effects. However, this is not a selective 5-HT provocative test, because marijuana affects several other neurotransmitter systems, including the acetylcholinergic system. A fascinating case report of a woman who developed body dysmorphic disorder following chronic abuse of cyproheptadine, a 5-HT antagonist, does make a serotonergic etiology intriguing (Craven and Rodin 1987).

Treatment

Previous case reports have documented some improvement in monosymptomatic hypochondriasis and dysmorphophobia with tricyclic antidepressants (Brotman and Jenike 1984) and monoamine oxidase inhibitors (MAOIs) (Jenike 1984), and in monosymptomatic hypochondriacal psychosis with pimozide (Munro and Chmara 1982).

In a report of two cases with disabling monosymptomatic hypochondriasis, there was improvement with tricyclic antidepressants (Brotman and Jenike 1984). One patient responded to doxepin, 200 mg/day, after 3 weeks, had an exacerbation when the dose was lowered, and improved again for 8 months on 200 mg/day. Another patient responded after 3 weeks of imipramine, 250 mg/day, a response that continued for 6 months of follow-up. In another single-case report, a dysmorphophobic patient failed to respond to neuroleptics and heterocyclic antidepressants, but responded completely after 4 days of tranylcypromine, 30 mg/day, a response that continued for 5 months of follow-up (Jenike 1984).

In a collection of 50 patients with monosymptomatic hypochondriacal psychosis, Munro and Chmara (1982) reported improvement in 80% of the patients who were administered pimozide. Pimozide was used in doses of 2 to 12 mg/day. If extrapyramidal side effects occurred, antiparkinsonian medication was added. Noncompliance was associated with a poor outcome. Improvement occurred after a few days in some cases, but after 6 to 8 weeks in others. If depression occurred while on pimozide, antidepressants were added. Despite successful treatment, a majority of patients retained a belief in the physical nature of their disorder.

A recent report has documented improvement in body dysmorphic patients following treatment with 5-HT reuptake inhibitors (Hollander et al. 1989c). Four of the five patients had failed to respond to previous vigorous therapeutic trials with agents that have some serotonergic action, such as tertiary amine tricyclic antidepressants, trazodone, and lithium. Nevertheless, all responded to the potent 5-HT reuptake inhibitor fluoxetine (80 mg/day) and/or clomipramine (60–300 mg/day), suggesting a more potent serotonergic effect or a possible differential mechanism of action of these agents. Although these findings raise the possibility of a common pathogenesis with OCD, a possible antidepressant effect of these agents in body dysmorphic disorder, or a relationship to affective illness, is not excluded.

Agents with potent 5-HT reuptake inhibition such as clomipramine and fluoxetine may prove to be the treatment of choice in body dysmorphic disorder. Use of these agents in body dysmorphic disorder would be similar to their use in OCD (for a detailed description, see Pato and Zohar, Chapter 2; Pigott, Chapter 3, this volume). Other treatments that have been reported as effective in case reports include tricyclic antidepressants and MAOIs. For those patients who develop delusional certainty about bodily defects, the addition of low-dose neuroleptics such as pimozide may be effective.

Case History (Body Dysmorphic Disorder)

Ms. A. is an attractive, intelligent, 25-year-old white female. Shortly after getting married and graduating from law school, she presented with the belief that vascular markings on her nose made her unattractive. She was fearful that these vascular markings would expand to cover her face, causing her husband to leave her. She used makeup to cover the imagined defect, avoided mirrors, and made multiple visits to dermatologists and plastic surgeons. There were no vegetative symptoms of major depression, but she was demoralized. After treatment with imipramine (150 mg/day) her outlook improved and she became less preoccupied with thoughts of her vascular markings. However, after looking in the mirror on one occasion while not wearing makeup to cover the defect, she deteriorated, with her overvalued belief developing into delusional certainty about the vascular markings. Addition of pimozide (2 mg/day) was effective for 2 months in altering this belief from a delusional certainty to a level of uncertainty. Nevertheless, overvalued concern about her face persisted, and new obsessional fears about possible damage to future babies as a result of medication developed. An increase in imipramine to 300 mg/day failed to result in additional improvement. The patient then agreed to a trial of fluoxetine, a selective 5-HT reuptake inhibitor. The pimozide and imipramine were discontinued. Six weeks after receiving fluoxetine, 80 mg/day, she reported a dramatic improvement in her over-valued concern about facial defects. She was able to resume socializing, made plans to resume her career, and overcame her avoidance of potential dermal traumatic agents such as sun and wind. This improvement continues at 5 months follow-up. Of note, there is a clear family history of OCD. The patient's sister has classic obsessions and compulsions regarding contamination, and she fears exposure of radiation to her family. The patient's father, a successful businessman, has subclinical symptoms of OCD, such as the need for symmetry and overconcern about the health of his children, but these symptoms are ego-syntonic and do not interfere with functioning.

Trichotillomania

Diagnostic Considerations

Trichotillomania, classified in DSM-III-R as an "impulse control disor-der not elsewhere classified," consists of recurrent failure to resist im-pulses to pull out one's own hair, resulting in noticeable hair loss. There is an increasing sense of tension immediately before pulling out the hair. There is also gratification or a sense of relief when pulling out the hair. The diagnosis is not made when hair pulling is associated with a preexist-ing inflammation of the skin or is in response to a delusion or hallucina-tion.

Rapoport and colleagues recently studied females with trichotillo-mania, or compulsive hair pulling. They propose that trichotillomania is closely related to OCD (Leonard 1989; Swedo et al. 1989). In addition, this group has proposed a fascinating model of neuroethological groom-ing behavior, with similar behavior patterns in dogs and parrots respond-ing to clomipramine treatment (J. L. Rapoport, unpublished observa-tions, 1989; see also Goldberger and Rapoport, in press; Rapoport 1990).

There are some differences between OCD and trichotillomanic pa-tients. While most trichotillomanic patients are women with childhood onset, there is an equal number of male and female OCD patients, and an excess of male childhood-onset OCD patients. Also, most trichotillomanic patients do not have other obsessions or rituals. In OCD, repetitive behaviors are seemingly purposeful and designed to prevent or produce some future event or situation. This is not the case with trichotillomania. Some patients describe a pleasurable aspect to the hair pulling, both in terms of tension reduction and a cleansing or purging, and in some ways similar to an orgasm. Finally, many clinicians in the field find a high rate of impulsive-style personality disorders (e.g., borderline personality disorder) in these patients.

However, there are several interesting similarities between the disorders. The hair pulling is often described as a habit or compulsion that is disturbing (ego-dystonic) and resisted against. There is also a similar treatment response in the two disorders, as is seen below.

Treatment

In both an open trial and a double-blind comparison of clomipramine and desipramine in eight trichotillomanic patients, clomipramine was superior to desipramine (Swedo et al., unpublished observations, cited in Leonard 1989 and Swedo et al. 1989). We have also studied five patients with trichotillomania in open treatment with fluoxetine. Four had a substantial improvement in hair pulling, but the other one became more impulsive and self-damaging (Hollander et al., unpublished observations, 1989).

Thus, while the available data are still limited, 5-HT reuptake inhibitors such as clomipramine and fluoxetine appear to be helpful in trichotillomania, both in terms of reducing anxiety and subjective tension and in reducing, and in some cases eliminating, the compulsive hair pulling. Effective doses appear equivalent to those used in the treatment of OCD. A possible cautionary note is that patients with a high degree of impulsivity may occasionally become even more impulsive on these agents. This side effect could be problematic if it interferes with the patient's judgment or ability to control these impulses. Discontinuation or adjustment of dose, or addition of neuroleptics or lithium, may occasionally be necessary to control impulsive behaviors.

Case History (Trichotillomania)

Ms. B. is a 31-year-old reporter with a 27-year history of trichotillomania. Onset began at age 4, when she began to pull out her eyelashes. She recalls that this occurred in response to hearing her doctor describe dandruff and her mother mention that false eyelashes looked "cheap." By age 18, she began to pull out and rub off her eyebrows. She used makeup to conceal her eyebrow hair loss. In addition, she wore glasses instead of contact lenses to hide her eyebrows. She wore false eyelashes to improve her appearance and to help prevent her from pulling her eyelashes. She also avoided swimming to prevent exposure of her problem. She reported feeling self-conscious and humiliated about her hair loss. The hair pulling increased prior to her menstrual periods and was also exacerbated by caffeine and alcohol. She also described a sense of pleasure associated with the hair pulling, or at least a release of tension and a sense of purging, similar to that of an orgasm or "popping" a pimple.

Family history is significant, including a maternal grandmother who compulsively picked at her face, a mother who uncontrollably cries and has tics, and a brother who compulsively rubs his lip with his hands.

Ms. B. saw a therapist briefly in the fifth grade, and for the past 5 years was seen in individual psychotherapy, but this problem was not discussed. She participated in a National Institute of Mental Health study, where she responded to a 6- to 8-week trial of clomipramine, which was then discontinued. On clomipramine, she experienced dry mouth, constipation, and fatigue. In addition, she had a hypomanic episode, which resulted in a job change and a move to another city to pursue a boyfriend. Following discontinuation of clomipramine she relapsed and again experienced compulsive hair pulling and compulsive eating.

Fluoxetine treatment was instituted at 20 mg/day and rapidly increased to 100 mg/day over 2 weeks. On fluoxetine, 100 mg/day, she felt an infusion of nervous energy, leg tapping, hand clenching, generalized stiffness, restless sleep, a feeling of being "revved up," and an urge to make animal noises to relieve tension. Fluoxetine was lowered to 60 mg/day, and the muscle stiffness, hand clenching, and "revved up" feeling resolved. Within 12 weeks she had a substantial reduction in hair pulling to a degree similar to that which occurred on clomipramine. The addition of fenfluramine at 20 mg/day resulted in almost complete resolution of hair pulling and no additional side effects.

Bowel Obsessions

Jenike et al. (1987) reported on four patients whose primary symptom was overwhelming fear of losing bowel control and having a bowel movement in public. They became progressively disabled, planned their lives around bowel movements, and spent many hours in the bathroom attempting to completely rid themselves of feces. All four patients had almost total resolution of symptoms after tricyclic antidepressant therapy. Treatment included imipramine, 50 to 150 mg/day, and doxepine, 150 mg/day, with improvement beginning 10 days to 1 month following onset of treatment.

While Jenike et al. (1987) initially postulated a link between bowel obsessions and OCD or social phobia, Lydiard et al. (1988) also noted similarities between bowel obsessions and panic disorder. In our experience, bowel obsessions occur both in OCD patients and in panic disorder patients, and respond to antipanic and antiobsessional medications. There are now two favorable case reports documenting improvement of bowel obsessions with low doses of the 5-HT reuptake inhibitor clomipramine (Caballero 1988; Kahne and Wray 1989). In these reports patients responded to 75 mg/day of clomipramine within 8 days, and this effect persisted for 3 months of follow-up. I have also had success with the 5-HT reuptake inhibitor fluoxetine in three patients with bowel obsessions at doses of 20 to 40 mg/day.

Depersonalization Disorder

Diagnostic Considerations

Depersonalization disorder is classified as a dissociative disorder in DSM-III-R. The essential feature is the occurrence of persistent or recurrent episodes of depersonalization sufficiently severe to cause marked distress.

The symptom of depersonalization involves alteration in the perception or experience of the self in which the usual sense of one's own reality is temporarily lost or changed. This is manifested by a feeling of detachment from and being an outside observer of one's mental processes or body, or of feeling like an automaton or as if in a dream. Various types of sensory anesthesia, and a sensation of not being in complete control of one's actions, including speech, are often present. All of these feelings are ego-dystonic, and the person maintains intact reality testing. The onset is usually rapid, and its disappearance is usually gradual.

Depersonalization is often reported in association with other syndromes, such as depression, schizophrenia, temporal-lobe epilepsy and complex partial seizures, anxiety disorders and phobic-anxiety depersonalization syndrome, migraines, and marijuana abuse, and even in some analogue and "normal" student populations. While the symptom of depersonalization is encountered with these other symptoms, the disorder is diagnosed only if the symptom is persistent or recurrent and causes distress.

According to DSM-III-R the diagnosis is not made when the symptom of depersonalization is secondary to any other disorder, such as panic disorder or agoraphobia without history of panic disorder. However, if depersonalization precedes or is independent of other disorders, it may be diagnosed.

Three of eight depersonalization disorder patients described by Hollander et al. (in press) had obsessions and/or compulsions. Previous studies have attempted to posit a link between obsessionalism and depersonalization. Depersonalization was viewed as a repetitive tendency toward self-observation. For example, an episode of unreality feelings in an obsessive personality could lead to the repetitive experience of the feeling as an obsessional focus (Torch 1978). Alternatively, an obsessional thought about the "self" could lead to feelings of depersonalization. Early analytic writers noted obsessional characters in depersonalized patients (Torch 1978). There was an 88% incidence and a 75% incidence of premorbid obsessional traits in two series of depersonalized patients (Roth 1959; Torch 1978).

Both OCD and depersonalization disorder patients experience repetitive ego-dystonic thoughts. In OCD the focus of these disturbing thoughts usually involves uncertainty and an exaggerated perception of future harm. In depersonalization disorder the disturbing thoughts center around discomfort and sensory perceptual distortions involving the self or body and its relation to the world.

Responsivity of depersonalization disorder to 5-HT reuptake inhibitors, co-occurrence with migraines (Comfort 1982), exacerbation with marijuana (Szymanski 1981), and overlap with OCD and panic disorder all indirectly implicate serotonergic involvement in depersonalization.

Treatment

Previous case reports have documented improvement of depersonalization symptoms with antidepressants (Walsh 1975), stimulants (Davison 1964), benzodiazepines, and antiepileptics (Greenberg et al. 1984). Davison (1964) described the use of intravenous methamphetamine, 10 to 20 mg, in four patients with episodic depersonalization. Complete abolition of the symptoms was produced in less than 1 minute, and the remission lasted for days, weeks, or months. Greenberg et al. (1984) described the use of carbamazepine, 400 mg tid, in one patient, with resolution of symptoms within 24 hours. Hypnosis, behavior modification, family therapy, ECT, and prefrontal leukotomy have also been reported to be effective in individual cases. There are also reports of exacerbation with relaxation techniques, and induction of mania with antidepressants and stimulants. Liebowitz et al. (1980) described the induction of mania in one depersonalization patient after discontinuation of a 2-week trial of dextroamphetamine (30 mg/day). The patient was subsequently treated with lithium and chlorpromazine, and her mood returned to baseline, with no recurrence of depersonalization. These authors also described another depersonalization patient treated with amitriptyline, 300 mg/day, for 2 weeks, then tapered off medication, who also developed mania that responded to lithium and chlorpromazine.

Hollander et al. (in press) have reported a preferential response of depersonalization symptoms or depersonalization disorder to agents that manifest potent 5-HT reuptake inhibition. Chronic depersonalization symptoms resolved in six of the eight patients treated with fluoxetine (5-80 mg/day) or fluvoxamine (300 mg/day). However, not all patients with depersonalization disorder responded to all 5-HT reuptake inhibitors. The co-occurrence of OCD in these patients was associated with a favorable response of depersonalization symptoms to 5-HT reuptake inhibitors. These patients also experienced at least partial resolution of obsessional symptoms as well.

Further work is needed to determine whether the antidepersonalization effect is really an antiobsessional effect or an effect due to some other mechanism. The chronicity of this disorder, coupled with a poor response to prior somatic and psychological treatments, makes the positive therapeutic response of depersonalization to 5-HT reuptake inhibitors noteworthy. In addition, the hierarchical exclusion of depersonalization in the presence of OCD and panic disorder may merit further discussion.

Gilles de la Tourette's Syndrome

Diagnostic Considerations

An association between recurrent motor and phonic tics and obsessive-compulsive symptoms was first reported by Gilles de la Tourette (Tourette 1885). More recently, several studies have examined psychiatric symptoms in patients with Tourette's syndrome, compared clinical characteristics of Tourette's syndrome and OCD patients, and examined the relatives of Tourette's syndrome patients for the presence of Tourette's syndrome, chronic motor tics, and OCD.

Several studies have reported rates of obsessive-compulsive symptoms in Tourette's syndrome patients as high as 68% (Nee et al. 1980) and 67% (Montgomery et al. 1982). These early studies, however, suffer from methodological limitations. Recently, a 63% incidence of OCD in subjects with Tourette's syndrome, and a 6% incidence of Tourette's syndrome and a greater than 35% incidence of tic disorders in subjects with OCD, have been reported (Pitman et al. 1987). However, this study also suffers some design limitations, such as the use of nonblind interviewers and family history data. Shapiro et al. (1988) used stricter criteria for a diagnosis of OCD, and their study is at present the only one that does not report an increased rate of OCD in Tourette's syndrome subjects.

Recent studies also show close family links between OCD and Tourette's syndrome (Pauls et al. 1986). The rate of OCD was elevated in relatives of Tourette's syndrome probands, both with and without OCD symptoms, compared with adoptive relatives. This finding suggested that Tourette's syndrome and OCD are etiologically related, at least within families of Tourette's syndrome patients, and that OCD may represent a different manifestation of the same underlying factor responsible for Tourette's syndrome. However, there is considerable disagreement in the field over conceptual issues, such as how to distinguish between a tic and a compulsion, that might influence the interpretation of these findings. The criterion of purpose (i.e., preventing some dreaded consequence) may distinguish compulsions from tics. Pitman and colleagues (1987, p. 1170) noted that "it was sometimes impossible to tell where one [the tic] ended and the other [the compulsion] began, supporting the notion of a symptomatic continuum from simple tic through complex tic to compulsion." Touching and symmetry behavior occurred more often in Tourette's syndrome than in OCD. This behavior was previously believed to be more common in men with OCD, and in those patients with an organic etiology. There was a high rate of tics in OCD patients and their relatives. The results, as Pitman and colleagues note (1987, p. 1171), suggest "symptomatic overlap tending to blur the two disorders as well as symptomatic poles tending to distinguish them. . . . the ease of differential diagnosis of a given patient would depend on his or her proximity to one of the poles."

Treatment

The standard treatment of Tourette's syndrome is the use of neuroleptics such as haloperidol and pimozide. It is important to begin with a very low dose, such as 1 mg/day of pimozide or 0.25 mg/day of haloperidol. Doses are gradually raised to an average of 8 to 13 mg/day for pimozide, and 2 to 10 mg/day of haloperidol. Antiparkinsonian medications are often used in conjunction with neuroleptics.

Possible side effects include dystonic reactions, akinesia, extrapyramidal parkinsonian effects, cognitive impairment, and depression. Shapiro et al. (1988) estimated that 25% of Tourette's syndrome patients have at least 70% reduction of symptoms at a low dose without adverse effects. Another 50% of patients develop adverse effects when treated with therapeutic doses of haloperidol, but these side effects can be managed over time. Another 25% become "treatment failures" on neuroleptics because adverse effects nullify therapeutic benefits. The development of depression on neuroleptics may be treated by lowering the dose or by addition of low-dose methylphenidate or antidepressant medication.

Although effective for motor and vocal tics, neuroleptics are not effective for associated obsessions or compulsions. Thus, 5-HT reuptake inhibitors may be added to neuroleptics for these patients.

There may also be an overlap in pharmacological responsiveness of obsessive symptoms to clonidine in both Tourette's syndrome (Cohen et al. 1980) and OCD (Hollander et al. 1988a, 1988b; Knesevich 1982). In Tourette's syndrome patients, initial reports with clonidine of 80% effectiveness (Cohen et al. 1980; Leckman et al. 1982) included improvement in both tics and obsessive-compulsive symptoms. More recent studies, including double-blind trials, have shown less positive results (Shapiro 1988).

In OCD patients, Seiver et al. (1983) found a blunted growth hormone response to clonidine, suggesting down-regulation of postsynaptic receptors. We have reported significant transient improvement in OCD symptoms following intravenous clonidine (Hollander et al. 1988b), but no evidence of blunted growth hormone response (Hollander et al. 1989a). While others have reported improvement in obsessions with orally administered clonidine treatment (Knesevich 1982), we have not found a sustained antiobsessional effect with chronic clonidine treatment (Hollander et al. 1988b). However, the addition of clonidine may be helpful for those OCD patients who experience considerable anxiety during initiation of 5-HT reuptake inhibitor treatment.

An open study of fluoxetine treatment in three Tourette's syndrome patients with concomitant obsessions and compulsions showed improvement in obsessive-compulsive symptoms with low doses of fluoxetine (20–40 mg/day) (Riddle et al. 1988). This finding parallels our report (Liebowitz et al., in press) and other reports (Fontaine and Chouinard 1986) of improvement in OCD in open trials of fluoxetine. Thirty-nine OCD patients completed at least an 8-week trial of fluoxetine (20–80 mg/ day) (Liebowitz et al., in press). Of these patients, 62% were judged to be "responders" and were rated as "much improved" or "very much improved" on obsessions and compulsions. Fluoxetine was well tolerated in this dose range. When used for treating Tourette's syndrome in combination with neuroleptics, we recommend using slightly lower doses (20–60 mg/day).

If Tourette's syndrome is accompanied by attention-deficit disorder (ADD), with or without hyperactivity, methylphenidate may be added, initially in doses of 2.5 mg/day, with gradual increase to an effective dose. Patients with Tourette's syndrome, OCD, and ADD may occasionally be effectively managed with low doses of pimozide, methylphenidate, and fluoxetine (or equivalent medications) for treatment of specific disabling symptoms. While it is widely believed that methylphenidate treatment will exacerbate tics, this is generally not the case.

Eating Disorders

Patients with anorexia nervosa and bulimia have well-characterized obsessions about food, body image, and food preparation. In addition, they have clear-cut rituals regarding diet, exercise, food preparation, and eating. However, some recent studies document very high rates of obsessive-compulsive behaviors, unrelated to food and weight and of sufficient severity to meet criteria for OCD, in a majority of anorexic patients (K. A.

Halmi, unpublished observations). In our clinical experience many patients may initially present with obsessional concerns regarding body image and food intake, and go on to develop other more classic obsessions regarding, for example, contamination, that would then meet criteria for OCD. There is also such a high degree of symptomatic overlap between body dysmorphic disorder and anorexia nervosa that DSM-III-R lists anorexia as a specific exclusion criterion in the diagnostic criteria for body dysmorphic disorder. Both disorders involve distortions of body image, but in anorexia this distortion always centers on weight.

A serotonergic role in appetite regulation and eating disorders has long been postulated. Feeding and dieting can affect the supply of the 5-HT precursor tryptophan to the brain and thereby affect 5-HT synthesis. In animals, tryptophan and fenfluramine, a 5-HT releaser and reuptake inhibitor, suppress appetite and feeding. Recent studies suggest that inhibitory 5-HT$_{1A}$ agonists increase eating, while 5-HT$_{1B}$ and 5-HT$_{1C}$ agonists acting on the paraventricular nucleus of the hypothalamus decrease eating in rats (Curzon 1989). In humans, cerebrospinal fluid studies of the 5-HT metabolite 5-hydroxyindoleacetic acid (5-HIAA) and blunted prolactin response to the orally administered 5-HT agonist m-CPP suggest diminished central serotonergic function associated with the binge-eating pattern of bulimia (Brewerton et al. 1989; Jimerson et al. 1989). Following weight gain the neuroendocrine responsivity of patients partially normalizes (Brewerton et al. 1989). Furthermore, in preliminary studies with oral m-CPP, we found exacerbation of obsessions and compulsive urges regarding food and body image in approximately 60% of eating disorder patients following orally administered m-CPP, with normalization of this effect following weight gain. There appear to be similar behavioral and neuroendocrine responses to oral m-CPP in OCD patients at baseline (Hollander et al. 1988a, 1989a; Zohar et al. 1987), such that both OCD and eating disorder patients show some behavioral sensitivity and neuroendocrine blunting. Chronic treatment with 5-HT reuptake inhibitors normalizes behavioral and neuroendocrine responses in OCD (Hollander et al. 1989b; Zohar et al. 1988), with changes in a direction similar to that found in eating disorder patients following weight gain.

Serotonergic drugs have long been administered for appetite control. Fenfluramine, a 5-HT releaser and reuptake inhibitor, has been administered to over 50 million patients around the world for appetite suppression (Derome-Tremblay and Nathan 1989). More recently, the 5-HT reuptake inhibitor fluoxetine has been noted to cause appetite suppression and weight loss; however, this effect appears to be transient. While several groups are now studying the effects of 5-HT reuptake inhibitors such as clomipramine and fluoxetine in the treatment of eating disorder patients, for controlling both the binge eating of bulimic patients and the distorted body image of anorexic patients, the results are not yet in.

Summary

This chapter addresses diagnostic considerations and treatment approaches for disorders related to OCD. While there is currently debate about which disorders are most closely related to OCD, the present evidence linking these disorders to OCD is presented. Body dysmorphic disorder, trichotillomania, bowel obsessions, depersonalization disorder, Tourette's syndrome, and eating disorders are discussed, and case management summaries for two disorders are described. A review of past and current treatment approaches to OCD-related disorders is presented, and common pitfalls are discussed. These findings, however, remain tentative given the limited amount of research to date.

References

American Psychiatric Association: Diagnostic and Statistical Manual of Mental Disorders, 3rd Edition. Washington, DC, American Psychiatric Association, 1980

American Psychiatric Association: Diagnostic and Statistical Manual of Mental Disorders, 3rd Edition, Revised. Washington, DC, American Psychiatric Association, 1987

Brewerton T, Murphy D, Jimerson DC: A comparison of neuroendocrine responses to L-TRP and m-CPP in bulimics and controls. Biol Psychiatry 25 (suppl):18A–21A, 1989

Brotman AW, Jenike MA: Monosymptomatic hypochondriasis treated with tricyclic antidepressants. Am J Psychiatry 141:1608–1609, 1984

Brotman AW, Jenike MA: Dysmorphophobia and monosymptomatic hypochondriasis (reply to letter by Thomas CA). Am J Psychiatry 142:1121, 1985

Caballero R: Bowel obsessions responsive to clomipramine (letter). Am J Psychiatry 145:650–651, 1988

Cohen DJ, Detlor J, Young J, et al: Clonidine ameliorates Gilles de la Tourette syndrome. Arch Gen Psychiatry 37:1350–1357, 1980

Comfort A: Out-of-body experiences and migraine (letter). Am J Psychiatry 139:1379–1380, 1982

Craven JL, Rodin GM: Cyproheptadine dependence associated with an atypical somatoform disorder. Can J Psychiatry 32:143–145, 1987

Curzon G: Serotonin and appetite. Paper presented at the Symposium on the Neuropharmacology of Serotonin, New York Academy of Sciences, New York, July 1989

Davison K: Episodic depersonalization: observations on seven patients. Br J Psychiatry 110:505–513, 1964

Derome-Tremblay M, Nathan C: Fenfluramine studies (letter). Science 243: 991, 1989

Flament MF, Rapoport JL, Berg CL, et al: Clomipramine treatment of childhood obsessive compulsive disorder: a double blind controlled study. Arch Gen Psychiatry 42:977–986, 1985

Fontaine R, Chouinard G: An open clinical trial of fluoxetine in the treatment of obsessive compulsive disorder. J Clin Psychopharmacology 6:98–101, 1986

Goldberger E, Rapoport J: Treatment of canine acral lick with clomipramine and desipramine. Journal of the American Animal Hospital Association (in press)

Greenberg DB, Hochberg FH, Murray GB: The theme of death in complex partial seizures. Am J Psychiatry 141:1587–1589, 1984

Hollander E, Fay M, Cohen B, et al: Serotonergic and noradrenergic function in obsessive-compulsive disorder: behavioral findings. Am J Psychiatry 145:1015–1017, 1988a

Hollander E, Fay M, Liebowitz MR: Clonidine and clomipramine in obsessive-compulsive disorder. Am J Psychiatry 145:388–389, 1988b

Hollander E, DeCaria C, Cooper T, et al: Neuroendocrine sensitivity in obsessive-compulsive disorder (abstract). Biol Psychiatry 25 (suppl):5A, 1989a

Hollander E, DeCaria C, Fay M, et al: Repeat m-CPP challenge during fluoxetine treatment in obsessive compulsive disorder: behavioral and neuroendocrine responses (abstract). Biol Psychiatry 25 (suppl):8A, 1989b

Hollander E, Liebowitz MR, Winchel R, et al: Treatment of body dysmorphic disorder with serotonin reuptake blockers. Am J Psychiatry 146:768–770, 1989c

Hollander E, Liebowitz MR, DeCaria C, et al: Treatment of depersonalization with serotonin reuptake inhibitors. J Clin Psychopharmacol (in press)

Insel TR, Akiskal HS: Obsessive-compulsive disorder with psychotic features: a phenomenological analysis. Am J Psychiatry 143:1527–1533, 1986

Insel TR, Murphy DL, Cohen RM, et al: Obsessive compulsive disorder: a double blind trial of clomipramine and clorgyline. Arch Gen Psychiatry 40:605–612, 1983

Jenike MA: A case report of successful treatment of dysmorphophobia with tranylcypromine. Am J Psychiatry 141:1463–1464, 1984

Jenike MA, Vitagliano HL, Rabinowitz J, et al: Bowel obsessions responsive to tricyclic antidepressants in four patients. Am J Psychiatry 144:1347–1348, 1987

Jimerson DC, Lesem MD, Kaye WH, et al: Serotonin and symptom severity in eating disorders. Biol Psychiatry 25 (suppl):141A–143A, 1989

Kahne GJ, Wray RW: Clomipramine for bowel obsessions (letter). Am J Psychiatry 146:120–121, 1989

Knesevich JW: Successful treatment of obsessive-compulsive disorder with clonidine hydrochloride. Am J Psychiatry 139:364–365, 1982

Leckman JF, Cohen DJ, Detlov J, et al: Clonidine in the treatment of Tourette syndrome and their neuroendocrine implications, in Advances in Neurology, Vol 35: Gilles de la Tourette Syndrome. Edited by Friedhoff AJ, Chase TN. New York, Raven Press, 1982, pp 391–401

Leonard HL: Drug treatment of obsessive-compulsive disorder, in Obsessive-Compulsive Disorder in Children and Adolescents. Edited by Rapoport JL. Washington, DC, American Psychiatric Press, 1989, pp 217–236

Liebowitz MR, McGrath PJ, Bush SC: Mania occurring during treatment for depersonalization: a report of two cases. J Clin Psychiatry 41:33–34, 1980

Liebowitz MR, Hollander E, Schneier F, et al: Fluoxetine treatment of obsessive-compulsive disorder: an open clinical trial. J Clin Psychopharmacol (in press)

Lydiard RB, Laraia MT, Fossey M, et al: Possible relationship of bowel obsessions to panic disorder with agoraphobia (letter). Am J Psychiatry 145:1324, 1988

Montgomery MA, Clayton PJ, Friedhoff AJ: Psychiatric illness in Tourette syndrome patients and first degree relatives, in Gilles de la Tourette Syndrome. Edited by Friedhoff AJ, Chase TN. New York, Raven Press, 1982, pp 335–339

Munro A, Chmara J: Monosymptomatic hypochondriacal psychosis: a diagnostic checklist based on 50 cases of the disorder. Can J Psychiatry 27:374–376, 1982

Nee LE, Caine ED, Polinsky RJ, et al: Gilles de la Tourette syndrome: clinical and family study of 50 cases. Ann Neurol 7:41–49, 1980

Pauls DL, Towbin KE, Leckman JF, et al: Gilles de la Tourette's syndrome and obsessive-compulsive disorder. Arch Gen Psychiatry 43:1180–1182, 1986

Pitman RK, Green RC, Jenike MA, et al: Clinical comparison of Tourette's disorder and obsessive-compulsive disorder. Am J Psychiatry 144:1166–1171, 1987

Rapoport JL: Treatment of behavioral disorders in animals (letter). Am J Psychiatry 147:1249, 1990

Riddle MA, Leckman JF, Hardin MT, et al: Fluoxetine treatment of obsessions and compulsions in patients with Tourette's syndrome (letter). Am J Psychiatry 145:1173–1174, 1988

Roth M: The phobic anxiety depersonalization syndrome. Journal of Neuropsychiatry 1:293–306, 1959

Seiver LJ, Insel TR, Jimerson DC, et al: Growth hormone response to clonidine in obsessive-compulsive patients. Br J Psychiatry 142:184–187, 1983

Shapiro AK, Shapiro ES, Young JG, et al: Gilles de la Tourette Syndrome, 2nd Edition. New York, Raven Press, 1988

Swedo SE, Rapoport JL, Leonard H, et al: Obsessive-compulsive disorder in children and adolescents: clinical phenomenology of 70 consecutive cases. Arch Gen Psychiatry 46:335–341, 1989

Szymanski HV: Prolonged depersonalization after marijuana abuse. Am J Psychiatry 138:231–233, 1981

Thomas CS: Dysmorphophobia: a question of definition. Br J Psychiatry 144:513–516, 1984

Thomas CS: Dysmorphophobia and monosymptomatic hypochondriasis (letter). Am J Psychiatry 142:1121, 1985

Thorén P, Åsberg M, Bertilsson L, et al: Clomipramine treatment of obsessive compulsive disorder, II: biochemical aspects. Arch Gen Psychiatry 37:1289–1294, 1980a

Thorén P, Åsberg M, Cronholm B, et al: Clomipramine treatment of obsessive compulsive disorder: a controlled clinical trial. Arch Gen Psychiatry 37:1281–1289, 1980b

Torch E: Review of the relationship between obsession and depersonalization. Acta Psychiatr Scand 58:191–198, 1978

Tourette G de la: Etude sur une affection nerveuse caraterisée par de l'incoordination motrice accompagnée d'echolalie et de coprolie. Archives of Neurology 9:19–42, 158–200, 1885

Walsh R: Depersonalization: definition and treatment (letter) Am J Psychiatry 132:873, 1975

Zohar J, Mueller EA, Insel TR, et al: Serotonergic responsivity in obsessive-compulsive disorder: comparison of patients and healthy controls. Arch Gen Psychiatry 44:946–951, 1987

Zohar J, Insel TR, Zohar-Kadouch RC, et al: Serotonergic responsivity in obsessive-compulsive disorder: effects of chronic clomipramine treatment. Arch Gen Psychiatry 45:167–172, 1988

Index

Contents

Contributors

Jane Eisen, M.D.
Associate Professor in Psychiatry, Brown University;
Associate Director of Admissions and Outpatient Services;
Assistant Director, OCD Clinic, Butler Hospital, Providence,
Rhode Island

Wayne K. Goodman, M.D.
Assistant Professor of Psychiatry, Department of Psychiatry,
Yale University School of Medicine; Chief, Obsessive
Compulsive Disorders Clinic, The Connecticut Mental Health
Center, Ribicoff Research Facilities, New Haven, Connecticut

David Greenberg, M.D.
Director, Jerusalem Mental Health Center, Hadassah Medical
School, Jerusalem, Israel

Eric Hollander, M.D.
Assistant Professor of Clinical Psychiatry, College of
Physicians and Surgeons, Columbia University; Director,
OCD Biological Studies Program, New York State Psychiatric
Institute, New York, New York

Thomas R. Insel, M.D.
Senior Scientist, Laboratory of Clinical Sciences, National
Institute of Mental Health, Bethesda, Maryland

Michael A. Jenike, M.D.
Associate Professor of Psychiatry, Harvard Medical School;
Research Psychiatrist and Director of Obsessive-Compulsive
Disorders Clinic and Research Unit, Massachusetts General
Hospital, Boston, Massachusetts

Marge C. Lenane, M.S.W.
Project Director, Child Psychiatry OCD Project, Child
Psychiatry Branch, National Institute of Mental Health,
Bethesda, Maryland

Henrietta L. Leonard, M.D.
Senior Staff Fellow, Child Psychiatry Branch, National
Institute of Mental Health, Bethesda, Maryland

Barbara Livingston Van Noppen, M.S.W.
Clinical Social Worker, OCD Clinic, Butler Hospital, Brown
University, Providence, Rhode Island

Lois McCartney, M.S.W.
Director of Social Work, Butler Hospital, Brown University,
Providence, Rhode Island

Michele Tortora Pato, M.D.
Assistant Professor; Director, OCD and Anxiety Disorder
Outpatient Research and Treatment Program, Department of
Psychiatry and Behavioral Sciences, State University of New
York at Stony Brook, Stony Brook, New York

Teresa A. Pigott, M.D.
Chief, Adult OCD Research Studies Unit, Laboratory of
Clinical Science, Section on Clinical Neuropharmacology,
National Institute of Mental Health, Bethesda, Maryland

Lawrence H. Price, M.D.
Associate Professor of Psychiatry, Department of Psychiatry,
Yale University School of Medicine; Director, Clinical
Neuroscience Research Unit, The Connecticut Mental Health
Center, Ribicoff Research Facilities, New Haven, Connecticut

Judith L. Rapoport, M.D.
Chief, Child Psychiatry Branch, National Institute of Mental
Health, Bethesda, Maryland

Steven A. Rasmussen, M.D.
Associate Professor in Psychiatry, Brown University;
Director, OCD Clinic; Director, Outpatient Services, Butler
Hospital, Providence, Rhode Island

Gail Steketee, Ph.D.
Assistant Professor, School of Social Work, Boston
University, Boston, Massachusetts

Susan E. Swedo, M.D.
Senior Staff Fellow, Child Psychiatry Branch, National
Institute of Mental Health, Bethesda, Maryland

L. Lee Tynes, Ph.D.
Clinical Instructor, Department of Psychiatry and Neurology,
Tulane University School of Medicine, New Orleans,
Louisiana

Eliezer Witztum, M.D.
Senior Staff Physician, Jerusalem Mental Health Center,
Hadassah Medical School, Jerusalem, Israel

Joseph Zohar, M.D.
Associate Professor, Department of Psychiatry, Ben Gurion
University; Director, Anxiety Clinic, and Deputy Director,
Beer Sheva Mental Health Centre, Beer Sheva, Israel

Introduction
to the Clinical Practice Series

Over the years of its existence the series of monographs entitled *Clinical Insights* gradually became focused on providing current, factual, and theoretical material of interest to the clinician working outside of a hospital setting. To reflect this orientation, the name of the Series has been changed to *Clinical Practice*.

The Clinical Practice Series will provide readers with books that give the mental health clinician a practical clinical approach to a variety of psychiatric problems. These books will provide up-to-date literature reviews and emphasize the most recent treatment methods. Thus, the publications in the Series will interest clinicians working both in psychiatry and in the other mental health professions.

Each year a number of books will be published dealing with all aspects of clinical practice. In addition, from time to time when appropriate, the publications may be revised and updated. Thus, the Series will provide quick access to relevant and important areas of psychiatric practice. Some books in the Series will be authored by a person considered to be an expert in that particular area; others will be edited by such an expert who will also draw together other knowledgeable authors to produce a comprehensive overview of that topic.

Some of the books in the Clinical Practice Series will have their foundation in presentations at an annual meeting of the American Psychiatric Association. All will contain the most recently available information on the subjects discussed. Theoretical and scientific data will be applied to clinical situations, and case illustrations will be utilized in order to make the material even more relevant for the practitioner. Thus, the Clinical Practice Series should provide educational reading in a compact format especially written for the mental health clinician–psychiatrist.

Judith H. Gold, M.D., F.R.C.P.(C)
Series Editor
Clinical Practice Series

Clinical Practice Series Titles

Treating Chronically Mentally Ill Women (#1)
Edited by Leona L. Bachrach, Ph.D., and Carol C. Nadelson, M.D.

Divorce as a Developmental Process (#2)
Edited by Judith H. Gold, M.D., F.R.C.P.(C)

Family Violence: Emerging Issues of a National Crisis (#3)
Edited by Leah J. Dickstein, M.D., and Carol C. Nadelson, M.D.

Anxiety and Depressive Disorders in the Medical Patient (#4)
By Leonard R. Derogatis, Ph.D., and Thomas N. Wise, M.D.

Anxiety: New Findings for the Clinician (#5)
Edited by Peter Roy-Byrne, M.D.

The Neuroleptic Malignant Syndrome and Related Conditions (#6)
By Arthur Lazarus, M.D., Stephan C. Mann, M.D., and Stanley N. Caroff, M.D.

Juvenile Homicide (#7)
Edited by Elissa P. Benedek, M.D., and Dewey G. Cornell, Ph.D.

Measuring Mental Illness: Psychometric Assessment for Clinicians (#8)
Edited by Scott Wetzler, Ph.D.

Family Involvement in Treatment of the Frail Elderly (#9)
Edited by Marion Zucker Goldstein, M.D.

Psychiatric Care of Migrants: A Clinical Guide (#10)
By Joseph J. Westermeyer, M.D., M.P.H., Ph.D.

Office Treatment of Schizophrenia (#11)
Edited by Mary V. Seeman, M.D., F.R.C.P.(C), and Stanley E. Greben, M.D., F.R.C.P.(C)

The Psychosocial Impact of Job Loss (#12)
By Nick Kates, M.B.B.S., F.R.C.P.(C), Barrie S. Greiff, M.D., and Duane Q. Hagen, M.D.

New Perspectives on Narcissism (#13)
Edited by Eric M. Plakun, M.D.

Foreword

As much as any branch of medicine, psychiatry is an empirical discipline. We may pride ourselves on our rich theories of etiopathology, but ultimately, faced with an individual patient, we do what works. And when something works, we reason backward to find an explanation, using successful results to develop a theory of cause. Treatments are thus the foundation on which theories are built, and as treatments expand, our entire system of thinking about patients and their disorders changes accordingly.

In psychiatry it is particularly intriguing how a new treatment almost seems to give birth to a new disorder. In the past three decades, each major psychopharmacological breakthrough has focused interest on an old disorder and recast it in an entirely new image. This happened in the 1960s with antipsychotic drugs and schizophrenia, in the 1970s with lithium and affective illness, and in the 1980s with new anxiolytic agents and anxiety disorders. The full scope of this phenomenon is worthy of study. It involves clinical fads, drug company hypes, trends in the society at large, and an undeniable advance in being able to help a well-defined patient group. And there is a predictable life cycle for this phenomenon. It starts with a contested discovery of a new treatment, then an exuberant acceptance of the treatment, then a report of treatment failures and side effects, and finally a realistic appraisal of the limitations of the treatment.

The syndrome of obsessive-compulsive disorder (OCD) is currently in the early phases of this phenomenon. Ten years ago, there was little research or clinical interest in this disorder, particularly in the United States, where promising European results with behavior therapy were not well known. OCD was considered a rare syndrome for which long-term dynamic psychotherapy was the treatment of choice. The emergence of specific antiobsessional therapies has recently refocused our image of this disorder, instilling therapeutic optimism and research interest. There has been nearly a threefold increase in the monthly number of research publications about OCD during this past decade. A book about OCD for a general audience (Rapoport JL: *The Boy Who Couldn't Stop Washing.* New York, Dutton, 1989) has recently been on the *New York Times* bestseller list (perhaps a first for any book about a psychiatric disorder). And specialty clinics for OCD patients, unheard of only 5 years ago, are becoming commonplace.

At the same time that psychiatry has rediscovered OCD, epidemiologic data have suggested that OCD is far more prevalent than we previously thought. The Epidemiologic Catchment Area study, sponsored by the National Institute of Mental Health, found OCD to be more common in the general population than schizophrenia, panic disorder, cognitive impairment, and anorexia nervosa (Karno M, Golding JM, Sorenson SB, et al: *Archives of General Psychiatry* 45:1094–1099, 1988; Robins LN, Helzer JE, Weissman MM, et al: *Archives of General Psychiatry* 45:450–457, 1984). However, almost all of these other disorders were more common than OCD in most psychiatric treatment settings. Apparently, many people with OCD have not sought treatment, or they have been diagnosed for a secondary disorder (e.g., dermatitis or depression) while the primary diagnosis of OCD has been missed. Either way, both the emergence of new treatments and the tremendous increase in publicity about OCD promise that psychiatrists will be spending more of their time with this intriguing group of patients.

Hence, the timeliness of this volume. This is a practical, problem-solving guide to treating OCD patients that tempers the exuberant acceptance of new treatments with a realistic appraisal of what to expect. Two examples are worth noting. With the surge of public interest in OCD, one might expect that many chronically impaired patients with a diverse array of symptoms (including obsessions) may formulate their problem as OCD. Although these patients are unlikely to respond to antiobsessional treatments any better than they have responded to other treatments, these patients whose treatment fails should not dilute our confidence in the usefulness of behavioral and pharmacological therapies. Several chapters here speak to the problem of treatment failure.

As a second example, this book drives home the point that the OCD patient who responds to treatment may look quite different than the successfully treated depressed or agoraphobic patient. Particularly with antiobsessional drugs, when the treatment works, the patient may have obvious residual symptoms, he or she may need to remain on medication indefinitely, and almost certainly he or she will need consistent follow-up. Even behavior therapy, which claims a more pervasive and lasting effect than medication, may need follow-up treatments and involvement of the family for improvement to be maintained.

This is a tough illness, as tenacious as the person suffering with it.

Although these new treatments are clearly useful, they are not cures. Nor are they the end of the line. The next decade will undoubtedly sharpen our focus further, teaching us about combining treatments, yielding predictors of who will respond to which treatments, and providing better guidelines for the diagnostic boundaries of OCD. Each clinician and each patient can be a part of this process, and, I believe, this book will prove a useful guide in getting started.

Thomas R. Insel, M.D.

Preface

Treatment of obsessive-compulsive disorder (OCD) is a dynamic discipline that requires broad understanding of diagnosis, therapy options, and unusual cases. The outlook for patients with OCD is being dramatically changed because of the introduction of effective pharmacological interventions such as fluoxetine, fluvoxamine, and clomipramine in the past decade. This volume is written as a practical, multidisciplinary update on the current effective treatments for OCD and related issues by some of the top researchers and clinicians in the field.

Our intention is for this book to be a practical manual for clinical psychiatrists who now have at their disposal effective treatments for a disorder that might be unfamiliar to them—a "how-to" manual for treating OCD. Thus, each chapter not only serves as a critical review of the available data but also addresses the advantages and pitfalls of each suggested treatment or approach. At the end of most chapters are several case histories illustrating the approach outlined in its pages, followed by a summary of the chapter. We hope that these case histories will provide a practical and pragmatic look at how the data put forth in the chapter unfold in clinical practice. From these case histories the reader can appreciate that treating OCD patients is an ongoing process. Many patients get significant improvement (40% to 70%), but few get "cured." For some patients even 10% or 20% improvement can make a significant difference in their life.

In Chapter 1, Drs. Zohar and Pato briefly review diagnostic considerations, emphasizing subtypes of the classification of OCD patients and differential diagnosis. Although identifying OCD subtypes can be helpful in making the diagnosis, thus far these subtypes have not proved consistently helpful in directing treatment, except perhaps in the case of purely obsessional patients, for whom behavioral treatment is more difficult to apply and thus seems less effective than pharmacological approaches. Throughout this first chapter the reader is directed to case histories in other chapters that illustrate these different presentations of OCD.

Drs. Pato and Zohar, Pigott, and Goodman and Price, in Chapters 2, 3, and 4, respectively, provide a detailed review of specific pharmacological treatments of OCD and present data on the efficacy of these agents.

Clomipramine, the most widely studied of these agents, was the first medication approved (in December 1989) by the U.S. Food and Drug Administration (FDA) for the treatment of OCD. Fluoxetine, although marketed as an antidepressant, has in the past 2 to 3 years gained increasing acceptance as an effective antiobsessional agent. Although still considered an investigational drug and not widely available, fluvoxamine offers hope as a third agent in the treatment of OCD. The authors outline the clinical use of these agents in considerable detail and make recommendations for dosage and duration of treatment.

The comparative efficacy of the behavioral treatment approach compared to pharmacological treatment is still in question, but the efficacy of behavioral treatment is well documented. In Chapter 5, Drs. Steketee and Tynes outline the theoretical underpinnings of this approach and provide case histories as practical examples of the application of behavioral treatment.

Drs. Leonard, Swedo, and Rapoport, leading researchers in the area, outline in Chapter 6 the similarities and differences in the presentation and treatment of children with OCD. In addition, they briefly present some of their landmark work in the neurobiology of OCD.

Authors Lenane and Livingston Van Noppen et al., in Chapters 7 and 8, respectively, present two types of family therapy approaches in the treatment of OCD. In Chapter 7, an approach with classic family therapy is outlined that can involve seeing the parents and patient, as well as other family members, together and separately. In Chapter 8, a new, innovative approach is described that brings together several families, including the patients, in a group setting for a prescribed, structured number of visits. Both chapters emphasize that OCD often affects not only the patient but family members, who may suffer from OCD to a greater or lesser extent.

Chapter 9 is a thorough review of what constitutes treatment resistance in OCD and how to approach the treatment of such patients. Dr. Jenike has drawn from his vast clinical experience and has provided a chapter that outlines the smooth application of a multidisciplinary approach to treating any OCD patient, whether or not he or she meets the definition of treatment resistance.

In Chapter 10, Drs. Greenberg and Witztum discuss the issue of religious practices in OCD. They address not only diagnosis but also treatment of such patients while allowing for the respect and maintenance of their patients' religious beliefs.

Finally, in Chapter 11, Dr. Hollander outlines in brief some rare and unusual symptoms that respond to serotonergic drugs. He terms these "OCD-related disorders" because although they do not fall into the classic DSM-III-R (American Psychiatric Association: *Diagnostic and Statistical Manual of Mental Disorders,* 3rd Edition, Revised. Washington, DC, APA, 1987) definition of OCD, the underlying drive or urge, perhaps obsessions and compulsions, that these patients describe to perform these behaviors and their response to similar antiobsessional agents would seem to put them in the realm of OCD.

In reading this book we hope the clinician is left not just with a knowledge of the available data on treating OCD patients but with a flavor and understanding of what these patients suffer and their earnestness to get well. We hope that for many clinicians this book will become a dog-eared reference manual on treating OCD patients.

We would like to thank our contributors for their thorough, careful preparation of their chapters. We dedicate this book to our loving spouses, Carlos Pato and Rachel Zohar-Kadouch, and to our children, Michael and Eric Pato and Karmit, Zeev, and Mishael Zohar.

Michele Tortora Pato, M.D.
Joseph Zohar, M.D.

Chapter 1

Diagnostic Considerations

Joseph Zohar, M.D.
Michele Tortora Pato, M.D.

*I*n the past not only was a diagnosis of obsessive-compulsive disorder (OCD) rare, but the clinician had little hope of effectively treating a patient with such a diagnosis. However, over the past 10 years this picture of OCD as a rare and treatment-resistant illness has greatly changed. The preliminary results of the National Institute of Mental Health (NIMH)–sponsored Epidemiologic Catchment Area (ECA) study (Robins et al. 1984) indicated that the prevalence rate of OCD is far from rare. A lifetime prevalence between 2% and 3% was noted rather than the 0.05% previously reported (Woodruff and Pitts 1964). Analysis of all five ECA sites agreed with these results, reporting 2% to 5% (Karno et al. 1988). Furthermore, other similar epidemiologic assessments in Edmonton, Canada, supported these findings (Bland et al. 1988a, 1988b), estimating a lifetime prevalence of 3%.

Perhaps more importantly, extensive research in the last 10 years has led to new and effective pharmacological and behavioral treatments of OCD and has begun to give us some understanding of the psychobiology of this illness (for review, see Zohar and Insel 1987b; Baxter et al. 1987). In this chapter we provide the therapist with an overview of OCD symptom clusters, differential diagnosis, and clinical course—an essential foundation before treatment can be considered.

Diagnosis of Obsessive-Compulsive Disorder

The diagnostic criteria for OCD on Axis I of DSM-III-R (American Psychiatric Association 1987) include the presence of recurrent, persistent, and unwanted thoughts, impulses, or images (obsessions) and/or the performance of repetitive, often seemingly purposeful, ritualistic behaviors (compulsions) (Table 1-1). These obsessions and compulsions are ego-

Table 1-1.   DSM-III-R diagnostic criteria for obsessive-compulsive disorder

A. Either obsessions or compulsions:

Obsessions: (1), (2), (3), and (4):

(1) Recurrent and persistent ideas, thoughts, impulses, or images that are experienced, at least initially, as intrusive and senseless, e.g., a parent's having repeated impulses to kill a loved child, a religious person's having recurrent blasphemous thoughts.
(2) The person attempts to ignore or suppress such thoughts or impulses or to neutralize them with some other thought or action.
(3) The person recognizes that the obsessions are the product of his or her own mind, not imposed from without (as in thought insertion).
(4) If another Axis I disorder is present, the content of the obsession is unrelated to it, e.g., the ideas, thoughts, impulses, or images are not about food in the presence of an eating disorder, about drugs in the presence of a psychoactive substance use disorder, or guilty thoughts in the presence of a major depression.

Compulsions: (1), (2), and (3):

(1) Repetitive, purposeful, and intentional behaviors that are peformed in response to an obsession, or according to certain rules or in a stereotyped fashion.
(2) The behavior is designed to neutralize or to prevent discomfort or some dreaded event or situation; however, either the activity is not connected in a realistic way with what it is designed to neutralize or prevent, or it is clearly excessive.
(3) The person recognizes that his or her behavior is excessive or unreasonable (this may not be true for young children; it may no longer be true for people whose obsessions have evolved into overvalued ideas).

B. The obsessions or compulsions cause marked distress, are time-consuming (take more than an hour a day), or significantly interfere with the person's normal routine, occupational functioning, or usual social activities or relationships with others.

Source. Reprinted, with permission, from *Diagnostic and Statistical Manual of Mental Disorders,* 3rd Edition, Revised. Washington, DC, American Psychiatric Association, 1987. Copyright 1987, APA.

dystonic, and, at some point in the illness, most patients make some attempt to resist them. This ego-dystonic nature of the illness, the attempt to resist, and interference with daily function not only are mandatory for the diagnosis but are clinically important in differentiating OCD from other diagnoses such as obsessive-compulsive personality disorder, schizophrenia, and phobic disorders.

Despite these straightforward criteria, in actual clinical practice the diagnosis of OCD is not always easy or obvious. For example, in a recent report by Rasmussen (1985), it was noted that patients were referred to dermatologists for dermatitis due to excessive hand washing, and thus potential OCD, but were never referred for psychiatric evaluation. In addition, until recently, many patients did not come for psychiatric care with the specific complaints of obsessive-compulsive symptoms; but rather they presented with other psychiatric symptoms, such as depression, phobic disorders, and panic disorder, which can occur concurrently with OCD (Goodwin et al. 1969; Jenike et al. 1986; Mellman and Uhde 1987). The embarrassment and consequent secretiveness that many OCD patients experience also explain why at least two studies have found a 7-year lag in seeking treatment from the time of symptom onset (Pollitt 1957; Rasmussen and Tsuang 1986). Furthermore, although OCD is an anxiety disorder, it differs in several ways from other anxiety disorders, which will be discussed below.

The clinical course of OCD may also contribute to some of the difficulty in making this diagnosis. Extensive longitudinal data on OCD do not exist, perhaps because until recently the high prevalence of this disorder was not known. However, the available studies indicate a waxing and waning clinical course (Goodwin et al. 1969; Grimshaw 1965; Rasmussen and Tsuang 1986; Zohar-Kadouch et al. 1989). Thus, many patients may only seek treatment during times of extreme symptom exacerbation, although clinical assessment may reveal periods of less severe illness during which time the patient might have benefited from treatment. As many as 50% of patients may have the onset of their OCD symptoms in childhood. Although in adulthood OCD is equally as likely to occur in females as it is in males, in childhood OCD is more common in boys (Rapoport 1989; Rasmussen and Tsuang 1986).

Symptom Clusters

Although initially struck by the diversity of the clinical presentations of OCD, the clinician will come to realize that the number and types of obsessions and compulsions are remarkably limited and stereotypical (Rasmussen and Tsuang 1986). As noted above, OCD patients are shocked when they hear that other OCD patients engage in the same behaviors (see Livingston Van Noppen et al., Chapter 8, this volume). Moreover, the basic types and frequencies of obsessive-compulsive symptoms have been found to be consistent across cultures and time (Akhtar et al. 1975; O'Kasha et al. 1968; Rasmussen and Tsuang 1986).

Many obsessive-compulsive symptoms fall into one of four major symptom clusters:

Washing. "Washers" are obsessed with dirt, contamination, germs, or bugs. These patients may spend several hours each day washing their hands, showering, or cleaning. Typically, they try to avoid sources of "contamination" such as door knobs, electric switches, and newspapers. Paradoxically, some of these patients are quite slovenly (see, for instance, the description of Howard Hughes [Bartlett and Steele 1979]).

Although these patients are cognizant that nothing will happen if they resist washing, they may refuse to touch even their own bodies, knowing that if they do, they will not be at ease unless they execute extensive washing rituals. (For case history examples, see Pato and Zohar, Chapter 2; Goodman and Price, Chapter 4; Leonard et al., Chapter 6; Jenike, Chapter 9, this volume.)

Checking. Patients in this symptom cluster are obsessed with a doubt, usually tinged with guilt, and frequently they are concerned that if they do not check carefully enough they will hurt others. Their checking, instead of resolving the uncertainty, often only contributes to even greater doubt, which leads to further checking. Often "checkers" will enlist the help of family and friends to ensure they have checked enough or correctly (for a case history see Leonard et al., Chapter 6, this volume). Ultimately, by some inscrutable means the patient resolves a particular doubt, only to have it replaced by a new obsessional doubt. Resistance, which in this case is the attempt to refrain from checking, leads to difficulty in concentrating and exhaustion from the never-ending assault of nagging uncertainties. Common examples of these concerns and doubts are a fear of causing a fire, which leads to checking the stove (even to the extent that the patient cannot leave home), or a fear of hurting somebody while driving, which leads to repetitive driving back over the same spot after hitting a bump in the road (for case histories see Pato and Zohar, Chapter 2; Steketee and Tynes, Chapter 5; Leonard et al., Chapter 6; Jenike, Chapter 9, this volume). Occasionally, checkers are not even certain why they are checking, expressing a vague feeling that they "just have the urge to do it."

Checkers may also engage in related compulsive behavior. In some cases, unsure that the checking is sufficient, patients may develop undoing type rituals such as counting to a certain number in their head, repeating things a certain number of times, or avoiding particular numbers. Hoarding behavior can be seen as corollary to checking behavior. Patients refuse to throw out junk mail, old newspapers, or used tissues, for example, because of doubt of throwing away something important in the process (for case histories see Pigott, Chapter 3; Leonard et al., Chapter 6, this volume).

Pure obsessions. A third clinical picture is of the pure obsessional patients. These patients experience repetitive, intrusive thoughts that are usually somatic, aggressive, or sexual, and always reprehensible. In the absence of what appears to be discrete compulsion, these obsessions may be associated with impulses (which have been called "horrific temptations") or fearful images. When the obsession is an aggressive impulse, it is most often directed at the one person most valuable to the patient. In addition, the obsession might be a fear that the patient will act on other impulses (e.g., to kill somebody, to rob a bank, to steal) or that he or she will be held responsible for something terrible (e.g., fire, plague). Often, however, there may be subtle rituals around these obsessive thoughts. For example, a mother who was afraid that she would stab her daughter struggled with this impulse by avoiding sharp objects, then by avoiding touching her daughter, and ultimately by leaving the house altogether, only to develop a new obsession that she might poison her boss. Although such avoidant behavior may not appear as an actual repetitive behavior or compulsion, it does share other properties of compulsion in that it is an intentional attempt to neutralize an obsession. Patients may seek treatment claiming they have phobias, when, in reality, their avoidance is motivated by obsessions. Often, careful examination of patient history will reveal other obsessions or compulsions as well.

Sexual obsessions include forbidden or perverse sexual thoughts, images, or impulses that might involve children, animals, incest, homosexuality, and so forth. Patients with aggressive and sexual obsessions might not reveal them, even if they are asked directly, fearing that they will be committed to "an institution forever." Psychiatrists can create an atmosphere that enables patients to disclose these types of obsessions by mentioning them as examples of possible obsessions and by assuring patients that these obsessions will not be acted on. Interestingly, violent antisocial behavior, suicide, and drug addiction are very uncommon in OCD patients (Goodwin et al. 1969).

Obsessional thoughts can often carry a religious rather than a sexual or violent theme. These thoughts might lead to repetitive silent prayer or confession or result in more obvious rituals such as repeated bowing or trips to church. Such behavior presents a particular problem to both clinicians and clergy as they try to draw the line between disorder and devotion. (See Greenberg and Witztum, Chapter 10, this volume, for a historically interesting and clinically practical discussion of this problem. For a further case study see Leonard et al., Chapter 6, this volume.) At times, the obsessive thoughts may take on a more nondescript quality. Examples include a need to know or remember what was eaten for breakfast, a need to say or not say a particular word or phrase, or a need to keep a certain musical phrase in one's head.

Obsessional slowness.   The clinical picture of obsessional slowness is dominated by an obsession to have objects or events in a certain order or position, to do and undo certain motor actions in an exact form, or to have things exactly symmetrical or "just right." These patients take an inordinate amount of time to complete even the simplest of tasks; thus, it may take them a couple of hours just to get dressed. Unlike most obsessive-compulsive patients, these patients do not resist their symptoms. Instead, they seem to be consumed with the obsession of how to complete their routine precisely. Although this subtype of OCD is quite rare, aspects of slowness often appear along with other obsessions and compulsions and may be the major source of interference in daily functioning.

Multiple Symptoms and Symptom Shifting

Many, if not most, OCD patients have a combination of symptoms, although one symptom type, be it washing, checking, pure obsessions, or obsessional slowness, may predominate. To date, there are few data supporting the clinical value of this differentiation, although some investigators have noted the treatment resistance of purely obsessional patients (see Steketee and Tynes, Chapter 5; Jenike, Chapter 9, this volume).

In addition to the lack of pure subtypes of OCD is the phenomenon of symptom shifting (Rapoport 1989; Zohar-Kadouch et al. 1989); at different points in the course of their illness, patients report that different OCD symptoms are predominant. Thus, a patient who in childhood may have predominantly had washing rituals may have checking rituals in adulthood. The most important point in noting this symptom shift is not in terms of treatment but in terms of diagnosis—that is, increasing the level of confidence in making the OCD diagnosis. When therapists must differentiate between OCD and other psychiatric illnesses such as phobic disorder, anxiety disorders, psychotic illness, and obsessive-compulsive personality disorder, knowledge of this prior history may be particularly helpful.

Differential Diagnosis

Obsessive-Compulsive Personality Disorder

There may be some similarities in the diagnosis of OCD (an Axis I disorder in DSM-III-R) and the diagnosis of obsessive-compulsive personality disorder (OCPD) (an Axis II disorder in DSM-III-R). Both disorders reveal a preoccupation with aggression and control; both use the defenses of reaction formation, undoing, intellectualization, denial, and isolation of affect. The psychoanalytic formulation suggests that OCD develops when these defenses fail to contain the obsessional character's anxiety (Salzman and Thaler 1981). In this view OCD is often considered to be on a continuum with OCPD pathology. Epidemiologic evidence, however, reveals that a concurrent diagnosis of OCPD is neither necessary nor sufficient for the development of OCD on Axis I in a considerable portion, if not the majority, of patients with OCD (Black et al. 1988; Lo 1967; Rasmussen and Tsuang 1986). Diagnostic confusion can be lessened if one remembers that symptoms in OCD patients are ego-dystonic, whereas compulsive character traits are ego-syntonic and rarely provoke resistance. It is sometimes difficult to differentiate between Axis I and Axis II disorders, and a trial of pharmacological or behavioral treatment may be warranted if the patient is willing to test whether any of the obsessions or compulsions improve.

Other Anxiety Disorders

Although OCD is classified as an anxiety disorder, it appears to be somewhat different from other anxiety disorders, as follows:

- **Age.** The age of onset for OCD patients is young compared with that for patients with panic disorder.
- **Sex distribution.** In OCD there is an equal distribution of males and females, whereas in other anxiety disorders females are more common.
- **Responses to anxiogenic and anxiolytic compounds.** OCD patients do not develop increased symptoms following administration of anxiogenic compounds such as lactate, yohimbine, and caffeine, whereas agoraphobic patients do (Zohar et al. 1990). OCD patients are also refractory to anxiolytic medications such as benzodiazepines. Moreover, patients with OCD are refractory to tricyclic antidepressants (with the exception of clomipramine), medications that are typically found to be effective in anxiety and panic disorder, as well as in major depression.
- **Selective responsivity of serotonergic medications.** Making the diagnosis of OCD can help the clinician to avoid the use of nonserotonergic medications, which will likely be ineffective. (See Pato and Zohar, Chapter 2; Pigott, Chapter 3; Goodman and Price, Chapter 4; Jenike, Chapter 9, this volume.)

Certain patients with OCD may seem to resemble simple or social phobic individuals. Patients with obsessions about contamination may even describe their problem as a "germ phobia." Although the distinction may be difficult to make in individual cases, many times the OCD patient's fear involves harm to others rather than harm to himself or herself. In addition, the OCD patient, when "phobic," is usually afraid of a stimulus that is unavoidable, such as a virus, germs, or dirt, as opposed to "classic" phobic objects like tunnels, bridges, or crowds.

Depression

Depression is the most common complication of OCD (Goodwin et al. 1969; Rapoport 1989). By recognizing this relationship between OCD and depression, DSM-III-R no longer excludes a diagnosis of OCD if depression is present, but stipulates that the obsession not be related in content to the guilt-ridden rumination of major depression. However, precisely defining the relationship between OCD and depression remains elusive. At the clinical level the illnesses often seem inseparable—one worsening or improving in synchrony with the other, as illustrated by numerous clinical trials (see Pato and Zohar, Chapter 2; Pigott, Chapter 3; Goodman and Price, Chapter 4, this volume) in which OCD and depressive symptoms both improved during the course of treatment. However, in other clinical cases, OCD symptoms may remain in remission while depression recurs (Pato et al. 1988). Researchers have reported some similarities in the biologic markers for depression and OCD, but differences have also been noted (for review see Zohar and Insel 1987b).

What seems most clinically relevant is that only those antidepressant medications that have serotonergic properties, namely clomipramine, fluoxetine, and fluvoxamine, to date, have consistent efficacy in decreasing OCD symptoms. On the other hand, many other serotonergic and nonserotonergic antidepressants are effective in treating depression.

Major Psychotic Syndromes

Unlike patients with major psychotic syndromes, patients with OCD retain some insight about their symptoms. Although in some cases the behavior of OCD patients may appear extremely bizarre, the obsessions or compulsions are recognized by the patients with OCD as internal as opposed to the psychotic "ideas of influence."

Another way to distinguish between obsession and delusion is that OCD patients try to resist the obsessions. However, in very severe cases of OCD, patients may briefly relinquish the struggle against their symptoms. At such times the obsession appears to shift from an ego-dystonic obsession to a psychotic delusion. It may be tempting to label such a patient schizophrenic, but follow-up data reveal that psychotic decompensations may occur in many truly obsessive patients who never develop schizophrenia, analogous to the psychotic features that may accompany major affective illness. For such patients, the term *obsessive-compulsive disorder with psychotic features* has been suggested (Insel and Akiskal 1986). (See Jenike, Chapter 9, this volume, for treatment of such patients.)

Pathological Gambling and Alcohol or Drug Abuse

Pathological gambling and alcohol or drug abuse might superficially resemble OCD as people engage in them excessively and with a sense of compulsion. However, in DSM-III-R these behaviors are distinguished from true compulsions because, to some degree, they are experienced as pleasurable, whereas compulsions are inherently not pleasurable.

OCD-Related Disorders

Based on clinical presentation, family history, and treatment response, there appears to be a group of disorders that might be called OCD-related disorders (see Hollander, Chapter 11, this volume). These disorders include body dysmorphic disorder, monosymptomatic hypochondriacal delusional disorder, hypochondriasis, trichotillomania, eating disorders, and perhaps bowel obsessions. (For case histories see Leonard et al., Chapter 6, this volume. Detailed diagnostic considerations regarding these patients are discussed in Hollander, Chapter 11, this volume.) Briefly, if these patients have multiple other obsessions or compulsions, then the diagnosis of OCD is appropriate. However, even if they do not have multiple obsessions or compulsions, some data still indicate that patients with OCD-related disorders respond to the same antiobsessional agents as do OCD patients. Exactly what this implies about the relationship between OCD, serotonin, and OCD-related disorders awaits further study.

Summary

OCD is a common, chronic, and disabling disorder marked by obsessions and/or compulsions that are ego-dystonic and cause marked distress to the patients and their families. Despite well-defined criteria, diagnosis of OCD can be complicated by patient secrecy, confusion with other psychiatric symptoms, and a waxing and waning clinical course. The recent dramatic advances in pharmacological and behavioral treatment for OCD emphasize the clinical importance of making an accurate diagnosis.

References

Akhtar S, Wig NH, Varma VK, et al: A phenomenological analysis of symptoms in obsessive-compulsive neuroses. Br J Psychiatry 127:342–348, 1975

American Psychiatric Association: Diagnostic and Statistical Manual of Mental Disorders, 3rd Edition, Revised. Washington, DC, American Psychiatric Association, 1987

Bartlett DL, Steele JB: Empire: The Life, Legend and Madness of Howard Hughes. New York, WW Norton, 1979

Baxter LR Jr, Phelps ME, Mazziotta JC, et al: Local cerebral glucose metabolic rates in obsessive-compulsive disorder: a comparison with rates in unipolar depression and normal controls. Arch Gen Psychiatry 44:211–218, 1987

Black DW, Yates WR, Noyes R, et al: Axis I/Axis II: comorbidity findings. Paper presented at the 141st annual meeting of the American Psychiatric Association, Montreal, Quebec, May 1988

Bland RC, Newman SC, Ora H: Lifetime prevalence of psychiatric disorders in Edmonton. Acta Psychiatr Scand 77 (suppl 338):24–32, 1988a

Bland RC, Newman SC, Ora H: Period prevalence of psychiatric disorders in Edmonton. Acta Psychiatr Scand 77 (suppl 338):33–42, 1988b

Goodwin DW, Guze SB, Robins E: Follow-up studies in obsessional neurosis. Arch Gen Psychiatry 20:182–187, 1969

Grimshaw L: The outcome of obsessional disorder: a follow-up study of 100 cases. Br J Psychiatry 111:1051–1056, 1965

Insel TR, Akiskal HS: Obsessive-compulsive disorder with psychotic features: a phenomenologic analysis. Am J Psychiatry 143:1527–1533, 1986

Jenike MA, Baer L, Minichiello WE: Obsessive-Compulsive Disorders: Theory and Management. Littleton, MA, PSG Publishing Company, 1986

Karno M, Golding JM, Sorenson SB, et al: The epidemiology of obsessive-compulsive disorder in five US communities. Arch Gen Psychiatry 45:1094–1099, 1988

Lo WH: A follow-up study of obsessional neurotics in Hong Kong Chinese. Br J Psychiatry 113:823–832, 1967

Mellman TA, Uhde TW: Obsessive-compulsive symptoms in panic disorder. Am J Psychiatry 144:1573–1576, 1987

O'Kasha A, Kamel M, Hassen R: Preliminary psychiatric observations in Egypt. Br J Psychiatry 114:949–956, 1968

Pato MT, Zohar-Kadouch R, Zohar J, et al: Return of symptoms after discontinuation of clomipramine in patients with obsessive-compulsive disorder. Am J Psychiatry 145:1521–1525, 1988

Pollitt J: Natural history of obsessional states. Br Med J 1:194–198, 1957

Rapoport JL: The Boy Who Couldn't Stop Washing. New York, Dutton, 1989

Rasmussen SE: Obsessive-compulsive disorder in dermatologic practice. J Am Acad Dermatol 13:965–967, 1985

Rasmussen SA, Tsuang MT: Clinical characteristics and family history in DSM-III obsessive-compulsive disorder. Am J Psychiatry 143:317–322, 1986

Robins LN, Helzer JE, Weissman MM, et al: Lifetime prevalence of specific psychiatric disorders in three sites. Arch Gen Psychiatry 41:949–958, 1984

Salzman L, Thaler FH: Obsessive-compulsive disorder: a review of the literature. Am J Psychiatry 138:286–296, 1981

Woodruff R, Pitts FN: Monozygotic twins with obsessional illness. Am J Psychiatry 120:1075–1080, 1964

Zohar J, Insel TR: Drug treatment of obsessive-compulsive disorder. J Affective Disord 13:193–202, 1987a

Zohar J, Insel TR: Obsessive-compulsive disorder: psychobiological approaches to diagnosis, treatment, and pathophysiology. Biol Psychiatry 22:667–687, 1987b

Zohar J, Murphy DL, Zohar-Kadouch RC, et al: Serotonin in obsessive-compulsive disorder, in Serotonin in Major Psychiatric Disorders. Edited by Coccaro EF, Murphy DL. Washington, DC, American Psychiatric Press, 1990, pp 99–125

Zohar-Kadouch R, Pato MT, Zohar J, et al: Follow-up of obsessive-compulsive patients. Paper presented at the 142nd annual meeting of the American Psychiatric Association, San Francisco, CA, May 1989

Chapter 2

Clomipramine in the Treatment of Obsessive-Compulsive Disorder

Michele Tortora Pato, M.D.
Joseph Zohar, M.D.

*A*ny discussion of the pharmacotherapy of obsessive-compulsive disorder (OCD) will most likely begin with clomipramine (Anafranil), made available in the United States as recently as February 1990. Marketed for many years outside the United States as an antidepressant, clomipramine's antiobsessional properties have made it a viable pharmacological option for treating OCD. In this chapter we review the properties of clomipramine that may be responsible for making it useful in treating OCD, its relationship to depression (in contrast to OCD), and its history of clinical use in the treatment of OCD. We then put forth clinical considerations—dosing, side effects, compliance, treatment response, and duration and discontinuation—to guide the thinking of psychiatrists considering the prescribing of this medication.

Clomipramine and Obsessive-Compulsive Disorder

Structure

Clomipramine is a tricyclic antidepressant virtually identical in structure to imipramine with the exception of a chloride substituted for a hydrogen at position 3. Consequently, its side effects are similar to those of imipramine, but, surprisingly, clomipramine behaves differently at the neurochemical level in significant ways. In particular, clomipramine is a much more potent serotonin (5-hydroxytryptamine [5-HI]) uptake inhibitor than is imipramine (Murphy et al. 1989); it is this characteristic that is believed to make clomipramine particularly useful in the treatment of OCD. In addition, one of the primary metabolites of clomipramine, desmethylclomipramine (DCMI), is a potent norepinephrine uptake blocker as well as an effective 5-HT uptake inhibitor. However, the parent compound, clomipramine, is at least 10 times as potent a 5-HT uptake inhibitor as its metabolite DCMI, and this fact may have some predictive value in terms of efficacy of treatment (Murphy et al. 1989; Träskman et al. 1979).

The Use of Clomipramine in the Treatment of OCD

Clomipramine has been commercially available outside the United States for over 20 years. The first studies of its use in the treatment of OCD appeared as early as 1967 (Fernandez and Lopez-Ibor 1967; Lopez-Ibor 1969; Renynghe de Voxrie 1968). At that time the drug was used with some success in open trials for obsessional patients and depressed patients with obsessional symptoms. In the 1970s a number of studies were undertaken on the use of clomipramine in the treatment of OCD and obsessional symptoms, some studies using intravenous administration and others using oral dosing (Jenike et al. 1986; Thorén et al. 1980b). In all, by 1980 there were 15 anecdotal studies of the use of clomipramine in the treatment of OCD. Summing these studies, 184 of 226 obsessive patients at doses of 75 mg to 300 mg of clomipramine received some relief of their symptoms (Ananth 1986).

The 1980s saw the beginning of controlled, double-blind studies of clomipramine in an attempt to objectify the efficacy of this agent in the treatment of OCD. There have been at least nine studies, some placebo-controlled and some comparing clomipramine with a myriad of other antidepressants, including desipramine, imipramine, clorgyline, nortriptyline, and amitriptyline. (Extensive review of these studies can be found elsewhere—see Ananth 1986; Insel 1984; Leonard et al. 1988; Murphy et al. 1989; Thorén et al. 1980b; Zohar and Insel 1987a, 1987b.) Clomipramine was found to be more effective than placebo alone in every case and more effective than desipramine, clorgyline, and amitriptyline. It also was suggested to have more probable efficacy over imipramine and nortriptyline. Clomipramine has even been compared with behavioral treatment. In a study by Marks et al. (1980) clomipramine administered in conjunction with behavioral treatment was found to be more effective in treating OCD than behavioral treatment alone. Unfortunately, this study did not include a treatment group of patients who received only clomipramine for the entire study period, so conclusions about the efficacy of this agent compared with that of behavioral treatment are limited.

Recently, a multicenter clinical trial was completed by the CIBA-Geigy Corporation (Summit, NJ). Thus far, the data of 384 patients have been analyzed. (DeVeaugh-Geiss et al. 1989). Of these 384 patients, 194 received clomipramine and 190 received placebo. By the end of the 10-week trial, patients on clomipramine had experienced a significant reduction in obsessive-compulsive symptoms. As measured by the Yale-Brown Obsessive Compulsive Rating Scale (Goodman et al. 1989a, 1989b), symptoms decreased by 40% to 45% ($P < .05$). Furthermore, symptom improvement was noted as soon as 2 weeks after initiation of the drug, and this improvement continued throughout the 10-week study. Doses up to 250 mg (and in rare cases 300 mg) were used. Unlike clinical trials in other disorders (e.g., depression), the placebo response rate of the OCD patients was extremely low, with the placebo group experiencing virtually no change in symptoms (less than 5%). In part of the multicenter trial, some patients having scores in the range of 17 to 21 on the Hamilton Rating Scale for Depression (Hamilton 1960) were included, but the severity of the depression of these patients did not affect their outcome (DeVeaugh-Geiss et al. 1989). This onset of improvement at 2 weeks but continuing throughout the 10 weeks is typical of clomipramine. Many authors have noted that although symptom improvement may be noted in the 4- to 6-week range (Ananth 1986; Ananth et al. 1981; Insel 1984; Insel et al. 1983; Mavissakalian and Michelson 1983), it may take 12 weeks or more to see the full benefit of the medication (Thorén et al. 1980b). In the case histories presented at the end of this chapter, we note continued gradual clinical improvement for 4 to 6 months.

Depression and OCD

A discussion of OCD and clomipramine must address the role of depression in OCD. Clomipramine was actually marketed beginning more than 20 years ago as an antidepressant and remains a popular antidepressant in many parts of the world. Currently, a number of convincing studies seem to conclude that the antiobsessional effect of clomipramine is separate from its antidepressant effect (Ananth et al. 1981; Insel et al. 1983; Mavissakalian et al. 1985; Montgomery 1980; Thorén et al. 1980a, 1980b; Zohar and Insel 1987a, 1987b). In particular, Mavissakalian et al. (1985) compared the five OCD patients with the highest depression scores to the five with the lowest depression scores and found no difference in the improvement of their OCD symptoms when treated with clomipramine. Clinically, we (Pato et al. 1988) reported one patient who had relief of her depression with amitriptyline but remission of both OCD symptoms and depression only when she was switched to clomipramine.

Clinical Considerations

Prescribing clomipramine to OCD patients requires a consideration of not only the nature of the drug but the nature of OCD. On the one hand, it has been our clinical experience that these patients are incredibly tolerant of side effects (see case histories at the end of this chapter). Perhaps this is because, as the patients themselves express it, they have suffered with their illness, often in secret, for so long that the improvement in their symptoms and in their overall level of functioning is well worth any amount of side effects. On the other hand, the nature of the illness means that these patients experience much doubt and apprehension. First, they often will obsess over actually taking the medicine at all and will require considerable encouragement and repeated explanation of its side effects. Second, these patients can often worry excessively about the possible side effects, often imagining the worst possible scenario; therefore, they need considerable reassurance. In the initial phases of treatment, doctor availability and slow, gradual increase in dose are particularly important in terms of the patient's long-term compliance. Because there are few commercially available medications that effectively treat OCD, extra effort should be made to avoid early rejection of the medication by the patient.

Unfortunately, there are no specific data on which patients respond best to clomipramine versus other antiobsessional agents. This lack of data is partially because until very recently, no other agents besides clomipramine were found to be consistently effective. However, Eisen and Rasmussen (1988) reported that among patients with psychotic features and OCD, those individuals with a paranoid or obsessional quality to their delusions had a better prognosis than did those with magical thinking or schizophrenia as part of their psychotic features. In Chapter 9, Jenike addresses treatment-resistant cases of OCD and presents data on the profile of better- and worse-prognosis patients. For example, patients with underlying schizotypal personality disorder are more treatment resistant.

Dosing

The starting dose of clomipramine should be low—25 mg to 50 mg the initial day—because there have been some reports of acute onset of nausea and vomiting requiring discontinuation (Ananth 1986). The dose can then be increased every 1 to 3 days by 25 mg to a maxium dose of 250 mg or until side effects become intolerable. Most studies have employed doses in the range of 75 mg to 300 mg (Ananth 1986).[1] Although some patients have shown responses at doses as low as 75 mg, traditionally a dose in the range of 150 mg to 250 mg seems to be most effective. We usually choose a once-a-day dosing, at bedtime, to allow for better compliance with taking the medication. In addition, we have found that this dosing approach minimizes the side effects in many cases, and that there is less complaint of sedation, one of the major side effects of clomipramine. Occasionally, patients cannot tolerate 200 mg or 250 mg of clomipramine at once, in which case the dose is split and given twice a day, in the morning and at bedtime, with a smaller dose given in the morning to minimize daytime sedation.

Of course, when considering clomipramine, as when prescribing any tricyclic antidepressant, therapists should use their clinical judgment and take into account differences in age response and dosing. (See Leonard et al., Chapter 6, this volume, for a discussion of treatment of children with OCD.) Until very recently, therapists could not use clomipramine in people over age 65 because of its status as an investigational drug in the United States. We have had some clinical experience with patients in their early 60s, most of whom were women weighing approximately 100 pounds who could suffice with 100 mg to 150 mg rather than the 250 mg we give most patients initially. In general, elderly patients may be able to get by with a smaller dose; they may, in fact, not tolerate the larger dose. Therapists need to be cognizant of several points when considering clomipramine for elderly patients, because these patients are more prone to side effects:

- Elderly patients are more prone to orthostatic hypotension and dizziness, which can result in falling when getting out of bed and risking a hip fracture. Therefore, clinicians should ask about these symptoms, check for orthostatic hypotension, and consider lowering the clomipramine dose.
- Constipation can be a side effect that can result in fecal impaction or

---

[1]A cautionary note in using clomipramine at doses greater than 250 mg must be made. The CIBA-Geigy Corporation has released a warning indicating that there is an increased instance of seizures in patients with a dose of 300 mg or more (2.1% [10 of 472 patients] versus 0.48% [12 of 2,514 patients] at doses of 250 mg or less). Thus, CIBA-Geigy has restricted the maximum dose to 250 mg a day (DeVeaugh-Geiss et al. 1989).

hemorrhoids; again, if the symptom is severe, lower the dose and/or add a stool softener or prune juice.

- Another side effect is a nondescript type of mental cloudiness that some patients describe as "not thinking as clearly or quickly" or as "being forgetful." Clinicians must not assume that this is dementia in elderly patients; decreasing the dose or a trial off medications might be helpful in making the differential diagnosis.

- Dehydration is likely to increase drug serum level and make the patient toxic. If an elderly patient becomes ill and dehydrated, the dose may need to be decreased until the patient rehydrates.

- Elderly patients are often on other, additional medications. Any potentially harmful interactions, such as risk of cardiac arrhythmias, should be assessed before starting clomipramine and monitored throughout treatment.

Side Effects

The side effects of clomipramine are typical of those seen with other tricyclic antidepressants. The literature disagrees on the relationship between side effects and plasma levels. Stern et al. (1980) found no relationship between side effects and serum level. However, Capstick (1977) felt that the side effects were dose dependent, although the side effects, as well as the therapeutic effects, varied from patient to patient. Our own clinical experience seems to indicate that there is a dose-dependent relationship in side effects but that there is considerable individual variability. In a systematic study of diminished dosing of clomipramine, we found that patients could tolerate a 40% drop in dose with no deterioration in symptom improvement and yet some decrease in side effects (Pato et al. 1990) (also see the second case history at the end of this chapter).

Despite the serotonergic and noradrenergic properties of clomipramine, most of the side effects are anticholinergic in nature (Stern et al. 1980). The most commonly reported side effects are dry mouth, constipation, tremor, increased appetite, weight gain, orthostatic hypotension, decreased sex drive, anorgasmia, increased sweating, lethargy, exercise intolerance, and mental cloudiness (J. DeVeaugh-Geiss, CIBA-Geigy Corp., personal communication, December 1989). Stern et al. (1980) noted that during the first 4 weeks of a study of clomipramine, patients reported significant side effects, including eye-focusing problems, constipation, dizziness, drowsiness, unsteady hands, dry mouth, and increased sweating. However, by the end of the 7-week study, only unsteady hands, dry mouth, and sweating maintained statistically significant severity.

In general, patients habituate to most of these side effects over time. Dry mouth is considered by some to be the most significant long-term side effect because of the effects of decreased saliva on dental health. Clinicians can recommend good oral hygiene and the avoidance of sugared candies to keep the mouth moist; instead, sugarless gum and candies are advised, and saliva substitutes might even be considered.

Constipation can often be handled by having patients stay well hydrated. We often recommend to our patients a minimum of eight glasses of fluid per day, increased fiber in their diet, and a regular schedule of exercise. If this does not work, a stool softener such as docusate sodium (Colace), 100 mg up to 300 mg per day, or psyllium hydrophilic mucilloid (Metamucil) is added.

Should the patient complain of nausea, the therapist can recommend taking the clomipramine with food.

Fatigue is also a problem, and for this reason we often give the full dose of medication at bedtime. If fatigue on awakening is noted, we move the evening dose from bedtime to 7:00 P.M. and then to 9:00 P.M., and this often helps. If this alone does not work, decreasing the dose or dividing it to twice a day or three times a day may help, although the major portion of the medicine is still taken at bedtime.

Occasionally, our patients, as with others on tricyclic antidepressants, develop urinary retention. This can usually be managed with a bethanechol derivative of 25 mg up to three times a day.

Mental cloudiness or mild memory deficit is a symptom that, although present in many of our patients, is usually well tolerated. Often, reassurance that the symptom is not permanent and is not the beginning of senile dementia is enough to put the patient at ease. Occasionally, a patient finds this side effect intolerable, in which case the dose must be decreased or the medication stopped.

Monteiro et al. (1987) reported a high incidence of anorgasmia in patients with OCD who were being treated with clomipramine. They noted that 22 of 24 male and female OCD patients with normal sexual function developed anorgasmia on clomipramine. This symptom occurred in most cases within 3 days of starting treatment at very low doses of 25 mg to 50 mg. Only 2 of the 22 patients found remission of this symptom within 2 to 3 months on clomipramine, although all patients had the return of normal sexual functioning within 3 days of stopping clomipramine. The authors point out that eliciting a history of this side effect was difficult. Patients were reticent to report it; in fact, in 36% of the cases it was not reported on a standardized questionnaire but only on direct questioning. To our knowledge this is the only systematic study of anorgasmia in treating OCD with clomipramine. In our clinical experience many patients experience some decrease in orgasm or sex drive, but we have found that decreasing the dose lessens the severity of this side effect in many patients (see case histories at the end of this chapter). In addition, we have found clomipramine to be helpful in those patients who experience premature ejaculation.

The standard recommendation for use during pregnancy holds for clomipramine as with any drug (Cohen et. al. 1989; Elia et al. 1987). Unless the illness poses a significant threat to the mental and physical well-being of the mother and the unborn child, medication during pregnancy should be avoided. In the case of OCD, especially with the proven efficacy of behavioral treatment, it is probably best to avoid the use of medication during pregnancy if possible. We have had only one patient who might have benefited from antiobsessional medication during pregnancy. In this patient her contamination fears became so great that she was unable to eat, and had marked decrease in her weight during the last trimester of pregnancy and became quite anemic.

Compliance Issues

Because of the considerable time lag between initial dosing and onset of significant improvement at 6 to 10 weeks, the patient will need a lot of encouragement to remain compliant with the treatment regimen. Because side effects often appear before any clinical improvement, patients are prone to early discouragement with clomipramine. Often, simply talking with the patient before the onset of side effects or improvement will considerably help compliance. Side effects can be at their worst when initially starting the clomipramine, but usually improve over time. Occasionally, one sees a mild exacerbation in OCD symptoms within the first few days of starting the medicine. This should not discourage continuation of the medicine. It may be helpful to discuss with some patients that this will happen, but with other patients this awareness may lead to increased obsessing and avoidance of the medication. Because this symptom worsening does not happen in every case, the clinician must judge on an individual basis what to tell the patient.

Treatment Response

Most studies have noted that although the onset of improvement may be noticeable by 4 weeks, often it is not significant until 6 to 10 weeks. Thorén et. al. (1980b) found that patients continued to improve even up to 12 weeks. Thus, most researchers recommend continuing treatment for up to 12 weeks before considering a patient a "nonresponder" (Volavka et al. 1985; Zohar and Insel 1987a, 1987b). Initially, patients should be warned they may not see much improvement. The first sign of improvement is usually not a disappearance of certain obsessions or compulsions but a subtle decrease in the intensity of the urge to perform them or an increase in ability to resist symptoms. Given that the response may be quite delayed, it is felt that maximizing the dose of medication allows for the least delay in improvement. It has been our clinical experience that patients may continue to have further gradual and consistent improvement for several months (see the second case history at the end of the chapter). As will be outlined below, some data show that patients can continue to do well on less medicine once they have achieved maximum improvement.

In clinical practice we do not often obtain blood levels unless 1) the patient remains unresponsive at high doses, 2) there is a question about compliance, or 3) the patient seems to be having side effects that are inconsistent with his or her dose of medication. There is considerable variability from laboratory to laboratory in the report of serum levels, and the clinician should be wary of comparing results from different laboratories. It has been established that clomipramine levels reach steady state within 7 to 14 days after a constant dose is maintained (Luscombe et al. 1980). Traditionally, doses are drawn about 12 hours after the last dose. Some have recommended aiming for plasma levels of 100 ng/ml to 250 ng/ml for clomipramine and 230 ng/ml to 550 ng/ml for DCMI (Stern et al. 1980), although the exact relation of these dosages to obsessive-compulsive symptom remission remains unclear.

Duration and Discontinuation of Clomipramine Treatment

Anecdoctal reports of recurrence of symptoms with discontinuation of clomipramine have been reported in the literature as has the occasional case of a patient staying symptom-free after clomipramine discontinuation (Ananth 1986; Åsberg et al. 1982; Capstick 1973; Flament et al. 1985; Leonard et al. 1989; Thorén et al. 1980b; Yaryura-Tobias et al. 1976). We recently reported a double-blind discontinuation study with clomipramine (Pato et al. 1988) and found that 17 of the 18 patients who completed the study had recurrence of their OCD symptoms of significant severity to require reinstitution of clomipramine. In 16 of these 18 patients, symptoms worsened significantly by the end of the 7-week study, and clomipramine was reinstituted in most patients. The duration of treatment prior to discontinuation (mean = 10.7 months ± 5.5 months) and serum levels of clomipramine and DCMI (mean = 194 ± 187 ng/ml and 351 ± 189 ng/ml, respectively) did not have an effect on recurrence. This study would seem to imply that clomipramine needs to be given for at least a year or more in most patients in order to maintain improvement. However, with some reports in the literature of patients remaining symptom-free after discontinuation of clomipramine, at least a trial off medication may be warranted (Pato 1990).

With the less-than-optimistic possibility of remaining symptom-free off clomipramine, another possible alternative is to minimize the dose of clomipramine used. Pato et al. (1990) reported an open trial in which OCD patients on clomipramine for a minimum of 10 ± 5 months were able to tolerate decreases in dose of 40% (from 270 mg ± 20 mg to 165 mg ± 19 mg) without deterioration in OCD symptom improvement. There is also hope that new agents other than clomipramine may provide a more permanent improvement in OCD symptoms (see Pigott, Chapter 3, this volume).

Case Histories

Case 1

P.J. is a 36-year-old, obese male, employed full time, who has had a history of OCD since childhood. Most of his many obsessions and compulsions centered around contamination. When he first entered our clinic his life seemed totally consumed with thoughts and rituals. He carried a plastic bag in his pocket filled with pieces of soapy, wet paper. When someone accidentally bumped into him in the subway or touched an item belonging to him, he had a set pattern of dabbing himself or the object to cleanse it. However, this ritual was often not enough; when returning from the grocery store, he sometimes felt compelled to wipe down the groceries after first taking a shower himself and then to throw away some groceries to ensure that those left were not contaminated. He would shower up to 10 times a day, or anytime he felt contaminated. There were certain articles and areas in his apartment he could not get adequately clean, so he would, for example, not sit on the sofa or touch his stereo. His eating was accompanied by the same urge to perform and ritualize as were his obsessions and compulsions. For instance, he would have to eat a certain number of yogurt containers at one sitting.

By the end of the first month of clomipramine at 300 mg/day, P.J. noticed improvement. Initial improvement took the form of an increased ability to resist and less depressed mood; but by the end of 6 weeks, he began to report actual reductions in obsessive-compulsive symptoms. His showers decreased to 1 to 2 times a day, and there was a noticeable decrease in the need to wipe things off at home and work. He also had less need to throw away groceries for fear they were contaminated. Unfortunately, P.J. also experienced some side effects. Most notable was carbohydrate craving, resulting in a 50-pound weight gain. He also had to tolerate dry mouth and increased sweating, for which he compensated by increasing his fluid intake. P.J. also had decreased ability to achieve orgasm and a mild elevation in liver serum glutamic-oxaloacetic transaminase (SGOT) and serum glutamic pyruvic transaminase (SGPT). He was more than willing to tolerate these side effects in exchange for his symptom improvement. However, because of the elevated liver transaminases, we decided on a trial off medication at 5 months.

Within 7 weeks of withdrawal, P.J. began to notice episodes of severe symptoms. For example, he would find that he had an increased urge to wipe and touch himself when he saw an indigent person on the subway, and he began to feel the urge to eat three containers of yogurt at one sitting. However, his side effects disappeared, and his weight began to drop, as did his levels of SGOT and SGPT, which returned to normal.

P.J. was restarted on clomipramine at 50 mg, which was quickly increased, by 50 mg every 2 to 3 days, to 300 mg. Again, he noticed improvement within 3 weeks. Within 7 weeks he was able to use items in his apartment that he previously had been unable to approach because of contamination fears. Unfortunately, his side effects also returned, including craving for sweets, sweating, and mild tremor. This time, however, sexual functioning remained normal. Within 6 months of restarting clomipramine, P.J. reported he was no longer throwing away groceries and no longer had to carry a plastic bag with wet paper towels in his pockets, although when the urge to wipe became very strong, he might spit on a piece of tissue and touch himself in the proper manner. The psychiatrist and patient global assessment at 250 mg of clomipramine was 50% improvement (Pato et al. 1988, 1990). Unfortunately, side effects at this time included decreased sex drive, increased appetite, weight gain, dry mouth, increased sweating, and elevated SGOT and SGPT levels. Evaluation by a hepatologist was inconclusive as to whether this elevation was due to fatty infiltration secondary to morbid obesity or a drug reaction. Because of the increase in liver transaminases, clomipramine was again discontinued.

Case 2

E.M. was a 42-year-old married man and amateur athlete with a 20-year history of OCD. His compulsions included a need to pick up glass and matches on the street because of a sense of overresponsibility that if he did not, a child would get hurt. He also had an obsession that his copy of the newspaper contained national secrets, and he had to destroy it, and that the plastic bag in which it came might suffocate a child. He would tear the paper and bag into little pieces and then throw them away. He would often avoid reading the newspaper in order not to be bothered by this obsession and its consequent compulsion. E.M. estimated that symptoms resulted in his functioning at 60% of his potential.

Within 2 months of starting clomipramine at 300 mg/day, his symptoms had reduced significantly. As he described it, "The medicine chokes off the anxiety so that the obsessions or compulsions don't have a chance to get started." The obsessions about the newspaper disappeared completely, and he had only an occasional need, not even daily, to pick up a match or piece of glass he saw on the street. His global assessment of his improvement was 80%. Side effects, however, included difficulty with orgasm and ejaculation, excessive sweating, 10- to 15-pound weight gain, mild dry mouth, and mild constipation. The side effect that was most bothersome to him was a sense of heaviness in his legs that resulted in decreased exercise tolerance. Thus, instead of being able to run 10 miles a day, he was down to 3 to 5 miles a day.

Clomipramine was discontinued in a double-blind fashion. Within 4 weeks, marked deterioration was noted. Obsessive thoughts about national secrets had returned almost to the point of causing panic attacks, and E.M. felt that it was taking a significant effort to resist the compulsions to pick up glass or matches. He also complained of some psychomotor agitation, increased appetite, and difficulty with sleep. Side effects improved, however. In particular, E.M. noticed improved exercise tolerance. Within 7 weeks of discontinuation, he had developed a new obsession: a fear that he had been contaminated by the AIDS virus even though his risk was quite low. He could also no longer resist the urge to pick up glass off the street. His sleep problems had subsided, and he reported no specific neurovegetative symptoms.

Clomipramine was reinstituted at only 150 mg/day in an attempt to minimize the exercise intolerance. Within 3 weeks, E.M. noted a remission of his symptoms—obsessions about national security in the newspaper and about AIDS, and compulsions to pick up matches and glass—which had virtually disappeared. He was still avoiding reading some parts of the newspaper, but his anxiety had diminished significantly. However, side effects, particularly increased sweating, dry mouth, and exercise intolerance, also returned. Within 3 months of restarting clomipramine, E.M. again reported global improvement of 75% to 80% on 150 mg/day, with less than 30 minutes combined per day of obsessions and compulsions and some days in which he was totally symptom-free. The side effects of marked increase in sweating, mild dry mouth, mild constipation, and problems with orgasm remained, as did some exercise intolerance, although it was less severe. At 4 months, clomipramine dosage was decreased further to 125 mg. This brought no deterioration in his symptom relief, which he now rated as 90% to 95% improved, but did further reduce his side effects. His constipation cleared completely, he had only minor dry mouth and much less sweating, and he felt that his ability to exercise was within 80% to 90% of his pretreatment level. At 10 months on clomipramine, a further decrease to 100 mg/day was attempted, but this was followed by mild but notable deterioration in improvement. Total time on obsessions and compulsions increased from 30 minutes to 90 minutes per day, with a more irritable and anxious mood. A return to 125 mg brought a quick remission of symptoms to the 90% to 95% improvement level within 4 weeks.

Summary

In our experience clomipramine is an effective and well-tolerated treatment for OCD. In most cases, doses close to 250 mg for a minimum of 10 weeks are required to obtain reasonable efficacy. The most bothersome side effects are dry mouth, constipation, decreased sex drive, and anorgasmia. The present data indicate that the antiobsessional effects of clomipramine are usually lost when the medication is discontinued. Studies of clomipramine with treatment duration for greater than 1 year are warranted.

References

Ananth J: Clomipramine: an antiobsessive drug. Can J Psychiatry 31:253–258, 1986

Ananth J, Pecknold JC, van den Steen N, et al: Double-blind comparative study of clomipramine and amitriptyline in obsessive neurosis. Prog Neuropsychopharmacol Biol Psychiatry 5:257–262, 1981

Åsberg M, Thorén P, Bertilsson L: Clomipramine treatment of obsessive disorder: biochemical and clinical aspects. Psychopharmacol Bull 18(3): 13–21, 1982

Capstick N: Psychiatric side-effects of clomipramine (Anafranil). J Int Med Res 1:444–448, 1973

Capstick N: Clinical experience in the treatment of obsessional states. J Int Med Res 5 (suppl 5):71–80, 1977

Cohen LS, Heller VL, Rosenbaum JF: Treatment guidelines for psychotropic drug use in pregnancy. Psychosomatics 30:25–33, 1989

DeVeaugh-Geiss J, Landau P, Katz R: Treatment of obsessive-compulsive disorder with clomipramine. Psychiatric Annals 19:97–101, 1989

Eisen JL, Rasmussen SA: Obsessive compulsive disorder with psychotic features, in 1988 New Research Program and Abstracts. Washington, DC, American Psychiatric Association, 1988, NR256, p 126

Elia J, Katz IR, Simpson GM: Teratogenicity of psychotherapeutic medications. Psychopharmacol Bull 23:531–586, 1987

Fernandez CE, Lopez-Ibor JJ: Monochlorimipramine in the treatment of psychiatric patients resistant to other therapies. Actas Luso Esp Neurol Psiquiatr Cienc Afines 26:119–147, 1967

Flament MF, Rapoport JL, Berg CJ, et al: Clomipramine treatment of childhood obsessive-compulsive disorder: a double-blind controlled study. Arch Gen Psychiatry 42:977–983, 1985

Goodman WK, Price LH, Rasmussen SA, et al: The Yale-Brown Obsessive Compulsive Scale, I: development, use, and reliability. Arch Gen Psychiatry 46:1006–1011, 1989a

Goodman WK, Price LH, Rasmussen SA, et al: The Yale-Brown Obsessive Compulsive Scale, II: validity. Arch Gen Psychiatry 46:1012–1016, 1989b

Hamilton M: A rating scale for depression. J Neurol Neurosurg Psychiatry 23:56–66, 1960

Insel TR: New Findings in Obsessive-Compulsive Disorder. Washington, DC, American Psychiatric Press, 1984

Insel TR, Murphy DL, Cohen RM, et al: Obsessive-compulsive disorder: a double-blind trial of clomipramine and clorgyline. Arch Gen Psychiatry 40:605–612, 1983

Jenike MA, Baer L, Minichiello WE: Obsessive Compulsive Disorders: Theory and Management. Littleton, MA, PSG Publishing Company, 1986

Leonard H, Swedo S, Rapoport JL, et al: Treatment of childhood obsessive-compulsive disorder with clomipramine and desmethylimipramine: a double-blind crossover comparison. Psychopharmacol Bull 24:93–95, 1988

Leonard H, Swedo SE, Rapoport JL, et al: Treatment of childhood obsessive-compulsive disorder with clomipramine and desmethylimipramine in children and adolescents: a double-blind crossover comparison. Arch Gen Psychiatry 46:1088–1092, 1989

Lopez-Ibor JJ: Intravenous perfusions of monochlorimipramine: technique and results, in The Present Status of Psychotropic Drugs. Edited by Cerletti A, Bove FJ. Amsterdam, Excerpta Medica Foundation, 1969, pp 519–521

Luscombe DK, Wright J, Stern RS, et al: Plasma concentrations of clomipramine and desmethylclomipramine in obsessive-compulsive neurosis. Postgrad Med J 56 (suppl 1):140–143, 1980

Marks IM, Stern R, Mawson D, et al: Clomipramine and exposure for obsessive-compulsive rituals. Br J Psychiatry 136:1–25, 1980

Mavissakalian M, Michelson L: Tricyclic antidepressants in obsessive-compulsive disorder: antiobsessional or antidepressant agents? J Nerv Ment Dis 171:301–306, 1983

Mavissakalian M, Turner SM, Michelson L, et al: Tricyclic antidepressants in obsessive compulsive disorder: antiobsessional or antidepressant agents? Am J Psychiatry 142:572–576, 1985

Monteiro WO, Noshirvani HF, Marks IM, et al: Anorgasmia from clomipramine in obsessive-compulsive disorder: a controlled trial. Br J Psychiatry 151:107–112, 1987

Montgomery SA: Clomipramine in obsessional neurosis: a placebo controlled trial. Pharmaceutical Medicine 1:189–192, 1980

Murphy DL, Zohar J, Benkelfat C, et al: Obsessive–compulsive disorder as a serotonin subsystem–related behavioral disorder. Br J Psychiatry 155 (suppl 8):15–24, 1989

Pato MT: When to discontinue treatment, in Obsessive-Compulsive Disorders: Theory and Management, 2nd Edition. Edited by Jenike MA, Baer L, Minichiello WE. Littleton, MA, PSG Publishing Company, 1990

Pato MT, Zohar-Kadouch R, Zohar J, et al: Return of symptoms after discontinuation of clomipramine in patients with obsessive-compulsive disorder. Am J Psychiatry 145:1521–1525, 1988

Pato MT, Hill JL, Murphy DL: A clomipramine dosage reduction study in the case of long-term treatment of obsessive-compulsive disorder patients. Psychopharmacol Bull 26:211–214, 1990

Renynghe de Voxrie GV: Anafranil (G-34586) in obsessive neurosis. Acta Neurol Belg 68:787–792, 1968

Stern RS, Marks IM, Mawson D, et al: Clomipramine and exposure for compulsive rituals, II: plasma levels, side effects and outcome. Br J Psychiatry 136:161–166, 1980

Thorén P, Åsberg M, Bertilsson L, et al: Clomipramine treatment of obsessive-compulsive disorder, II: biochemical aspects. Arch Gen Psychiatry 37:1289–1294, 1980a

Thorén P, Åsberg M, Cronholm B, et al: Clomipramine treatment of obsessive-compulsive disorder, I: a controlled clinical trial. Arch Gen Psychiatry 37:1281–1285, 1980b

Träskman L, Åsberg M, Bertilsson L, et al: Plasma levels of chlorimipramine and its desmethyl metabolite during treatment of depression: differential biochemical and clinical effects of two compounds. Clin Pharmacol Ther 26:600–610, 1979

Volavka J, Neziroglu F, Yaryura-Tobias JA: Clomipramine and imipramine in obsessive-compulsive disorder. Psychiatry Res 14:83–91, 1985

Yaryura-Tobias JA, Neziroglu F, Bergman L: Chlorimipramine for obsessive compulsive neurosis: an organic approach. Curr Ther Res 20:541–547, 1976

Zohar J, Insel TR: Drug treatment of obsessive-compulsive disorder. J Affective Disord 13:193–202, 1987a

Zohar J, Insel TR: Obsessive-compulsive disorder: psychobiological approaches to diagnosis, treatment, and pathophysiology. Biol Psychiatry 22:667–687, 1987b

Chapter 3

Fluoxetine in the Treatment of Obsessive-Compulsive Disorder

Teresa A. Pigott, M.D.

*F*luoxetine is the first antidepressant with selective serotonin (5-hydroxytryptamine [5-HT]) uptake inhibition properties to be widely utilized and commercially available in the United States. In addition, perhaps because of this selective property that is similar to clomipramine's ability to inhibit 5-HT uptake, fluoxetine has been found to exhibit some antiobsessive properties, suggesting that it may prove to be useful in the treatment of obsessive-compulsive disorder (OCD) (Fontaine and Chouinard 1986). In this chapter we present information concerning the clinical efficacy of fluoxetine in the treatment of OCD, including several case histories. Also included is some information concerning dosage, side effects, and potential drug interactions in fluoxetine treatment.

Fluoxetine: Structure, Mechanism of Action, Pharmacokinetics, and Dosage

Fluoxetine is a straight-chain phenylpropylamine compound that is distinct from the tricyclic antidepressants in both pharmacology and structure (Dista Products Company 1988). It is in fact a "bicyclic" antidepressant that is a selective inhibitor of the uptake of 5-HT into presynaptic neurons, with a specific ability to block the action of the 5-HT transport system that removes 5-HT from the synaptic cleft between nerve cells. This blockade results in an increase in the amount of active 5-HT within the cleft and the 5-HT receptor sites, initially causing an increased stimulation of 5-HT receptors. However, the chronic presence of increased amounts of 5-HT in the synaptic cleft may well result in longer-term adaptive changes in receptor number and sensitivity.

Investigators have proposed that OCD patients may have 5-HT receptors that are either exquisitely sensitive to 5-HT or increased in number, or both, and that the chronic effect of agents such as clomipramine or fluoxetine is to decrease the number or sensitivity (i.e., "down-regulate") 5-HT receptors (Zohar and Insel 1987). This effect would then result in a "re-regulation" of the receptors, with a subsequent diminution in OCD behaviors, which were perhaps contributed to by a relative 5-HT excess. Hence, the net effect of fluoxetine would not be to increase overall availability of 5-HT in the brain, but instead to reset the central serotonergic system back into equilibrium with its appropriate feedback mechanisms. The etiology of OCD and/or the initial event that dysregulates the serotonergic system and its usual intricate modulation remain elusive.

Regardless of the exact mechanism of action, the effects of fluoxetine on the metabolic pathway of 5-HT are implicated in both its antidepressant and its probable antiobsessive properties. Several studies have shown that fluoxetine exhibits virtually no affinity for 5-HT receptors (5-HT_1 and 5-HT_2), suggesting that fluoxetine's effects are limited to its inhibition of the 5-HT uptake mechanism rather than to direct or indirect agonist effects on 5-HT receptors (Richelson 1988). Unlike clomipramine, which is metabolized to a metabolite with noradrenergic properties, fluoxetine is metabolized to the active metabolite norfluoxetine, which also produces potent, 5-HT–specific uptake inhibition (Lemberger et al. 1985). While maximum plasma concentrations of fluoxetine occur approximately 6 to 8 hours after the initial dose (Stark et al. 1985), both fluoxetine and its active metabolite have extended half-lives: 2 to 3 days and 7 to 9 days, respectively (Lemberger et al. 1985). These extended half-lives result in equilibration of steady-state plasma concentrations only after 2 to 4 weeks of a fixed-dose regimen (Stark et al. 1985). Consequently, rapid escalation of dose secondary to lack of efficacy at lower dosages before 2 to 3 weeks of treatment at a specific dose is probably unwarranted.

Fluoxetine's long half-life is helpful in that occasional missed doses have minimal clinical effects and can also allow for more liberal dosage strategies, including less-than-daily dosage strategies in patients with enhanced sensitivity to drug side effects. In fact, in depressed patients, Montgomery (1986) recently reported that fluoxetine could be effective if given in 20-mg once-a-week doses after an initial 7 days of treatment with 60 mg/day in depressed patients. However, fluoxetine's half-life has also contributed to considerable controversy concerning plasma level determinations and adequate therapeutic doses for selective antidepressant, antibulimic, or antiobsessive responses. Preliminary studies in depression indicated that fluoxetine doses of 20 mg/day were as effective, and better tolerated, than daily dosages of 40 to 60 mg/day (Fabre and Putman 1987; Wernicke et al. 1987). However, our initial experience has suggested that daily dosages in the 60- to 80-mg per day range appear to be more efficacious in treating OCD than do lower dosage schedules. Certainly, further controlled studies utilizing different fixed doses of fluoxetine are needed to clarify this important issue. While commercial assays for monitoring fluoxetine levels are available, their use is limited by the lack of studies correlating clinical efficacy with drug plasma levels.

Fluoxetine is absorbed well after oral administration, and its absorption appears to be unaffected by food ingestion (Lemberger et al. 1985). Its primary site of metabolism is the liver, and it is eliminated from the kidneys as conjugated metabolites. Consequently, fluoxetine's metabolism may be affected in patients with impaired hepatic function (Dista Products Company 1988) or potentially in patients receiving multiple drug therapy. Initial studies failed to show significant renal effects from fluoxetine usage, including a lack of significant difficulties in renally impaired patients (Aronoff et al. 1984), although fluoxetine's long half-life suggests that appropriate precautions should be utilized during chronic fluoxetine administration in patients with compromised renal function.

Fluoxetine Trials in Treatment of Obsessive-Compulsive Disorder

Fontaine and Chouinard (1985) reported the use of fluoxetine in seven OCD patients in an open trial in 1985. They reported that six of the seven patients responded to fluoxetine at doses of 60 to 90 mg/day and concluded that it was as effective as clomipramine, which had previously been administered to these patients. They also noted that the patients tolerated fluoxetine "more easily." In a more expanded version of this study, Fontaine and Chouinard (1986) reported the detailed results of the 9-week trial in OCD patients (40–80 mg/day), which indicated significant improvement on the Comprehensive Psychopathological Rating Scale (CPRS) (Åsberg et al. 1978), but no correlation between improvement of depressive symptoms and improvement of obsessional symptoms.

Since that initial report there have been numerous anecdotal reports of the antiobsessive properties of fluoxetine, but only one controlled trial of fluoxetine has been reported, and this one was conducted in a single-blind, although placebo-controlled, fashion (Turner et al. 1985a). Ten OCD patients who received 10 weeks of fluoxetine treatment (20–80 mg/day) were reported to maintain significant "subjective" improvement on the patient-rated Symptom Checklist-58 obsessive-compulsive subscale (SCL-58-OC) (Derogatis et al. 1974). A correlation between pretreatment levels of depression and eventual reduction of obsessive-compulsive symptoms was also reported.

Fontaine and Chouinard (1989) have reported the results of another open trial of fluoxetine in the treatment of OCD that involved 50 patients with OCD. They reported that 43 of the 50 patients (86%) responded to fluoxetine (dosage range = 60–100 mg/day) as measured by improvement of at least two points on the seven-point Clinical Global Impression (CGI) scale of severity of OCD; moreover, after 12 months of fluoxetine treatment, there were significant decreases in three OCD scales (CPRS, CGI scale, and SCL-58-OC subscale) over the next several months of treatment. Jenike and colleagues (1989) reported a 12-week open trial of fluoxetine in 61 patients with OCD and found significant reductions in depressive and obsessive-compulsive symptoms.

In light of these considerations, we (Pigott et al., in press) felt that it was particularly important in OCD patients to perform a double-blind trial of fluoxetine and compare the efficacy of fluoxetine to clomipramine in a controlled fashion. We also assessed the side effects of fluoxetine and compared them to clomipramine's side effects by administering biweekly a self-rating physical symptom checklist scale that rated 32 potential side effects from 0 (none) to 3 (severe) throughout the 26-week controlled trial.

Thirty-two patients meeting DSM-III-R criteria for OCD were enrolled in the controlled trial in which clomipramine was compared with fluoxetine in the treatment of OCD. The patients consisted of two cohorts: a randomized group ($n = 11$) and a nonrandomized group ($n = 21$) of patients who had originally been stabilized on clomipramine and had voluntarily elected to be "crossed over" for a fluoxetine trial. All patients were serially assessed by experienced raters using several rating scales, including the Hamilton Depression Rating Scale (HDRS) (Hamilton 1960), the Yale-Brown Obsessive-Compulsive Scale (Y-BOCS) (Goodman et al. 1989), and the National Institute of Mental Health (NIMH) Obsessive-Compulsive Scale (NIMH-OC Scale) (Insel et al. 1983b) during the double-blind, crossover study. Patients in the randomized group were medication-free for at least 3 weeks prior to entering a 2-week placebo-controlled washout period followed by the 24-week random assignment crossover portion that consisted of two 10-week periods of active drug treatment separated by a 4-week interval of medication taper and placebo substitution.

Ten of the 11 randomized OCD patients completed 10 weeks of clomipramine treatment (209 ± 13 mg/day) and 10 weeks of treatment with fluoxetine (75 ± 4 mg/day). Analysis of data using repeated-measures ANOVA revealed that both drug treatments resulted in equal and significant reductions in rating scores. Patients reported a consistently higher incidence or worsening of most physical symptoms on clomipramine as compared with fluoxetine treatment. There were significant increases in OCD and depressive ratings associated with drug (clomipramine or fluoxetine) discontinuation and placebo substitution, and both medications were also associated with substantial lags in therapeutic efficacy (6–10 weeks), despite previous substantial responses with the first medication (clomipramine or fluoxetine) administered.

The nonrandomized group received 10 weeks of double-blind fluoxetine after a baseline-blinded clomipramine period and a 1-week placebo period. Twenty of the 21 patients completed 10 weeks of treatment with fluoxetine (80 mg/day). ANOVA with repeated measures and associated paired and Student's *t* tests revealed a significant drug effect with time: by 10 weeks of fluoxetine treatment, all scores had decreased to values equal to, or below, the level of the baselines on clomipramine, indicating equal or better efficacy of fluoxetine compared with clomipramine. Moreover, these analyses also showed significant increases in OCD scores over the first 6 weeks of fluoxetine treatment. Significant (>95%) reductions in platelet 5-HT concentrations were found after both clomipramine and fluoxetine treatment.

In summary, in two OCD patient subgroups ($n = 32$), treatment with fluoxetine for 10 weeks was found to produce therapeutic effects equivalent to those of randomized treatment with clomipramine for 10 weeks ($n = 10$) and of previous nonrandomized treatment with clomipramine for 15 months ($n = 21$). In addition, most patients (85%) in the larger, long-term clomipramine treatment subgroup achieved similar reductions in obsessive-compulsive symptoms and in depression after 10 weeks of fluoxetine treatment, suggesting that responders to clomipramine treatment are often responders to fluoxetine treatment. In both patient subgroups, relapses in obsessive-compulsive symptoms were precipitated by drug tapering and placebo substitution following both clomipramine and fluoxetine administration, and both clomipramine and fluoxetine were associated with equivalent and significant time lags in the attainment of therapeutic efficacy as measured by OCD symptom reduction. That is, immediate antecedent drug treatment and/or response (clomipramine or fluoxetine) did not accelerate the length of time necessary to achieve equivalent obsessive-compulsive or depressive response with the second drug (clomipramine or fluoxetine), despite the fact that both clomipramine and fluoxetine are thought to act by a common mechanism (i.e., 5-HT uptake inhibition). Fewer side effects were reported during fluoxetine than clomipramine treatment in both patient subgroups, although sexual dysfunction was reported frequently with both drugs.

Further, an antidepressant response apparently does not necessarily correlate with an antiobsessive response in patients with OCD (Mavissakalian and Michelson 1983; Mavissakalian et al. 1985) (see the case histories at the end of this chapter). This lack of correlation can be a particularly frustrating experience for both the patient and the clinician. It has been estimated that approximately 70% of patients with OCD will also experience at least one depressive episode (Goodwin et al. 1969), and concomitant anxiety disorders are also seen in approximately 30% of OCD patients (Rasmussen and Eisen 1989; Vaughan 1976). While depression commonly complicates OCD as a secondary phenomena, it is important also to assess the patient's affective symptoms as an additional primary disorder. Many people have posited that OCD may represent a form of depression (i.e., an affective-spectrum disorder) based upon several interesting findings, including 1) the very frequent occurrence of depression in OCD; 2) the finding that OCD patients exhibit some abnormal biologic markers similar to those exhibited by depressed patients (nonsuppression on the dexamethasone suppression test) (Åsberg et al. 1982; Cottraux et al. 1984; Insel et al. 1982b), shortened REM latency during sleep tracings (Insel et al. 1982a), and low platelet tritiated-imipramine binding sites (Weizman et al. 1986), among others; and 3) some evidence to suggest that relatives of patients with OCD exhibit higher than expected prevalence rates of affective disorders, alcoholism, and eating disorders (Insel et al. 1983a; Rasmussen and Eisen 1989). The dissociation of antidepressant and antiobsessive response to treatment with clomipramine and other 5-HT–selective uptake inhibitors suggests that OCD is not a form of depression, or perhaps that OCD represents a more recalcitrant form of mood disorder that requires higher antidepressant dosages or a more sustained duration of treatment than seems to be required in patients with mood disorders alone. This remains a controversial issue, but certainly one worth further systematic evaluation.

The issues of medication regimen, dosage, and duration of treatment in OCD remain rather elusive ones. Clomipramine does appear to have more efficacy at higher dosages (maximum = 250 mg/day), and patients often require extended treatment duration (8–12 weeks) before exhibiting improvement in their obsessions and compulsions. Previous studies with fluoxetine in depression failed to show that increasing the dosage of fluoxetine over the starting dose of 20 mg/day was of significant benefit; in fact, antidepressant responses at 20 mg/day were the same as those at 40 to 60 mg/day (Fabre and Putman 1987; Wernicke et al. 1987). Controlled, fixed-dose trials of fluoxetine in OCD have not yet been reported. However, it has been our impression that many OCD patients seem to respond more completely to dosages of 60 to 80 mg/day, particularly in terms of OCD symptoms. Some patients will even experience reemergence of their symptoms at lower dosages (see the first case history at the end of this chapter). Of course, this may well reflect these patients' effective therapeutic plasma level of medication rather than a simple dose-dependent regimen. However, assays for plasma fluoxetine concentrations are available commercially, but effective or therapeutic blood level guidelines have not yet been established for either depression or OCD. It has been our experience that fluoxetine also requires a longer duration of treatment for antiobsessive response than for antidepressant response, with many patients not having a significant reduction in their symptoms until 6 to 10 weeks of treatment.

There are many unanswered questions concerning the use of fluoxetine in OCD, including further studies of its comparable efficacy with clomipramine, and more complete information on treatment response rates and patterns. In addition, more information is needed on the long-term use of fluoxetine and its potential side effects, and on the rate of relapse of OCD after discontinuation of treatment with fluoxetine. This last issue is particularly critical, especially given the high rate of relapse reported by Pato et al. (1988) after the discontinuation of clomipramine treatment in OCD patients. Pato and colleagues reported that 16 of 18 OCD patients had substantial recurrence of OCD symptoms by the end of the 7-week placebo period, and 11 of the 18 patients had a significant increase in depressive symptoms. In contrast, Fontaine and Chouinard (1989) recently reported that only 8 of 35 OCD patients (23%) treated with fluoxetine relapsed within the first year of follow-up without medication. This is indeed an astonishing finding and one that suggests sustained long-term antiobsessive efficacy for fluoxetine in OCD. Hopefully, controlled studies will yield similar optimistic results.

The Side Effect, Drug Interaction, and Safety Profiles of Fluoxetine

The side-effect profile of fluoxetine is significantly different than that for most tricyclic antidepressants; this may be related to fluoxetine's relative neurotransmitter specificity, which includes a lack of anticholinergic effects (Feighner 1985). In extensive clinical trials (Dista Products Company 1988), the most commonly reported side effects associated with therapeutic doses of fluoxetine were nausea (21%), anxiety/excitation (10%–15%), and insomnia (14%). Other side effects that occurred in more than 10% of the patients treated with fluoxetine included headache (20%), drowsiness (12%), and diarrhea (12%); however 15.5% and 6.3% of the placebo-treated patients also reported headaches, and diarrhea was reported by 7% of placebo-treated patients in these comparison trials. Very few of these side effects led to drug discontinuation, although the manufacturers do recommend discontinuation of fluoxetine if rash or urticaria develop (Dista Products Company 1988). In comparative clinical trials, rash was observed in only 4% of the patients given fluoxetine as compared with 4% of those given tricyclic antidepressants and 2% of the patients given placebo (Dista Products Company 1988).

Perhaps most promising in terms of potential side effects is the lack of weight gain associated with fluoxetine therapy. This finding is in marked contrast to the findings with tricyclic antidepressants, which are often implicated in weight gain (Berken et al. 1984). In fact, fluoxetine has been associated with modest weight loss in depressed patients (Feighner and Cohn 1985) and is currently under investigation as an anorectic agent in the treatment of obesity (Ferguson 1986). Fluoxetine has also been found to be relatively safe in overdosage, without significant morbidity or mortality. There have been two deaths reported after fluoxetine overdosage (Wernicke 1985), but both patients ingested multiple medications including other antidepressants. Fluoxetine has limited cardiovascular effects (Fisch 1985), and its rate of seizure induction (Wernicke 1985) is similar to that of other marketed antidepressants (approximately 0.2%). As previously noted (Pigott et al., in press), fluoxetine treatment appears to be associated with substantial sexual dysfunction in patients being treated for OCD.

Fluoxetine is highly protein-bound in the plasma, and as such it has a significant potential for inducing drug interactions, particularly with medications that are also highly protein-bound via displacement effects. Clinical trials involving concomitant administration of secobarbital, chlorothiazide, tolbutamide, cimetidine, oral contraceptives, thyroid hormones, beta-blockers, or antacids, however, have failed to show significant drug interactions or adverse effects (Dista Products Company 1988). There are a number of reports implicating fluoxetine as a cause of increased plasma tricyclic antidepressant concentrations (Aranow et al. 1989; Downs et al. 1989; Vaughan 1988); this interaction can occur when two antidepressants are utilized concurrently or when a patient is being transferred from one antidepressant to fluoxetine. Particularly important has been the occurrence of adverse effects when monoamine oxidase inhibitor (MAOI) therapy was started 16 days after fluoxetine withdrawal (Sternbach 1988). The manufacturer's current recommendation is that a waiting period of 5 weeks should be allowed when switching from fluoxetine to an MAOI (Dista Products Company 1988). There also has been a report of adverse effects in a small number of patients treated with tryptophan and fluoxetine (Steiner and Fontaine 1986); consequently, such a combination is probably contraindicated.[1] Fluoxetine may reduce the clearance of diazepam (Rowe et al. 1985), although the clinical significance, if any, of this interaction is not known. Fluoxetine has not been shown to have additive effects when combined with alcohol; furthermore, in rats fluoxetine has been shown to lead to a decrease in alcohol consumption (Miksic et al. 1982). There have been several reports of fluoxetine inducing mania in susceptible patients (Lebegue 1987; Settle and Settle 1984; Turner et al. 1985b).

As with all new medications, there has been an outpouring of anecdotal reports of the emergence of "new" side effects and/or potential toxicities. Schatzberg (1989) mentioned the emergence of "increased bruising" in several female patients on fluoxetine who were subsequently found to have normal coagulation studies. We have also noted the emergence of this complaint in a very small percentage of women as well as occasional complaints of decreased libido in both men and women. Interestingly, our OCD patients have complained more of sedation than excitation with fluoxetine treatment. It is unclear whether this may repre-

---

[1]Because the use of L-tryptophan has recently (Fall 1989) been implicated in an increased incidence of eosinophilia, the authors advise against the prescribing and use of this agent, as discussed in this book, until the issue is resolved.

sent a differential drug sensitivity seen in OCD patients in contrast to depressed patients, or whether this instead reflects a dose-dependent characteristic. In general, fluoxetine is very well tolerated and offers a considerable advantage to those patients who have significant difficulties with weight gain during treatment with other antidepressants.

Case Histories

Case 1

Ms. J. was a 48-year-old divorced white female who had an approximately 12-year history of OCD. At the time of her initial visit, she complained of a variety of compulsive behaviors—notably, repeated checking, hoarding of trash, and obsessions concerning fears of contamination, with subsequent cleaning rituals. She was seriously incapacitated in her job as a secretary because of her pervasive obsessive-compulsive symptoms, which would result in her repeatedly checking her typing and spelling for errors, and her inability to perform any task at work without wiping her glasses a circumscribed number of times to "remove dirt." She estimated that she spent approximately four times as long as other coworkers on letters because she would have to check each line that she typed at least five times "for correctness." She had great difficulty sorting through the mail, because she was often unable to throw away any paper: "I am always afraid that I will throw something away that will be very important or that letters might contain money or checks that I missed." She noted that she often stayed several hours longer than her coworkers because she would feel obliged to check and recheck everything that she had typed that day and would also feel compelled to recheck the trash for "important items." She readily noted that these behaviors were irrational, but felt unable to resist them without overwhelming anxiety.

Ms. J.'s behaviors were not confined to her workplace; she described a similar world of private torment at home. She was paradoxically very concerned with germs and contamination at her home, yet was forced to live in relatively squalid surroundings because of her inability to wash clothes or dishes as a result of her contamination fears, and her hoarding of trash. In fact, her house was filled with overflowing trash bags containing papers and other items that she was unable to throw away because of her fear of "losing something important." Interestingly, she related that her mother had similar behaviors, although her mother refused psychiatric treatment, and Ms. J. recalled that her family moved to another house when she was an adolescent because her mother had collected "so many bags of trash and paper that there was no room for us to live there."

Ms. J. had been taking imipramine and perphenazine for several years prior to her entry into protocol. She felt that these medications were helpful in treating some of her depressive symptoms and anxiety, but denied any demonstrable antiobsessive effects. She entered a research protocol and received 6 weeks of treatment with the anxiolytic agent buspirone followed by 6 weeks of clomipramine treatment; both medications were administered under double-blind, placebo-controlled conditions. She experienced mild antidepressant and antianxiety effects, but only mild antiobsessive effects from the buspirone trial. She reported, however, substantial improvement (an estimated 50% reduction) in her OCD symptoms, affect, and anxiety during the 6-week clomipramine treatment trial. She received clomipramine at 200 mg/day on an open basis for the next 5 months. After 5 months of clomipramine treatment, her scores on the rating scales indicated that her OCD symptoms were reduced by approximately 60% from her pretreatment baseline ratings. She was spending much less time checking and proofreading at work and had begun to leave work at the same time as her coworkers. She continued to be fairly symptomatic at home, although she was able to do several loads of laundry for the first time in 6 months. She was also able to throw away approximately 30% of the trash bags in her home; this was the first time in 10 years that she had been able to throw anything away at home. Ms. J. did have some side effects from the clomipramine—notably, dry mouth, constipation, and a significant decrease in libido. Most troubling to her, however, was the presence of a significant fine tremor in her hands that occurred daily and was fairly disruptive at her workplace.

Because of this persistent tremor it was mutually decided to attempt to taper Ms. J. off clomipramine and institute a trial of fluoxetine. This was subsequently done, and Ms. J. was stabilized on a daily dosage of fluoxetine at 80 mg/day administered over a 6-week period. She reported that fluoxetine was also significantly effective in reducing her OCD symptoms after approximately 8 weeks of treatment. By 6 months of fluoxetine treatment, her OCD symptoms were reduced by approximately 60% to 70% from her pretreatment baseline ratings. She reduced her cleaning compulsions at work and was able to further reduce the amount of trash bags in her home. She did not experience any substantial side effects from the fluoxetine, including tremor, except for some complaints of vague lethargy. Ms. J. reported an antidepressant and antianxiety response comparable to her response on clomipramine. She has remained on fluoxetine at 80 mg/day for approximately 9 months; several attempts to decrease her dosage have resulted in an exacerbation of her OCD symptoms and reemergence of depressive affect.

Case 2

Mr. H. was a 40-year-old married male with an approximately 10-year history of OCD. He had been tried on a variety of psychotropic medications, including diazepam, imipramine, and amitriptyline, without significant benefit. At the time of his initial interview, he reported a number of OCD symptoms, most of which were focused around irrational, intrusive thoughts that he had inadvertently harmed someone, especially young children. In order to rid himself of these horrific doubts, he engaged in many compulsive activities designed to convince himself that he had not harmed anyone. For instance, he was unable to drive because of his concerns that he might "run over young children," and he spent hours per day checking drawers, doors, and bottles to make sure that he had not "trapped any young children inside." He knew that his fears were unfounded, but could not bear to tolerate the concomitant anxiety that would arise if he refused to give in to his fears and to repeatedly check his environment. He avoided parking lots and public places so that he would not be exposed to children and subsequently become overwhelmed by fears that he would harm them or jeopardize their safety. On his weekly visits to the OCD clinic, which were generally scheduled for an hour, he often spent hours at the hospital because of his hypervigilant behaviors designed to prevent imagined catastrophes. For example, he would spend hours picking up every piece of paper or trash on the floor because he feared that "some child might slip on the paper, fall, and die." He spent many hours stalking the halls looking for potential fires, leaks, construction problems, and elevator mishaps; he would promptly report any possible irregularities to the maintenance department, such that he would average approximately three to five calls to the maintenance department per outpatient visit to the clinic.

Mr. H. entered a research protocol and received 10 weeks of clomipramine followed by 10 weeks of fluoxetine treatment, under double-blind, placebo-controlled conditions. During the clomipramine phase, he experienced a dramatic antiobsessive response, with an approximately

70% reduction in his OCD symptoms on 250 mg/day of clomipramine. He also reported a variety of side effects including dry mouth, constipation, sedation, and decreased libido with impotence while on clomipramine, but felt such remarkable improvement in his overall level of anxiety and OCD symptoms that he felt that "the side effects were worth the benefits." However, during the fluoxetine phase, he did very poorly and apparently obtained no antiobsessive response from fluoxetine treatment; in fact, he returned to his pretreatment baseline of OCD symptom severity and became very depressed. He continued to experience some side effects on fluoxetine, notably sedation and decreased libido. At the completion of 10 weeks of fluoxetine treatment at 80 mg/day, he was restarted on the clomipramine and achieved his previous level of symptom reduction after approximately 6 weeks of clomipramine treatment at 250 mg/day. Mr. H. reported that he was again able to drive without substantial fears of running someone over, and he no longer was forced to stay in the OCD clinic past his scheduled appointment time because of the resolution of his fears that "something terrible would happen" if he did not report potential mishaps or accidents to the maintenance department. He remained at this level of improvement after 6 months of therapy with clomipramine.

Summary

While there have been only two (Pigott et al., in press; Turner et al. 1985) controlled trials of fluoxetine in the treatment of OCD, there is considerable optimism concerning its potential efficacy in OCD and evidence to suggest that fluoxetine may posses efficacy similar to that of clomipramine (Pigott et al., in press). Because of its minimal side-effect profile, its lack of associated weight gain, and its relative safety in overdosage, fluoxetine may well represent an advance in OCD treatment comparable to the discovery of clomipramine as the first medication shown to be efficacious in OCD in controlled trials. In addition, there have been several reports of augmentation of fluoxetine's antiobsessive properties by the use of other psychotropic medications, including buspirone (Markovitz et al. 1989). The advent of fluoxetine and other highly selective 5-HT uptake inhibitors argues well for the continuing development of increasingly effective and safe medications for OCD, and may also provide more evidence regarding the etiology and pathogenesis of this intriguing disorder.

References

Aranow RB, Hudson JI, Pope HG, et al: Elevated antidepressant plasma levels after addition of fluoxetine. Am J Psychiatry 146:911–913, 1989

Aronoff GR, Bergstrom RF, Pottratz ST, et al: Fluoxetine kinetics and protein binding in normal and impaired renal function. Clin Pharmacol Ther 36: 138–144, 1984

Åsberg M, Thorén P, Bertilsson L: Clomipramine treatment of obsessive disorder: biochemical and clinical aspects. Psychopharmacol Bull 18(3):13–21, 1982

Åsberg M, Montgomery SA, Perris C, et al.: A comprehensive psychopathological rating scale. Acta Psychiatr Scand 271:5–27, 1978

Berken GH, Weinstein DO, Stern WC: Weight gain: a side-effect of tricyclic antidepressants. J Affective Disord 7:133–138, 1984

Cottraux JA, Bouvard M, Claustrat B, et al: Abnormal dexamethasone suppression test in primary obsessive-compulsive patients: a confirmatory report. Psychiatry Res 13:157–165, 1984

Derogatis LR, Lipman RS, Covi L, et al.: The Hopkins Symptom Checklist (HSCL): a self-report symptom index. Behav Sci 19:1–15, 1974

Dista Products Company: Prozac: Comprehensive Monograph. Indianapolis, IN, Eli Lilly and Company, 1988

Downs JM, Downs AD, Rosenthal TL, et al.: Increased plasma tricyclic antidepressant concentrations in two patients concurrently treated with fluoxetine. J Clin Psychiatry 50:226–227, 1989

Fabre LF, Putman HP: A fixed-dose clinical trial of fluoxetine in outpatients with major depression. J Clin Psychiatry 48:406–408, 1987

Feighner JP: A comparative trial of fluoxetine and amitriptyline in patients with major depressive disorder. J Clin Psychiatry 46 (no 3, sec 2):369–372, 1985

Ferguson JM: Fluoxetine-induced weight loss in overweight, nondepressed subjects (letter). Am J Psychiatry 143:1496, 1986

Fisch C: Effect of fluoxetine on the electrocardiogram. J Clin Psychiatry 46 (no 3, sec 2):42–44, 1985

Flament MF, Rapoport JL, Berg CJ, et al: Clomipramine treatment of childhood obsessive-compulsive disorder: a double-blind controlled study. Arch Gen Psychiatry 42:977–983, 1985

Fontaine R, Chouinard G: Fluoxetine in the treatment of obsessive-compulsive disorder. Prog Neuropsychopharmacol Biol Psychiatry 9:605–608, 1985

Fontaine R, Chouinard G: An open clinical trial of fluoxetine in the treatment of obsessive-compulsive disorder. J Clin Psychopharmacol 6:98–101, 1986

Fontaine R, Chouinard G: Fluoxetine in the long-term maintenance treatment of obsessive-compulsive disorder. Psychiatric Annals 19:88–91, 1989

Goodman WK, Price LP, Rasmussen SA: The Yale-Brown Obsessive Compulsive Scale, I: development, use, and reliability. Arch Gen Psychiatry 46:1006–1011, 1989

Goodwin DW, Guze SB, Robins E: Follow-up studies in obsessional neurosis. Arch Gen Psychiatry 20:182–187, 1969

Hamilton M: A rating scale for depression. J Neurol Neurosurg Psychiatry 23: 56–62, 1960

Insel TR, Gillin JC, Moore A, et al: The sleep of patients with obsessive-compulsive disorder. Arch Gen Psychiatry 39:1372–1377, 1982a

Insel TR, Kalin NH, Guttmacher LB, et al: The dexamethasone suppression test in patients with primary obsessive-compulsive disorder. Psychiatry Res 6:153–160, 1982b

Insel TR, Hoover C, Murphy DL: Parents of patients with obsessive-compulsive disorder. Psychol Med 13:807–811, 1983a

Insel TR, Murphy DL, Cohen RM, et al: Obsessive-compulsive disorder: a double-blind trial of clomipramine and clorgyline. Arch Gen Psychiatry 40:605–612, 1983b

Jenike MA, Buttolph L, Baer L, et al: Open trial of fluoxetine in obsessive-compulsive disorder. Am J Psychiatry 146:909–911, 1989

Lebegue B: Mania precipitated by fluoxetine (letter). Am J Psychiatry 144: 1620, 1987

Lemberger L, Rowe H, Carmichael R, et al: Fluoxetine, a selective serotonin uptake inhibitor. Clin Pharmacol Ther 23:421–429, 1978

Lemberger L, Bergstrom RF, Wolen RL, et al: Fluoxetine: clinical pharmacology and physiologic disposition. J Clin Psychiatry 46 (no 3, sec 2):14–19, 1985

Markovitz PJ, Stagno SJ, Calabrese JR: Buspirone augmentation of fluoxetine in obsessive-compulsive disorder. Biol Psychiatry 25:186A, 1989

Mavissakalian M, Michelson L: Tricyclic antidepressants in obsessive-compulsive disorder: antiobsessional or antidepressant agents? J Nerv Ment Dis 171:301–306, 1983

Mavissakalian M, Turner SM, Michelson L, et al: Tricyclic antidepressants in obsessive-compulsive disorder: antiobsessional or antidepressant agents? Am J Psychiatry 142:572–576, 1985

Miksic SL, Barry H, Krimmer EC: Increased serotonin activity reduces alcohol preference in rats (abstract). Alcohol Clin Exp Res 6:149, 1982

Montgomery SA: 5HT uptake inhibitors in the treatment of depression. Paper presented at the World Psychiatric Association Regional Symposium, 1986

Pato MT, Zohar-Kadouch R, Zohar J, et al: Return of symptoms after discontinuation of clomipramine in patients with obsessive-compulsive disorder. Am J Psychiatry 145:1521–1525, 1988

Pigott TA, Pato MT, Bernstein SE, et al: Controlled comparisons of clomipramine and fluoxetine in the treatment of OCD: behavioral and biological results. Arch Gen Psychiatry (in press)

Rasmussen SA, Eisen JL: Clinical features and phenomenology of OCD. Psychiatric Annals 19:67–73, 1989

Richelson E: Synaptic pharmacology of antidepressants: an update. McLean Hosp J 13:67–88, 1988

Rowe H, Lemberger L, Bergstrom R, et al: The effect of co-administration of fluoxetine and diazepam on psychomotor and physiologic responses (abstract). Pharmacologist 27:196, 1985

Schatzberg AF: Update on fluoxetine. Currents in Affective Illness 8:5–11, 1989

Settle EC, Settle GP: A case of mania associated with fluoxetine. Am J Psychiatry 141:280–281, 1984

Stark P, Fuller RW, Wong DT: The pharmacologic profile of fluoxetine. J Clin Psychiatry 46 (no 3, sec 2):7–13, 1985

Steiner W, Fontaine R: Toxic reaction following the combined administration of fluoxetine and L-tryptophan: five case reports. Biol Psychiatry 21:1067–1071, 1986

Sternbach H: Danger of MAOI therapy after fluoxetine withdrawal (letter). Lancet 2:850–851, 1988

Turner SM, Jacob RG, Beidel DC, et al: Fluoxetine treatment of obsessive-compulsive disorder. J Clin Psychopharmacol 5:207–212, 1985a

Turner SM, Jacob RG, Beidel DC, et al: A second case of mania associated with fluoxetine (letter). Am J Psychiatry 142:274–275, 1985b

Vaughan DA: Interaction of fluoxetine with tricyclic antidepressants (letter). Am J Psychiatry 145:1478, 1988

Vaughan M: The relationships between obsessional personality, obsessions in depression, and symptoms of depression. Br J Psychiatry 129:36–39, 1976

Weizman A, Carmi M, Hermesh H, et al: High-affinity imipramine binding and serotonin uptake in platelets of eight adolescent and ten adult obsessive-compulsive patients. Am J Psychiatry 143:335–339, 1986

Wernicke JF: The side effect profile and safety of fluoxetine. J Clin Psychiatry 46 (no 3, sec 2):59–67, 1985

Wernicke JF, Dunlop SR, Dornseif BE, et al: Fixed-dose fluoxetine therapy for depression. Psychopharmacol Bull 23:164–168, 1987

Zohar J, Insel TR: Obsessive-compulsive disorder: psychobiological approaches to diagnosis, treatment, and pathophysiology. Biol Psychiatry 22:667–687, 1987

Zohar J, Mueller EA, Insel TR, et al: Serotonergic responsivity in obsessive-compulsive disorder: comparison of patients and healthy controls. Arch Gen Psychiatry 44:946–951, 1987

Chapter 4

Fluvoxamine in the Treatment of Obsessive-Compulsive Disorder

Wayne K. Goodman, M.D.
Lawrence H. Price, M.D.

*E*fficacy studies and the weight of clinical experience suggest that antidepressant drugs—in particular, the potent inhibitors of serotonin (5-hydroxytryptamine [5-HT]) reuptake, should be the mainstay of the drug treatment of obsessive-compulsive disorder (OCD) (see Ananth et al. 1981; Baxter 1985; Foa et al. 1987; Insel et al. 1983; Leonard et al. 1988; Prasad 1985; Thorén et al. 1980; Zohar and Insel 1987). A number of double-blind studies have shown that the potent 5-HT reuptake inhibitor clomipramine is more effective than placebo in the treatment of OCD (DeVeaugh-Geiss et al. 1989; see Pato and Zohar, Chapter 2, this volume). Moreover, in recent double-blind trials in OCD outpatients, clomipramine was significantly better than the relatively selective norepinephrine reuptake inhibitor desipramine (Leonard et al. 1988; Zohar and Insel 1987). Together, these drug response data support the hypothesis that the 5-HT reuptake properties of an antidepressant drug are relevant to its efficacy as an antiobsessive-compulsive agent. However, because a major metabolite of clomipramine is a potent blocker of norepinephrine reuptake (Träskman et al. 1979), it is unclear if the efficacy of clomipramine in the treatment of OCD is related solely to its effects on 5-HT transport.

In recent years, trials have been conducted in OCD patients with a newer generation of antidepressants that are both potent and selective

Studies of fluvoxamine were supported in part by National Institute of Mental Health Grants MH-25642, MH-30929, and MH-40140, and by the State of Connecticut. Fluvoxamine was generously provided by Reid-Rowell, Inc., Marietta, Georgia. The authors thank the research, clinical, and clerical staffs of the Clinical Neuroscience Research Unit of the Ribicoff Research Facilities, New Haven, CT, for their assistance.

blockers of 5-HT reuptake (e.g., fluvoxamine, zimelidine, sertraline, venlafaxine, and fluoxetine). Unlike clomipramine, none of these medication lose their selectivity for blocking 5-HT reuptake in vivo (Fuller and Wong 1987). Also, in contrast to tricyclic antidepressants like clomipramine, these newer drugs lack significant affinity for cholinergic, alpha-adrenergic, and histaminic receptors. This may explain the relatively lower incidence of anticholinergic and cardiovascular side effects and sedation with the newer agents. Except for fluoxetine (Prozac) [approved for depression] and clomipramine (Anafranil) [approved for OCD in 1990], the potent 5-HT reuptake inhibitors are currently available in the United States on an investigational basis only. (Zimelidine was withdrawn from clinical testing because of adverse neurological events.) Recent studies suggest that these drugs may offer new options in the treatment of OCD, as well as furnish clues to its pathophysiology. In this chapter we review the relative role of fluvoxamine in the treatment of OCD.

Fluvoxamine in the Treatment of OCD: A Review of Studies

Fluvoxamine was originally developed in Europe as an antidepressant. In most published double-blind trials in depressed patients, fluvoxamine has been shown to be significantly better than placebo and equal in efficacy to tricyclic antidepressants such as imipramine and clomipramine (Benfield and Ward 1986). On the basis of its monoamine reuptake–blocking properties, several groups have conducted trials of fluvoxamine in patients with OCD (Goodman et al. 1989a, 1989b, 1989c; Jenike et al. 1990; Price 1988).

In a single-blind study of fluvoxamine, 6 of 10 inpatients with severe OCD were "responders" on the basis of a clinical rating of "much" or "very much improved" on a modified version of the Clinical Global Impression (CGI) scale (Price et al. 1987). On this conservative measure of clinical outcome, patients who were rated as "somewhat improved" were classified as "nonresponders." Most of the patients in this study were previously refractory to adequate trials of other antidepressant medications. These encouraging findings are further supported by two double-blind studies of fluvoxamine in outpatients with OCD.

In a study conducted at the University of Wisconsin, 16 OCD patients completed a 20-week randomized crossover trial that compared fluvoxamine to placebo (Perse et al. 1988). Patients received active fluvoxamine treatment for 8 weeks. There was a 2-week single-blind placebo period prior to the start of treatment, and between treatments ("wash-out" period). Fluvoxamine was found to be effective on several different measures of OCD. For example, marked clinical improvement in OCD was associated only with the active drug phase, with 9 of 16 (56%) patients classified as "better" during fluvoxamine treatment.

Similar findings were obtained in a parallel-groups–design study conducted jointly at Yale and Brown (Goodman et al. 1989c). Forty-two OCD patients were randomly assigned to 6 to 8 weeks of treatment with either fluvoxamine (up to 300 mg daily) or placebo. Patients received supportive psychotherapy and were encouraged to "resist" their obsessive-compulsive symptoms. All patients had a principal diagnosis of OCD (according to DSM-III [American Psychiatric Association 1980]), but approximately 50% of the sample had coexisting major depression. Weekly assessment of severity of OCD and depression was based on semistructured patient and clinician ratings. The principal outcome measure for OCD was the Yale-Brown Obsessive Compulsive Scale (Y-BOCS), a 10-item clinician-rated questionnaire (Goodman et al. 1989d). (Each item is rated on a 5-point scale from 0 = "no symptoms" to 4 = "extreme symptoms"; total score range = 0 to 40.)

In this study fluvoxamine was superior to placebo on four different measures of OCD (Goodman et al. 1989c). For example, on the basis of mean Y-BOCS scores, analysis of variance with repeated measures revealed significant changes from baseline beginning week 2 of fluvoxamine treatment. In contrast, there were no significant changes in mean total Y-BOCS scores for any week following baseline in the placebo-treated group. Similarly, analysis of response category data showed that fluvoxamine was effective in reducing the severity of obsessive-compulsive symptoms. In the fluvoxamine-treated group, 9 of 21 patients were responders (as defined above according to CGI scores), whereas none of the 21 placebo-treated patients were rated as responders. This remarkably low placebo response rate seems characteristic of outpatient OCD studies and contrasts with a much higher placebo rate typically seen in drug trials in depressed outpatients.

Antidepressant or Antiobsessional?

The design of the Yale-Brown study also allowed us to examine whether the antiobsessive-compulsive effects of fluvoxamine could be differentiated from its antidepressant action. Patients with a range of severity in secondary depressive symptoms were entered in the study, and rating instruments were selected to optimize separation of response of obsessive-compulsive versus response of depressive symptoms. The Y-BOCS, in particular, lends itself to examination of selective changes in obsessive-compulsive symptoms, since it was constructed to exclude items concerning severity of depressive symptoms. Analysis of the relationship between measures of improvement in OCD (including the Y-BOCS) and measures of depression disclosed that the antiobsessive-compulsive effects of fluvoxamine were independent of baseline levels of depression (Goodman et al. 1989c). For example, there was no significant correlation between fluvoxamine-induced improvement in Y-BOCS scores and baseline ratings of depression (based on the Hamilton Rating Scale for Depression [HAM-D] [Hamilton 1967]). If fluvoxamine was primarily acting as an antidepressant, then OCD patients with concurrent major depression might be predicted to have the best response. This was not the case in this study. Of the nine responders to fluvoxamine, three were classified at initial presentation as depressed, but six were nondepressed. In fact, according to baseline HAM-D ratings, the most depressed and the least depressed OCD patients were both rated as responders to fluvoxamine treatment.

The University of Wisconsin group had similar findings for the relationships between the antidepressant and antiobsessive-compulsive responses to fluvoxamine. Perse and her colleagues (1988) found that improvement in obsessive-compulsive symptoms was unrelated to severity of depression at baseline. This experience with fluvoxamine in OCD mirrors that of most studies that have attempted to distinguish the antiobsessive-compulsive from the antidepressant actions of other antidepressants in the treatment of OCD (Insel and Zohar 1987). In all but one study of clomipramine in the treatment of OCD (Marks et al. 1980), coexisting depression was not a prerequisite to an antiobsessive-compulsive response (Mavissakalian et al. 1985). Multicenter, double-blind, placebo-controlled trials of fluvoxamine in nondepressed OCD outpatients are currently in progress in North America.

Magnitude and Time Course of Clinical Response

Although in our outpatient study we found statistically significant mean group effects of fluvoxamine on obsessive-compulsive symptoms after only 2 weeks of treatment, clinically meaningful changes were generally not apparent until at least 4 to 6 weeks of treatment (Goodman et al. 1989c). In fact, of seven patients that were considered only partial responders by week 6, five converted to full responders after 2 additional weeks of fluvoxamine at week 8. Also, mean total Y-BOCS scores for the fluvoxamine-treated group continued to decrease throughout the trial. Mean Y-BOCS scores were decreased 25% from baseline at 8 weeks compared with 20% from baseline at 6 weeks of fluvoxamine treatment. Thus, it appears that with fluvoxamine, and perhaps with other antidepressants in OCD, at least 8 weeks may be needed for an adequate treatment trial.

In the nine fluvoxamine responders, the mean Y-BOCS scores at the conclusion of treatment were 42% below baseline ratings. This degree of improvement represented major gains in social and vocational functioning. The mean Y-BOCS score of this responder group at the end of the trial was 14 ± 7 (± SD), which corresponds to a global severity in the mild-to-moderate range. Thus, these patients were much improved but not entirely free of symptoms. In fact, no patient had a Y-BOCS score of 0 at the end of the double-blind trial. Similar results have been obtained for clomipramine in OCD with respect to rate and degree of treatment response (DeVeaugh-Geiss et al. 1989; Thorén et al. 1980).

Implications

The efficacy studies reviewed here suggest that fluvoxamine possesses clinically significant antiobsessive-compulsive properties. These findings also support the hypothesis that potency of 5-HT reuptake inhibition may be critical to the antiobsessive-compulsive efficacy of a drug. However, since significant 5-HT reuptake inhibition is achieved after a single dose of a 5-HT reuptake inhibitor, yet a therapeutic response usually requires weeks of drug treatment, other mechanisms may be responsible for the antiobsessive-compulsive action of fluvoxamine. One possibility is that fluvoxamine-induced adaptive changes in 5-HT autoreceptor sensitivity, which take several weeks to develop, may be more directly related to antiobsessive-compulsive efficacy (Blier et al. 1987). Alternatively, although several lines of preclinical and clinical evidence suggest that chronic 5-HT reuptake inhibitor administration has important effects on brain 5-HT function (e.g., increased 5-HT transmission in electrophysiological studies) (Blier et al. 1987), there is preclinical evidence that other monoaminergic systems may be indirectly affected by chronic fluvoxamine. For example, in laboratory animals, chronic administration of fluvoxamine has been associated with down-regulation of beta-adrenergic receptors (Bradford and Schipper 1985). There is also ample preclinical evidence for important anatomical and functional interactions between serotonergic and dopaminergic systems (Crespi et al. 1988). Hence, it is conceivable that chronic fluvoxamine treatment induces compensatory alterations in other neurochemical systems that are more directly tied to the reduction of obsessive-compulsive symptoms.

Guidelines to Drug Treatment

Choice of Antidepressant

In general, the choice of a drug treatment depends on consideration of its relative efficacy, side effects (safety), and availability.

Relative efficacy. As reviewed here and elsewhere (see Pato and Zohar, Chapter 2, this volume), there is a wealth of published evidence that clomipramine is effective in the treatment of OCD (DeVeaugh-Geiss et al. 1989). Less data are available on fluoxetine, yet recent clinical experience suggests it is also beneficial in OCD (see Pigott, Chapter 3, this volume; Fontaine and Chouinard 1985, 1989). As discussed above, several studies support the superiority of fluvoxamine over placebo. A recent study also suggests that fluvoxamine is more effective than desipramine in the treatment of OCD (Goodman et al. 1989a). Unfortunately, the relative antiobsessive-compulsive efficacy of fluvoxamine to other potent 5-HT reuptake inhibitors, such as clomipramine and fluoxetine, has not been directly studied. Comparison of response rates across independent placebo-controlled studies suggests that fluvoxamine and clomipramine are roughly equivalent, with a slight advantage in favor of clomipramine. Because of the recent availability of fluoxetine, we have attempted to substitute fluoxetine for fluvoxamine in some OCD patients chronically maintained and improved on fluvoxamine. In most cases we have been successful in making this change without apparent loss of efficacy. However, because these changes were conducted in an open fashion, and without the benefit of a placebo control, it is not possible to draw firm conclusions about comparative efficacy.

Side effects. In our hands, the most commonly reported side effects for fluvoxamine, in order of decreasing frequency, are daytime drowsiness, nausea, insomnia, headache, tremors, and delayed orgasm. Nausea, tremor, and sexual dysfunction (particularly delayed or absent orgasm) seem to be common side effects of all the potent 5-HT reuptake inhibitors. Most patients on fluvoxamine, and other 5-HT reuptake inhibitors, develop tolerance to nausea. If nausea is severe it may be necessary to maintain the patient at the lowest possible daily dose until signs of tolerance develop. Unlike many other antidepressants, fluoxetine does not seem to induce weight gain and, in some cases, may actually result in weight loss (Price 1988). Studies are needed to determine whether this effect on weight is sustained during long-term use. Our own experience suggests that in some OCD patients, appetite and weight may increase moderately after approximately 6 months of treatment with either fluoxetine or fluvoxamine (Goodman et al., unpublished data, 1989). However, in evaluating these possible late side effects, it is difficult to separate direct pharmacological actions from the secondary effects of reduced obsessive-compulsive symptoms and improved mood on appetite and eating habits. Also based on our anecdotal experience, we have observed that the side-effect profiles of fluvoxamine and fluoxetine are different in some respects, with fluvoxamine producing more sedation and fluoxetine causing more insomnia (Goodman et al., unpublished data, 1989). In general, there are fewer side effects with fluvoxamine and fluoxetine than with clomipramine. The side-effect profile of clomipramine includes symptoms typical of both potent 5-HT reuptake inhibitors (e.g., nausea and delayed orgasm) and tricyclic antidepressants. Anticholinergic side effects (e.g., dry mouth, constipation, urinary retention), orthostatic hypotension, sedation, and weight gain are common with clomipramine and other tricyclics (see Pato and Zohar, Chapter 2, this volume).

The seizure incidence of clomipramine has been reported to be somewhat higher than that of other tricyclics (Goodman 1988). However, recent studies by the manufacturer suggest that the risk of seizures associated with clomipramine may be dose-related, with the majority occurring above 250 mg daily. (See Chapter 2, this volume, for further discussion of side effects.) Rash and systematic signs of drug sensitivity (e.g., fever, arthralgias, edema, carpal tunnel syndrome) have been reported by approximately 4% of patients receiving fluoxetine. Reversible elevations in liver transaminases have been reported with fluvoxamine, fluoxetine, and clomipramine.

Availability.   Clomipramine is the first drug marketed in the United States with a specific indication for OCD. Until recently, of the potent and selective 5-HT reuptake inhibitors, only fluoxetine (marketed for depression) was available on a general prescription basis in the United States. Fluvoxamine is investigational in the United States but is available in several European countries, including England, The Netherlands, and Spain. Sertraline, buspirone, and venlafaxine are currently undergoing testing for treatment of OCD.

Adequacy of Trial

A working definition of an adequate drug trial includes parameters for duration of treatment, dose, and bioavailability (e.g., a reliable measure of the drug level actually attained in plasma or brain). For the treatment of depression an adequate antidepressant trial is usually 4 to 6 weeks; in the treatment of OCD a minimum of 6, and as many as 8 to 10, weeks of antidepressant drug treatment may be required. Fluvoxamine is prescribed up to a maximum daily dose of 300 mg, as tolerated; however, there are presently no published data on the relationship between fluvoxamine dose (or plasma levels) and clinical outcome in OCD. To help ensure compliance, it is useful to educate the patient regarding the expected time course and magnitude of response to fluvoxamine.

When assessing outcome, it is important to differentiate responses of depressive and obsessive-compulsive symptoms. Clear identification of the target obsessive-compulsive symptoms is critical to this assessment. Weekly administration of a structured rating instrument for OCD, such as the Y-BOCS, should facilitate monitoring of clinical response to treatment.

Patients with OCD frequently report that benzodiazepines "take the edge off" their symptoms, but the benefit is rarely enduring. Fluvoxamine was effective in treating both obsessive-compulsive and depressive symptoms despite the patients' previous failed trials on other antidepressant drugs. It should be noted, however, that significant improvement in obsessive-compulsive symptoms may not be observed until more than 6 weeks of treatment. Depressive symptoms usually seem to respond earlier and more completely than do obsessive-compulsive symptoms. Patients may continue to show clinically significant improvement on fluvoxamine alone. In one study, with OCD patients treated with fluvoxamine for 6 weeks, further improvement after 2 additional weeks of treatment (total of 8 weeks of fluvoxamine) was noted (Goodman et al.

1989c). In practice, we now administer fluvoxamine alone for at least 8 weeks prior to considering combination treatment strategies (see case history at the end of this chapter). It is not clear in the case described at the end of this chapter whether addition of lithium acted to augment the patient's treatment response to fluvoxamine. Except for some weight gain and mild drowsiness, drug treatment has been well tolerated and clinical response has been maintained on follow-up.

In most patients, fluvoxamine-induced improvement in OCD seems to be maintained during chronic treatment. We routinely encourage patients who have had good symptom control for 6 to 9 months to begin a gradual (3-month to 6-month) taper of the medication. Although we have not conducted formal drug discontinuation studies, some of these patients continue to do well off fluvoxamine.

The Treatment-Refractory Patient

To our knowledge there has been no controlled evaluation of a systematic approach to OCD patients who have not responded to an adequate trial of a 5-HT reuptake inhibitor alone. For example, it is not clear whether the first step in the treatment algorithm should involve a trial with another 5-HT reuptake inhibitor or an augmentation strategy. We can think of examples of individual OCD patients who had failed trials with two 5-HT reuptake inhibitors (e.g., clomipramine and fluoxetine), and then had a robust response to a third 5-HT reuptake inhibitor (e.g., fluvoxamine), in all three possible permutations. Although a systematic evaluation of this approach is needed, in clinical practice it seems justified to try fluvoxamine in OCD patients who have failed trials with other 5-HT reuptake inhibitors.

In depressed patients one approach to treating nonresponders or partial responders has been to add lithium (which may augment 5-HT function [Blier and deMontigny 1985]) to antidepressant drug treatment. Some OCD patients may improve when lithium is added to chronic treatment with potent 5-HT reuptake inhibitors (e.g., clomipramine [Eisenberg and Asnis 1985; Rasmussen 1984] or fluvoxamine [Price et al., unpublished data]), but this strategy seems generally less effective in OCD than it is in depression. Addition of L-tryptophan, the amino acid precursor of 5-HT, has been reported to be helpful in an OCD patient on clomipramine (Rasmussen 1984), but ineffective in OCD patients on trazodone (Mattes 1986).[1] Large supplements of tryptophan are contraindicated in patients on fluoxetine because of reports of neurological side effects with this combination (Steiner and Fontaine 1986). In an open case series, some OCD patients seemed to benefit from the addition of low doses of antipsychotic medication to fluvoxamine treatment (McDougle et al. 1990). More detailed studies of antidepressant-antipsychotic combination therapy in OCD are needed.

It is conceivable that OCD is pathophysiologically heterogeneous and that putative clinical subtypes of OCD may be differentially responsive to one or another type of antidepressant. For example, it has been suggested on the basis of anecdotal experience that OCD patients with a history of panic disorder may respond well to monoamine oxidase inhibitors (MAOIs) (Jenike et al. 1983). In a retrospective study, OCD coexisting with schizotypal personality disorder was associated with a very poor treatment outcome (Jenike et al. 1986). These findings deserve further study. However, at present, there are no known reliable clinical or biological predictors of response of OCD patients as a whole, or individually, to antidepressant drug treatment. Finally, there is reason to believe that a combination of drug and behavioral treatment might best optimize outcome. (See Jenike, Chapter 9, this volume, for a more thorough discussion of the treatment-resistant patient.)

Case History

Ms. A., a 39-year-old divorced mother of two, was admitted to the research unit with the chief complaint that "I am constantly washing my hands and changing my clothes . . . for fear of . . . getting people sick by spreading contamination." The patient dated the onset of her current symptoms to approximately 8 months prior to admission after learning that she had made an error at work. By forgetting to place a stamp on an envelope containing a $10.00 filing fee, the fee was late and an important business deal fell through. Following this incident, the patient began checking and rechecking all her current and past work. In the process the patient discovered some minor mistakes that reinforced her compulsion to check. She experienced difficulty falling asleep, dysphoric mood,

---

[1]Because the use of L-tryptophan has recently (Fall 1989) been implicated in an increased incidence of eosinophilia, the authors advise against the prescribing and use of this agent, as discussed in this book, until the issue is resolved.

marked anxiety, insomnia, a diminished appetite, and a 5- to 10-pound weight loss. A psychiatrist prescribed clorazepate (7.5 mg qid), which was initially helpful in reducing symptoms of anxiety and insomnia. Further worsening of Ms. A.'s obsessive-compulsive and depressive symptoms and deterioration in her level of functioning led to several psychiatric hospitalizations, where she received the following medications: diazepam (up to 20 mg qd), alprazolam (dose unknown), thioridazine (150 mg qd), amitriptyline (150 mg qd) alone and in combination with perphenazine (16 mg qd), and trazodone (600 mg qd). After showing no improvement she was transferred to our facility for a trial of fluvoxamine.

At the time of admission Ms. A.'s obsessions involved primarily the fear she would be responsible for inadvertently harming others. The patient feared that germs might be spread by her bodily wastes and secretions. Her compulsions principally involved cleaning rituals and checking. She washed her hands, on the average, 12 times a day (5 to 10 minutes per washing), and she restricted her dietary intake to avoid urinating or moving her bowels. She inspected reflective spots on the floor for evidence of metal fragments or slivers of glass, out of concern that they might be accidently transferred into someone's food. She spent more than 8 hours a day scanning her environment for potential hazards or reviewing instances where she may have caused others harm. Pathological doubting was a prominent feature of her presentation; staff reassurance only momentarily allayed her anxiety. The patient readily acknowledged the irrationality of her fears and excessiveness of her behaviors, except during times of extreme anxiety. She made little effort to actively resist her compulsive behaviors and exhibited no control over them. Depressive symptoms were prominent.

Fluvoxamine was administered at a starting dose of 50 mg at bedtime and subsequently increased in divided doses (up to 300 mg daily by the end of week 2), with the bulk in the late P.M. Mild nausea was reported during the first week of treatment, and some sedation persisted throughout fluvoxamine treatment. After 6 weeks of fluvoxamine treatment (300 mg daily for 4 weeks), the patient experienced a marked improvement in obsessive-compulsive symptoms. Approximately a 60% reduction in severity was noted in obsessive-compulsive symptoms with respect to the time they occupied, the distress and interference they produced, and the patient's willingness and ability to control them. However, Ms. A. continued to have occasional intrusive thoughts that were similar in intensity to those experienced at the outset of treatment. Depressive symptoms were nearly absent except for dysphoric mood when obsessive-compulsive symptoms were present. Because of these persistent symptoms, lithium carbonate (900 mg daily) was added to the fluvoxamine. After 2 weeks of combination treatment obsessive-compulsive symptoms were present for less than 1 hour per day and were no longer significantly interfering with functioning. Depression was resolved. The patient was discharged on this combination treatment.

At 1 year follow-up, the patient was only on fluvoxamine (300 mg daily). Discontinuation of lithium 6 months earlier did not result in apparent worsening of symptoms. There was no evidence of either obsessive-compulsive or depressive symptoms. The patient had returned to gainful employment. She reported carbohydrate craving and a 10- to 15-pound weight gain compared to her premorbid baseline. She also complained of mild daytime drowsiness, particularly when in a nonstimulating environment (e.g., a boring business meeting) or while driving long distances. No laboratory abnormalities have been noted. Out of fear of losing her excellent response, she declined a recommendation to begin a slow taper of the medication.

Summary

On the basis of five published studies (including Cottraux 1989 and Jenike et al. 1990), the potent and selective 5-HT reuptake inhibitor fluvoxamine has been found to be an effective treatment for OCD. At least 8 weeks of treatment may be required for an adequate trial. Response to the antiobsessive-compulsive effects of fluvoxamine was independent of severity of depression at baseline. However, approximately one-third of OCD patients showed no significant improvement with fluvoxamine, and few patients were completely asymptomatic. Nonetheless, these findings are roughly comparable to the rate of improvement shown in similar studies with clomipramine treatment of OCD, the current standard for antiobsessive-compulsive drug treatment. In addition, lack of efficacy of clomipramine does not predict response to fluvoxamine. One possible explanation for these findings is that OCD is heterogeneous, and that only certain subtypes of OCD may be responsive to treatment with 5-HT reuptake inhibitors alone. Until reliable predictors of outcome are identified or studies have been conducted in which the antiobsessive-compulsive efficacy of the different 5-HT reuptake inhibitors can be compared directly, the initial choice of a medication treatment for an individual patient with OCD may be based mostly on its side-effects profile and availability.

References

American Psychiatric Association: Diagnostic and Statistical Manual of Mental Disorders, 3rd Edition. Washington, DC, American Psychiatric Association, 1980

Ananth J, Pecknold JC, van den Steen N, et al: Double-blind comparative study of clomipramine and amitriptyline in obsessive neurosis. Prog Neuropsychopharmacol Biol Psychiatry 5:257–262, 1981

Baxter LR: Two cases of obsessive-compulsive disorder with depression responsive to trazodone. J Nerv Ment Dis 173:432–433, 1985

Benfield P, Ward A: Fluvoxamine: a review of its pharmacodynamic and pharmacokinetic properties, and therapeutic efficacy in depressive illness. Drugs 32:313–334, 1986

Blier P, deMontigny C: Short-term lithium administration enhances serotonergic neurotransmission electrophysiological evidence in the rat CNS. Eur J Pharmacol 113:69–79, 1985

Blier P, deMontigny C, Chaput Y: Modifications of the serotonin system by antidepressant treatments: implications for the therapeutic response in major depression. J Clin Psychopharmacol 7:24S–35S, 1987

Bradford LD, Schipper J: Biochemical effects in rats after long term treatment with fluvoxamine and clovoxamine: postsynaptic changes. Paper presented at the annual meeting of the Society for Neuroscience, Dallas, TX, November 1985

Cottraux J: Predictive factors in the treatment of obsessive-compulsive disorders with fluvoxamine or behaviour therapy. Paper presented at the Symposium on Serotonin, Florence, Italy, 1989

Crespi F, Martin KF, Marsden CA: Simultaneous in vivo voltammetric measurement of striatal extracellular DOPAC and 5-HIAA levels: effect of electrical stimulation of DA and 5-HT neuronal pathways. Neurosci Lett 90:285–291, 1988

DeVeaugh-Geiss J, Landau P, Katz R: Treatment of obsessive-compulsive disorder with clomipramine. Psychiatric Annals 19:97–101, 1989

Eisenberg J, Asnis G: Lithium as an adjunct treatment in obsessive-compulsive disorder. Am J Psychiatry 142:663, 1985

Foa EB, Steketee G, Kozak MJ, et al: Effects of imipramine on depression and obsessive-compulsive symptoms. Psychiatry Res 21:123–136, 1987

Fontaine R, Chouinard G: Fluoxetine in the treatment of obsessive-compulsive disorder. Prog Neuropsychopharmacol Biol Psychiatry 9:605–608, 1985

Fontaine R, Chouinard G: Fluoxetine in the long-term maintenance treatment of obsessive compulsive disorder. Psychiatric Annals 19:88–91, 1989

Fuller RW, Wong DT: Serotonin reuptake blockers in vitro and in vivo. J Clin Psychopharmacol 7:36S–43S, 1987

Goodman WK: Clomipramine for obsessive-compulsive disorder. Med Lett Drugs Ther 30:102–104, 1988

Goodman WK, Delgado PL, Price LH, et al: Fluvoxamine versus desipramine in OCD (abstract NR343), in New Research Program and Abstracts, 142nd annual meeting of the American Psychiatric Association, San Francisco, CA, May 1989a, p 186

Goodman WK, Price LH, Charney DS: Fluvoxamine in obsessive-compulsive disorder. Psychiatric Annals 19:92–96, 1989b

Goodman WK, Price LH, Rasmussen SA, et al: Efficacy of fluvoxamine in obsessive-compulsive disorder: a double-blind comparison with placebo. Arch Gen Psychiatry 46:36–44, 1989c

Goodman WK, Price LH, Rasmussen SA, et al: The Yale-Brown Obsessive Compulsive Scale, I: development, use, and reliability. Arch Gen Psychiatry 46:1006–1011, 1989d

Hamilton M: Development of a rating scale for primary depressive illness. Br J Soc Clin Psychol 6:278–296, 1967

Insel TR, Zohar J: Psychopharmacologic approaches to obsessive-compulsive disorder, in Psychopharmacology: The Third Generation of Progress. Edited by Meltzer HY. New York, Raven Press, 1987, pp 1205–1210

Insel TR, Murphy DL, Cohen RM, et al: Obsessive-compulsive disorder: a double-blind trial of clomipramine and clorgyline. Arch Gen Psychiatry 40:605–612, 1983

Jenike MA, Surman OS, Cassem NH, et al: Monoamine oxidase inhibitors in obsessive-compulsive disorder. J Clin Psychiatry 144:131–132, 1983

Jenike MA, Baer L, Minichiello WE, et al: Concomitant obsessive-compulsive disorder and schizotypal personality disorder. Am J Psychiatry 143: 530–532, 1986

Jenike MA, Hyman S, Baer L, et al: A controlled trial of fluvoxamine in obsessive-compulsive disorder: implications for a serotonergic theory. Am J Psychiatry 147:1209–1215, 1990

Leonard H, Swedo SE, Rapoport JL, et al: Treatment of childhood obsessive-compulsive disorder with clomipramine and desmethylimipramine: a double-blind crossover comparison. Psychopharmacol Bull 24:93–95, 1988

Marks IM, Stern RS, Mawson D, et al: Clomipramine and exposure for obsessive-compulsive rituals: I. Br J Psychiatry 136:1–25, 1980

Mattes JA: A pilot study of combined trazodone and tryptophan in obsessive-compulsive disorder. Int Clin Psychopharmacol 1:170–173, 1986

Mavissakalian M, Turner SM, Michelson L, et al: Tricyclic antidepressants in obsessive-compulsive disorder: antiobsessional or antidepressant agents? Am J Psychiatry 142:572–576, 1985

McDougle CJ, Goodman WK, Price LH, et al: Neuroleptic addition in fluvoxamine-refractory obsessive-compulsive disorder. Am J Psychiatry 147:652–654, 1990

Perse TL, Greist JH, Jefferson JW, et al: Fluvoxamine treatment of obsessive-compulsive disorder. Am J Psychiatry 144:1543–1548, 1988

Prasad A: Efficacy of trazodone as an anti-obsessional agent. Pharmacol Biochem Behav 22:347–348, 1985

Price LH: Fluvoxamine for depression. Med Lett Drugs Ther 30:45–47, 1988

Price LH, Goodman WK, Charney DS, et al: Treatment of severe obsessive-compulsive disorder with fluvoxamine. Am J Psychiatry 144:1059–1061, 1987

Rasmussen SA: Lithium and tryptophan augmentation in clomipramine-resistant obsessive-compulsive disorder. Am J Psychiatry 141:1283–1285, 1984

Steiner W, Fontaine R: Toxic reaction following the combined administration of fluoxetine and L-tryptophan: five case reports. Biol Psychiatry 21:1067–1071, 1986

Thorén P, Åsberg M, Cronholm B, et al: Clomipramine treatment of obsessive-compulsive disorder, I: a controlled clinical trial. Arch Gen Psychiatry 37:1281–1285, 1980

Träskman L, Åsberg M, Bertilsson L, et al: Plasma levels of chlorimipramine and its desmethyl metabolite during treatment of depression. Clin Pharmacol Ther 26:600–610, 1979

Zohar J, Insel TR: Obsessive-compulsive disorder: psychobiological approaches to diagnosis, treatment, and pathophysiology. Biol Psychiatry 22:667–687, 1987

Chapter 5

Behavioral Treatment of Obsessive-Compulsive Disorder

Gail Steketee, Ph.D.
L. Lee Tynes, Ph.D.

*T*raditional psychodynamic and hospital-milieu forms of psychotherapy have proven only moderately effective in alleviating obsessive-compulsive symptomatology; improvement rates have ranged from 20% to 40%, with slightly higher figures found in outpatient settings (Black 1974). Improvement in the prognostic picture emerged with the use of behavioral techniques that were derived from a conceptualization of obsessive-compulsive disorder (OCD) based upon the function of obsessions and compulsions with respect to anxiety. Treatment based on this model included procedures to reduce anxiety associated with obsessions as well as to prevent ritualistic behavior. The learning theory conceptualization of OCD and the effects of behavioral treatments based on this model are presented below.

Theoretical Conceptualization

Learning theory models of human and animal responses on which behavioral treatments are based presume that behavior (and, for the most part, cognitions) follow certain basic laws. That is, behaviors persist because they are reinforced by their consequences (operant conditioning). Certain events or situations lead automatically to certain responses (e.g., pain and withdrawal follow contact with a hot stove). Positive or negative emotional responses (e.g., happiness or fear) become attached or "conditioned" to certain situations because of the person's prior experience in that context or similar ones (respondent or classical conditioning). Thus, behaviors and emotions are learned and can also be unlearned, the task of the behavior therapist.

Using a behavioral model, Foa and Tillmanns (1980) defined OCD according to the functional relationship between obsessive-compulsive symptoms and anxiety. Obsessions or ruminations are viewed as thoughts, images, impulses, or actions that generate anxiety. Compulsions are seen as attempts to reduce anxiety aroused by the obsession and can be manifest as overt actions or as covert mental events. Both types of responses are functionally equivalent in that both reduce fear (Rachman 1976). Anxiety-provoking obsessions may be prompted by external (environmental) or internal (thoughts, images) fear cues, with or without fears of potential disasters (e.g., disease, death, going to hell). To relieve anxiety, individuals may simply avoid the feared situation or stimuli (passive phobic-like avoidance) or perform overt or covert rituals (active avoidance) to restore safety or prevent harm (Rachman 1971). This definition is consistent with a behavioral model of OCD discussed below and with behavioral interventions derived from it.

Mowrer's two-stage theory for the acquisition and maintenance of fear and avoidance behavior has been commonly employed to explain phobic and obsessive-compulsive disorders (Dollard and Miller 1950; Mowrer 1960). This theory postulates that in the first stage a neutral stimulus becomes associated with fear because it is paired with an event that by its nature provokes discomfort or anxiety. Through this association, concrete objects, as well as thoughts and images, become capable of producing discomfort. In stage two, escape or avoidance responses are developed and maintained because they reduce anxiety or discomfort evoked by stimuli conditioned in stage one. Because many of the fear-provoking situations of obsessive-compulsive patients cannot readily be avoided, passive avoidance behaviors are inadequate in controlling anxiety. Ritualistic behaviors are then developed to prevent or reduce discomfort.

Evidence supporting the fear-acquisition stage of this model is inadequate in that many patients cannot recall specific aversive events associated with symptom onset. However, onset does often follow stressful life events, and such events may serve to sensitize the individual to cues that have an innate tendency to elicit fear (Watts 1971) or may provoke early learned anxiety reactions (Teasdale 1974). Similarly, Rachman (1971) proposed that an individual might experience heightened arousal when specific thoughts have special cultural or historical significance. Thus, high physiological arousal combined with general stressors and specific fear cues may produce OCD symptoms.

With regard to how OCD symptoms are maintained, the evidence suggests clearly that obsessions increase both subjective and physiological anxiety and discomfort, and compulsions reduce it (Boulougouris et al. 1977; Hodgson and Rachman 1972; Hornsveld et al. 1979; Rabavilas and Boulougouris 1974; Roper et al. 1973). In general, then, the two-stage theory is supported more with respect to maintenance of OCD than to its onset.

Assessment of Obsessive-Compulsive Disorder Symptoms

Before beginning treatment it is important for the clinician to gain a full picture of the OCD symptoms and their function for the patient. A complete assessment of symptomatology consists of both interview data (from the patient and, if applicable, from family and friends) and psychometric assessment instruments. These methods will be outlined briefly below. (Refer to Steketee and Cleere [1989] for a more detailed description of assessment approaches for OCD.)

Ideally, measurement of obsessive-compulsive symptomatology should assess obsessions and compulsions separately, along with mood state and general functioning. Assessment of obsessions should include information about external sources of fear, internal triggers for fear (thoughts, images, or impulses), and fears of disastrous consequences that may follow failure to carry out compulsions. Assessment of compulsions should include behavioral rituals, the amount of passive-avoidance behavior associated with obsessional thoughts, and cognitive compulsions. An exhaustive list of specific rituals, overt and covert compulsions, and avoidance behaviors, as well as the thoughts or events that precipitate them, will be needed when behavior therapy is initiated.

For behavioral measures of the frequency and duration of ritualistic behavior, the patient is typically requested to record the number of minutes spent on compulsive activity (Emmelkamp and van Kraanen 1977; Foa and Tillmanns 1980). Despite problems of reliability and validity for research purposes, daily completion of a self-monitoring form provides useful clinical insight into the patient's daily routine and may help generate hypotheses about external influences on compulsive behavior. Such hypotheses can be investigated during interviews and used to design behavioral exposure treatments.

Although several standardized instruments to assess obsessional fear, anxiety, avoidance, and compulsions have been developed, reliability and validity have been investigated for only a few. Of these, the assessor-administered Leyton Obsessional Inventory (LOI) (Cooper 1970) has been the most widely used until recently. However, because of its inadequacy in assessing intrusive thoughts and washing rituals, it is less valid than other questionnaires. The Maudsley Obsessional Compulsive Inventory (MOCI) (Hodgson and Rachman 1977) is a 30-item true/false questionnaire that yields a total score and several subscales, of which the checking and cleaning subscales are most used. Adequate in validity and reliability (Rachman and Hodgson 1980), it has been useful in measuring treatment outcome and may provide the clinician with a sense of severity of the patient's symptoms vis-à-vis other OCD patients. It provides little information about specific obsessions and compulsions beyond the interview data.

The Compulsive Activity Checklist (CAC) (Philpott 1975), now shortened to 38 items (Freund et al. 1987; Marks et al. 1977) and employed as either an assessor- or self-rated measure, can detect changes following treatment (Freund et al. 1987; Marks et al. 1980) and has acceptable validity but unfortunately does not have reliability criteria (Cottraux et al. 1988; Freund et al. 1987). Despite this drawback, it is the most behaviorally descriptive and specific of the instruments and therefore most clinically useful in obtaining additional information. At present, it is undergoing further revision. The interviewer-administered Yale-Brown Obsessive Compulsive Scale (Y-BOCS) (Goodman et al. 1989a, 1989b) has satisfactory reliability and validity. Because it is based directly on DSM-III-R criteria (American Psychiatric Association 1987) without reference to the type of obsessions or compulsions, it is helpful as a diagnostic instrument, but provides information only about severity rather than types of obsessions and compulsions. Two new scales, the Padua Inventory (Sanavio 1988) and the Obsessive Thoughts Checklist (G. Cottraux et al., manuscript in preparation, 1989), have not yet received adequate psychometric evaluation and so cannot be assessed.

Cognitive Features and Treatment of OCD

It is apparent from the phenomenology and description of OCD that patients with this disorder exhibit disturbances in cognitive functioning. Obsessional content typically includes exaggerations of normal concerns regarding health, death, others' welfare, sex, aggression, religious matters, among others. Cognitive theorists have noted the tendency of OCD individuals to overestimate the risk of negative consequences for a variety of actions (Carr 1974; Foa and Kozak 1986; Guidano and Liotti 1983), as well as to hold various erroneous beliefs, including ideas that one must be perfectly competent (Guidano and Liotti 1983; McFall and Wollersheim 1979), that failure to do so should be punished, and that certain actions can prevent catastrophes (McFall and Wollersheim 1979).

Guidano and Liotti (1983) have suggested that if these individuals devalue their ability to deal adequately with such threats, these ideas result in feelings of pervasive uncertainty, discomfort, and helplessness. Rituals are viewed by the patient as the only available coping method, since other more appropriate ones are lacking. In line with this conceptualization, Beech and Liddell (1974) proposed that ritualistic behaviors are maintained not only to reduce immediate discomfort but also to address the obsessive-compulsive individual's need for certainty before terminating an activity. Experimental findings lend some support to the above assertions, particularly with respect to the overspecification and need for certainty evident in OCD patients (Makhlouf-Norris and Norris 1972; Makhlouf-Norris et al. 1970; Milner et al. 1971; Persons and Foa 1984; Reed 1968; Volans 1976).

Foa and Kozak (1986) have proposed that, unlike normal individuals, most obsessive-compulsive individuals base their beliefs about danger on the absence of evidence that guarantees safety rather than on the presence of danger cues. Further, these individuals fail to assume *general* safety from specific experiences of exposure to feared situations in which no harm occurred. Consequently, although rituals are performed to reduce the likelihood of harm, they can never really provide safety and therefore must be repeated. Evidence supporting these intriguing suggestions is needed, since they bear on possible cognitive treatments that might enhance exposure outcome.

Despite the seeming theoretical importance of cognitive treatments for OCD, the few studies that have applied cognitive theories regarding dysfunctional thought processes have proved to be only minimally helpful. Most of these studies employed interventions that attempted to modify thoughts and irrational beliefs using a conversational format. Emmelkamp et al. (1980) compared graded exposure in vivo with exposure preceded by self-instructional training. Both treatments produced significant improvement in both groups, but the cognitive technique did not appear to enhance the efficacy of exposure. A study by Bleijenberg

(1981; reported in Emmelkamp 1982) indicated that disputing irrational beliefs and analyzing obsessional fears rationally did not improve OCD symptoms or alter cognitions.

A recent comparison of rational emotive therapy (RET) and self-controlled exposure in vivo (Emmelkamp et al. 1988) showed that both treatments improved OCD symptoms equally and that RET also decreased depression and irrational beliefs. This is the first study to show that a cognitive treatment alone was clinically beneficial for OCD. Perhaps this treatment was more appropriate for the cognitive dysfunctions found in OCD, such as perfectionism, errors in beliefs about danger, and avoidance of risk.

The above cognitive treatments may not have been tailored specifically for correcting cognitive distortions believed to be typical of OCD. However, research must first establish which cognitions are important in the development or maintenance of OCD symptoms. Then we can begin to determine whether needed cognitive changes are best achieved via cognitive treatments or by other (e.g., behavioral) methods.

Behavioral Treatment

Variants of exposure and blocking procedures have been used for both obsessional patients and overtly ritualizing patients. Exposure techniques, such as systematic desensitization, paradoxical intention, flooding, and satiation, require the patient to confront fearful or disturbing ideas or situations, either in vivo or in imagination. Blocking methods interrupt the patient's ruminations or ritualistic behaviors via such strategies as thought stopping, aversive stimulation, distraction, and response prevention.

Early Exposure and Blocking Procedures

Attempts to reduce obsessional fear have been based on the assumption that once obsessional cues no longer generate anxiety, compulsive behaviors will automatically extinguish because they will no longer be reinforced by their ability to reduce anxiety. Several procedures to alleviate anxiety were studied in OCD patients.

Systematic desensitization consisted of brief presentations of mild but increasingly anxiety-evoking items when the subject was deeply relaxed. Imaginal desensitization led to improvement in only 30% to 40%

of cases in multiple-case studies (Beech and Vaughn 1978; Cooper et al. 1965). Results of in vivo desensitization were somewhat better, with 7 of 11 (64%) improved to some extent. Systematic desensitization, then, does not appear to be a treatment of choice for OCD, although a clinical report by Walton and Mather (1963) has indicated that desensitization may be quite useful for those with recent symptom onset. Nonetheless, to date we have no information suggesting that desensitization is more advantageous for OCD than other exposure procedures.

Variants of prolonged exposure have also been employed with OCD patients. Via paradoxical intention and satiation, patients are instructed to try to deliberately increase or repeat their obsessional fears. Early single-case reports of successful outcomes using these methods were supplanted by later findings that 50% or fewer of a series of patients improved (for paradoxical intention see Solyom et al. 1972; for satiation see Emmelkamp and Kwee 1977; Stern 1978). Thus, variations of prolonged exposure had limited effects on obsessions and on ritualistic behavior (which was not directly targeted).

Theoretically, if compulsions persist because they decrease discomfort, then they should extinguish if they are paired with an increase, rather than a decrease, in discomfort. The use of aversion procedures (electrical shock) following ritualistic behavior led to some improvement in case studies (e.g., Kenny et al. 1978), but one report indicated that relapse occurred in some cases (Walton 1960). Aversion methods have also been applied to obsessional thoughts, with successful outcomes in most of the single cases reported (e.g., Kenny et al. 1973, 1978; McGuire and Vallance 1964). The use of another blocking method, thought stopping, on obsessional thoughts led to mixed results: some single cases improved (e.g., Mahoney 1971; Stern 1970; Yamagami 1971), whereas only one-third of multiple-case reports and controlled studies benefited from this procedure (Emmelkamp and Kwee 1977; Stern 1978; Stern et al. 1975). In comparisons of exposure and blocking treatments, equivalent effects were found with prolonged exposure (satiation or imaginal flooding) compared to thought stopping (Emmelkamp and Kwee 1977; Stern 1978).

The conclusions that can be derived from this body of research are at best equivocal, given the wide variation in the types of exposure and blocking interventions and the failure to distinguish between effects of the treatment on obsessions and on ritualistic behavior. Further, much of the available information has been derived from single-case studies rather than controlled comparisons. When information from case reports is not included, the rather sparse body of literature on the treatment of ritualizing patients with exposure procedures is disappointing. For obsessional patients neither blocking nor exposure techniques resulted in satisfactory outcomes.

The conceptualization of OCD described earlier suggests that procedures that reduce anxiety should be applied specifically to obsessional content, whereas blocking strategies are appropriate for cognitive and behavioral rituals. Both strategies should be necessary for patients with obsessions and compulsions. In the above research, rarely were treatments applied differentially and simultaneously. Thus, for example, desensitization for obsessive thoughts may be useful in combination with aversion treatment for cognitive and overt rituals, but such combinations of treatment techniques have not been attempted.

Treatment by Exposure and Response Prevention

The combining of exposure for obsessions with response prevention for compulsions was first employed by Meyer in 1966 with patients who used washing and cleaning rituals. In this program compulsions were prevented while the patient was required to repeatedly touch objects that evoked anxiety about "contamination" and consequent urges to wash. Of 15 patients treated in this way, 10 were rated much improved or symptom-free and the remaining 5 were moderately improved (Meyer and Levy 1973; Meyer et al. 1974). Only two of the patients relapsed after 5 to 6 years. These remarkable results brought considerable interest in this combined treatment program. Results of controlled trials using exposure and response prevention for obsessions and compulsions are summarized below.

Studies conducted on inpatients at the Maudsley Hospital in London provide much of the available data about these procedures. Variants of exposure in vivo were compared with relaxation training, both in conjunction with response prevention, for 20 obsessive-compulsive inpatients (reviewed in Rachman and Hodgson 1980). After 15 sessions of the exposure regimen, 75% of the patients were much improved or moderately improved; by contrast, relaxation training had no effect. At a 2-year follow-up, improvement was maintained or increased, and only 25% of the patients were unchanged (Marks et al. 1975). Similar results with 10 "washers" were reported by Roper et al. (1975). At the end of treatment,

8 of the patients were much improved or somewhat improved and 2 remained unchanged. These results persisted at follow-up. In two studies conducted in Greece, an average of 11 sessions of in vivo and imaginal exposure plus response prevention produced good results: 13 patients improved and only 2 remained unchanged after treatment (Boulougouris and Bassiakos 1973; Rabavilas et al. 1976). However, a long-term follow-up indicated that 6 of the 15 patients failed to show gains (Boulougouris 1977).

In Holland, Emmelkamp and his colleagues conducted three studies with OCD outpatients using 10 to 15 sessions of in vivo exposure and blocking of compulsions. Overall, about 70% to 80% of 41 patients improved, and most remained so at follow-up, although some patients required additional treatment sessions (Boersma et al. 1976; Emmelkamp and van Kraanen 1977; Emmelkamp et al. 1980). In discussing their results, the authors suggested that 10 sessions of treatment might not adequately protect patients against future relapse. Further support for the effectiveness of exposure and response prevention was provided by Julien et al. (1980): of their 20 patients, 12 were much improved, 5 moderately, and 1 was unchanged. Some relapse was evident at follow-up. Catts and McConaghy (1975) reported that all of their 6 OCD patients improved, with further improvement in both rituals and obsessions evident at follow-up evaluation. Hoogduin and Duivenvoorden (1988) treated 60 patients with 10 sessions (one every other week) of exposure and response prevention without therapist supervision. Weekly discussion groups were also held. Forty-seven subjects (78%) demonstrated improvement of greater than 30%.

More detailed information about the effects of exposure and response prevention on obsessions and compulsions separately was provided by Foa and Goldstein (1978). After 10 sessions of combined imaginal and in vivo treatment, 18 of their 21 patients were symptom-free on measures of rituals, 2 improved, and 1 remained unchanged. At follow-up, only 3 relapsed to various degrees. With regard to obsessions, 12 of the patients were asymptomatic after treatment, 8 were mildly to moderately symptomatic, and 1 failed to change. At follow-up, 2 patients relapsed on obsessions. These findings indicate that treatment was somewhat more effective with compulsions than with obsessions, results that have been borne out in subsequent studies of both exposure therapy and pharmacotherapy.

Although "purely obsessional" patients (OCD patients without overt rituals) have traditionally been considered more difficult to treat with exposure and response prevention, recent studies suggest that careful application of this behavioral treatment may result in substantial improvement for some patients. For instance, Hoogduin et al. (1987) treated 26 obsessive patients with a systematic program of deliberate evoking of obsessional thoughts (exposure) with strategies for refraining from neutralizing thoughts and cognitive rituals (response prevention). Nineteen subjects (73%) showed improvement of greater than 30%, and 61% of these individuals maintained their gains at a 1-year follow-up. Salkovkiis and Westbrook (1989) outlined some helpful approaches to invoking an exposure with response prevention treatment paradigm with purely obsessional patients, including the use of tape-recorded obsessional thoughts to effect proper exposure. The authors also presented four case studies to illustrate successful treatment. Clearly, more investigation of these applications is needed, and with cautious optimism it can be said that effective behavioral treatment of purely obsessional patients may indeed be forthcoming.

To date, prolonged exposure and response prevention have been used to treat over 200 OCD patients. Most of these data have been derived from group studies rather than single-case reports, adding confidence to the findings. The remarkable convergence of results from studies conducted in many centers with numerous therapists further attests to the generalizability of the treatment effects. It seems, then, that exposure and response prevention can be considered the psychological treatment of choice for OCD (see case history at the end of this chapter).

Variants of Exposure and Response Prevention

Meyer's original treatment consisted of two basic components: exposure to discomfort-evoking stimuli and prevention of ritualistic responses. Subsequent studies have investigated the ways in which these two procedures should be administered.

Imaginal versus in vivo exposure.   Early reports on the effect of the modality in which exposure was delivered to OCD patients were conflicting. Stampfl (1967) successfully treated a patient with imaginal exposure, yet Rachman et al. (1970) concluded that implosion had no therapeutic effect on washing rituals, in contrast with exposure in vivo, which produced good results. Subsequently, Rabavilas et al. (1976) demonstrated in a controlled trial that in vivo treatment was significantly more effective in reducing obsessive-compulsive symptoms than exposure in fantasy.

Most of these studies have focused on the modality rather than the content of exposure and its relevance to the patient's symptomatology. When exposure in fantasy merely mimics exposure in vivo, it is not surprising that the latter is typically more effective. However, for OCD patients as well as other anxiety-disordered patients, anxiety can be generated not only by tangible environmental cues but also by thoughts of possible disasters that may follow exposure (e.g., death, disease, burglary, house burning). Foa et al. (1980b) have demonstrated that when imaginal exposure to feared disasters is added to exposure in practice, it enhances long-term outcome in patients with checking rituals who fear the disastrous consequences. Inclusion of exposure to feared disasters affects maintenance of gains, although not immediate treatment outcome, and appears to be a valuable addition to treatment for patients who report such fears.

Duration of exposure.   Prolonged exposure to fear provoking stimuli is superior to brief exposure, according to studies of both animal and volunteer subjects. Rabavilas et al. (1976) examined the differential effects of long versus short exposure in fantasy and in vivo on OCD. Eighty minutes of continuous in vivo exposure proved superior to eight 10-minute segments. When exposure was conducted in fantasy, the duration did not affect outcome. In vivo exposure, then, should be conducted for prolonged uninterrupted periods whenever possible.

Gradual versus rapid exposure.   The speed of presentation of the most disturbing stimuli has not proved to be salient in the treatment of OCD. Hodgson and Rachman (1972) exposed patients gradually to discomfort-evoking situations after they watched the therapist model each step. Other patients were exposed immediately to the most feared situation, again after watching the therapist model exposure. The two procedures were equally effective, although, not surprisingly, patients reported feeling more comfortable with the gradual approach. In clinical practice, then, patients are exposed to increasingly fearful situations.

Modeling.   A combination of participant modeling (patient copies the therapist-demonstrated exposure) and response prevention yielded considerably better results than passive modeling (patient only observes the therapist) in a study by Roper et al. (1975). However, this study was confounded by the inclusion of response prevention instructions with the participant modeling but not with the passive modeling. Rachman et al. (1973) compared flooding in vivo with and without modeling and found that modeling did not improve outcome. Similar results were obtained in a study by Boersma et al. (1976), who found that therapist demonstration of exposure conferred little added benefit. As noted by Marks and his colleagues (1975), this lack of improvement does not imply that certain individuals cannot benefit from modeling. Indeed, some patients have reported that observing the therapist assisted them in overcoming their resistance and avoidance of exposure.

The therapist's role

Therapist qualities of warmth, genuineness, and empathy have long been recognized as important components of any psychotherapeutic intervention (e.g., Truax and Carkuff 1967). Informal observations led Marks et al. (1975) to suggest that exposure and response prevention treatment requires a good therapeutic relationship and often a sense of humor. Research findings by Rabavilas et al. (1979) indicated that therapists who were respectful, understanding, interested, encouraging, challenging, and explicit were able to achieve greater gains in patients than those who gratified dependency needs, were permissive, or were tolerant. In practice, a combination of support, encouragement, and firm insistence that the patient follow therapeutic instructions for exposure and ritual prevention appears to be optimal.

Although the personal style of the therapist seems to be an important variable, his or her presence during exposure may not be required, at least in some cases. Emmelkamp and van Kraanen (1977) compared 10 sessions of self-controlled in vivo exposure with an equivalent number of sessions in which the therapist controlled the exposure. No differences in outcome were found on obsessive-compulsive symptomatology, although the therapist-controlled treatment subjects required more treatment sessions at follow-up than did the other group. The authors suggested that the self-controlled exposure patients may have gained greater independence in handling their fears. Marks and his colleagues (1988) observed that adding therapist-aided exposure after 8 weeks of self-exposure instructions conferred only transient benefits that were lost at week 23. The findings of these studies do not suggest that therapists are dispensable, but they do indicate that in vivo exposure may be implemented without the therapists' immediate presence. Whether this is especially true for patients with moderate, rather than severe, symptoms remains to be tested.

The failure to detect differences between variants of exposure may be due to a ceiling effect produced by the powerful effects of exposure–response prevention treatment in studies using relatively small sample sizes. Thus, these results cannot be interpreted as evidence that variables such as therapist presence, rapidity of presentation, and modeling do not impact at all on treatment outcome. However, these variables do not appear to be critical. Additionally, response prevention was implemented simultaneously with deliberate exposure and may have further obscured differences among variants of exposure. From a clinical standpoint the research suggests that therapists may begin treatment by conducting some exposure in the office and then assign more between sessions. Only if the patient has serious difficulty with "homework" should the therapist insist on being present throughout the process. Most patients are likely to prefer graduated exposure, but some circumstances may require more rapid confrontation. Modeling may be used whenever patients feel it would be helpful.

Response prevention variants.   By contrast with exposure treatment, relatively little attention has been directed at variants of response prevention. Some studies (e.g., Foa and Goldstein 1978; Meyer et al. 1974) have utilized very strict restriction or prevention of rituals, whereas others have been more lenient. Is the former more effective? Supervised response prevention versus mere instructions to refrain from ritualizing were compared in five OCD "washers" (Mills et al. 1973). Instructions alone reduced compulsions, but complete elimination of rituals did not occur until supervised treatment was implemented. Marks et al. (1975) attributed most of their failures to patients' inadequate compliance with response prevention instructions. We conclude that although strict supervision may not be necessary for most patients, it may facilitate adherence to the treatment regimen for some and result in a more complete elimination of ritualistic behavior.

Concomitant treatments.   Although severe marital problems are often seen in conjunction with OCD, Marks (1981) has noted that the presence of marital problems does not make exposure treatment inadvisable. In fact, exposure improved both OCD symptoms and marital problems, whereas marital treatment alone improved only the couple relationship (Cobb et al. 1980). With respect to social dysfunction, the use of assertiveness training produced favorable results with patients who had obsessions about harming others, and was found to be at least as effective as thought stopping (Emmelkamp and van der Heyden 1980). However, because thought stopping was not strongly effective, the comparability of assertiveness training does not recommend it as an effective strategy. Clinical impression suggests that assertiveness training and marital therapy may provide useful adjuncts to exposure and response prevention procedures (e.g., Queiroz et al. 1981) but that they cannot be substituted for the latter.

Differential Effects of Exposure and Response Prevention

Exposure and response prevention have usually been employed in tandem, and, therefore, the separate effect of each procedure could not be ascertained. Theoretically, exposure should be necessary to reduce anxiety associated with obsessions. Ritualistic behavior should be blocked, because it terminates confrontation with the fearful stimuli, thus preventing extinction of anxiety. The research data support these assumptions. In case studies compulsions were reduced by response prevention, but not by exposure (Mills et al. 1973; Turner et al. 1980). Obsessional anxiety declined somewhat with response prevention and more so after flooding. Foa et al. (1980a, 1984) conducted two studies comparing exposure alone with response prevention alone, and with combined treatment. As expected, exposure reduced anxiety more than rituals, which were affected more by response prevention. Combined treatment led to the best results. These studies support the theoretical notion that separate mechanisms operate in the two treatment modalities and that both are necessary for effective treatment of ritualizing patients. Clinically, therapists should implement graduated exposure to feared obsessional situations in combination with prevention of rituals that are directly related to the exposed fears.

Combined Behavioral and Pharmacological Treatment

Studies in which pharmacological and behavioral treatments are compared are reviewed elsewhere in this volume and are therefore not presented in detail here. In most of these studies serotonergic antidepressant drugs (clomipramine, fluoxetine, and fluvoxamine) had both antidepressant and antiobsessive effects (e.g., Cottraux et al. 1989; Marks et al. 1980). By contrast, other antidepressants (such as imipramine) affected only depressive symptoms (Foa et al., submitted for publication). In these studies behavior therapy also led to improvement in both depressive and OCD symptoms, with the changes in the latter appearing to be at least equivalent to those produced by clomipramine or fluvoxamine (for review see Steketee and Cleere 1989). A meta-analysis of treatment studies collected from screening 120 recent research reports assessed statistically the relative efficacy of behavioral versus tricyclic antidepressant treatment for OCD (Christensen et al. 1987). Results indicated that behavior therapy was generally more effective than tricyclic pharmacotherapy, although both therapies demonstrated efficacy for the treatment of OCD.

Thus far, the combination of pharmacotherapy and behavior therapy has shown relatively little advantage over behavior therapy alone in the few trials in which the combination has been tested. Both serotonergic drug treatments and behavioral treatment via exposure and response prevention appear to be consistently effective in reducing OCD symptoms. Some writers have suggested that behavioral treatment leads to greater and more lasting reduction in symptomatology than do antiobsessional drugs (Steketee and Cleere 1989), but measurement differences across studies conducted to date make comparisons difficult. It stands to reason that the learning of coping skills and tolerance of obsessional anxiety that inevitably occurs during exposure treatment may assist patients in maintaining gains when faced with urges to ritualize at times of stress. Nonetheless, drug treatment appears to enable many patients to control their symptoms without additional behavior treatment. Others who are initially too fearful to enter a behavioral treatment may find that the partial improvement and anxiety reduction that they experience from pharmacotherapy renders them more amenable to formal behavioral treatment. For those who refuse behavioral treatment, clearly the serotonergic antidepressants are the treatment of choice.

Predictors of Outcome

Treatment by exposure and response prevention has led to improvement in approximately 65% to 75% of OCD patients who undertake it. Some information about those who remain unaffected or relapse over time has been collected.

It is not surprising that noncompliance with treatment instructions has led to poor outcome (Rachman and Hodgson 1980), since uncooperative patients receive only partial treatment. Examination of demographic variables has not provided helpful information regarding prognosis nor have severe symptoms been identified as a risk factor, although this may be due to the restricted range on this variable in most studies (for review see Steketee and Cleere 1989). Although high levels of pretreatment depression appeared problematic in early research (e.g., Foa et al. 1983; Marks et al. 1980), subsequent studies have failed to find an association (e.g., Mavissakalian et al. 1985; Steketee et al. 1985; M. Basoglu, T. Lax, Y. Kasvidis, unpublished manuscript, 1986). One study indicated that high levels of depression at posttreatment were related to poorest long-term outcome (Steketee 1987).

With respect to social variables, patients with more cohesive marriages fared better after treatment (Hafner 1982). However, spouse assistance in treatment led to only transient benefits over therapy conducted without the spouse's assistance (Emmelkamp and DeLange 1983), perhaps because not all of the marriages were positive relationships. General social support did not lead to better outcome or to less relapse, but family members' critical, angry responses or beliefs that patients could control their symptoms if they chose to were positively associated with relapse (Steketee 1987).

When patients ask whether they are likely to benefit from behavioral therapy for OCD, the clinician should consider the severity of their symptoms and degree of familial support available to them. It is wise, however, not to discourage the patient, but to advise them that thoughts of an obsessive nature and urges to ritualize are likely to continue to occur occasionally, even if treatment is highly successful. It is often helpful to note that nearly everyone has disturbing thoughts from time to time, but they provoke relatively little or only brief discomfort and are readily dismissed. After behavioral treatment, patients should not be alarmed by the experience of mild obsessional symptoms, particularly in times of stress, but merely allow themselves to experience the obsessive thought until fear declines, without engaging in ritualistic efforts.

Case Histories

Case 1

The following case is typical of patients with obsessions about contamination and washing rituals. This patient received no concurrent pharmacotherapy, but continued her psychodynamic psychotherapy of several years duration that she had found helpful for relationship issues, although it had never focused on her OCD symptoms and, indeed, had not led to improvement in these symptoms.

Ms. C., a single Catholic-educated white woman, 34 years of age, who lived alone, presented with fears of touching objects in or associated with public places and especially rest rooms (trash cans, money, faucets, door handles, toilet seats), her own and other's body fluids (including urine, feces, menstrual blood, touching the genital area, semen), places frequented by the public and homeless people (the subway floor, seats), and certain objects in her own home and in her parents' home (a lamp that had once fallen into the toilet, old clothes, garbage cans). She avoided touching "contaminated" objects with her right hand, but used her left if avoidance was impossible. Similarly, she avoided touching objects in her purse (pens, credit cards, cosmetics) unless her hands were "clean."

Her fears appeared related to a period during her early teens when she felt frustrated with her rigid, domineering mother and began to engage in various rituals, including pulling out pubic hairs, repeating the rosary over and over, repeating other actions, and compulsive hand washing after genital contact. She sought treatment for the first time at age 18 for the hair pulling and washing rituals. Although she stopped pulling pubic hairs, washing and repeating rituals continued for some time. Eventually, she began to check calculations and words repeatedly, to be perfectionistic in filling out forms or handing in papers for schoolwork, and to check her doctoral thesis repeatedly for errors. Sexual contact with her boyfriend required immediate disposal of birth control materials and washing to remove "contamination." Surprisingly, she felt he did not realize why she washed—she had never discussed her problem with him.

Ms. C.'s treatment included exposure to a hierarchy of obsessional objects and situations, along with gradual prevention of washing and cleaning. No medications were employed. Sessions were held twice weekly for 60 to 90 minutes, with homework assigned daily to repeat and vary the previous session's exposure situations. Exposure began with touching counters, faucets, and flushers in "nice" bathrooms without allowing washing afterward, and progressed to trash, subway stop floors, less clean and eventually "dirty" bathrooms, toilet seats, locker-room floors, her own genitals and urine, and finally items "contaminated" from various sources from several years ago in her own home and her parents' home. She agreed to shower every other day and to wash her hands for 20 seconds or less after contact with items higher on her hierarchy, but had to "recontaminate" with the worst items from the previous exposure treatment immediately after washing of any kind. In touching a contaminant she rubbed it on her hands, her face, and her hair, and immediately touched her "clean" pens and other contents of her purse. At times she deliberately dropped her clean things on the floor or in the trash to make sure they were "contaminated." Cleaning was reduced to the minimum essential to maintain her household.

Ms. C.'s progress was slow but steady, and she remained committed to the exposure and washing restrictions, noting to the therapist any situations that disturbed her that she had forgotten to mention, as well as "mini" rituals like wiping her hands on her clothes to remove contamination. In a typical session her anxiety level might peak at 75 subjective units of disturbance (SUDS) and drop to 55 by the end of the hour. After 8 weeks of treatment, anxiety about the highest items reduced rapidly with exposure to 25 to 30 SUDS, and she found herself forgetting that she was contaminated in more and more situations. Progress continued during the third month until all items had reduced substantially and sessions were reduced to once weekly and then every other week until treatment ended 4 months later. She remained in psychotherapy, continuing to address other interpersonal problems for several months thereafter, with continued maintenance of improvement in OCD symptoms.

Case 2

Mr. A. was a 35-year-old married male who presented for inpatient treatment with the chief complaint that "I feel my physical presence affects others in an adverse way." Further questioning revealed an obsession with the possibility of causing harm to others. This obsession led the patient eventually to be housebound and unable to work or drive for almost 2 years preceding hospitalization. Mr. A. was only able to venture out of his home at night because of his intense fear that, during the day, automobile drivers might be distracted by his presence and run off the road or cross over into oncoming traffic. Even at night, he was quite cautious about not dropping any thread of lint from his clothes onto the sidewalk or street, he was unable to extinguish a cigarette on the ground, and he would often return from a trip to the mailbox with his pockets full of rocks, paper, nails, and other objects that he picked up to prevent harm from befalling others. He was extremely cautious not to allow loud noises in the house (e.g., television) or to permit glass or mirrored objects near the windows, lest passing drivers be distracted. Mr. A. had given up driving because of his compulsive checking and circling back to assure himself that he had not caused an accident. At one point, a 20-minute trip took over 2 hours to complete. Although housebound, the patient religiously checked the news and police logs of the local newspapers to assure himself that none of his family members had been present near the location and time of any accidents in his town.

Psychometric data included a Maudsley Obsessional Compulsive Inventory score of 21 (checking subscore of 5, washing subscore of 8), a Yale-Brown Obsessive Compulsive Scale score of 32 (obsession subtotal of 16, compulsion subtotal of 16) and a 17-item Hamilton Depression Scale score of 16. In Mr. A.'s case, the Compulsive Activity Checklist did not indicate a high score because his obsessional and ritualistic symptoms were not specifically included on this measure.

The patient's obsessive compulsive symptoms could be traced back to the sixth grade, but did not cause significant interference in the patient's life until shortly before his marriage. A list of 16 discrete compulsive behaviors was created by the patient and therapist working together. These included items relatively low in anxiety-evoking potential (e.g., "standing in a window in full view of passing cars"), medium items (e.g., "crossing the street with a car in sight"; "purposefully putting a rock, bottle cap, string, etc., in the street"), and high anxiety-evoking items (e.g., "leaving coins in a chair"; "riding as a passenger in a car without being able to turn around and double-check the road"). The items were then rated from 0 to 100, with 0 equaling "no anxiety" and 100 equaling "the worst imaginable anxiety."

In the treatment of Mr. A. the list of discrete compulsive behaviors and their subjective ratings of distress was used to take a graduated approach to exposure with response prevention. In other words, sessions (and homework) began with a focus on the less anxiety-producing items and, as the patient became successful with preventing compulsive behavior in those situations, gradually moved on to more intense items. Accordingly, the first session began with standing in front of a window in full view of passing cars. Because the patient's anxiety could be relieved by compulsively checking after the car as it drove by, he was instructed to spot a car in full view and then turn and walk away from the window without the compulsive checking. Anxiety was allowed to dissipate for a few minutes and the task repeated. It is instructive to note that, initially, the therapist accompanied Mr. A. as he stood at the window waiting for a car to pass. It soon became obvious, however, that the clinician's presence greatly reduced the anxiety of the task. The patient explained that he knew a "health care provider" would respond in a responsible manner if he observed an accident happen, thereby relieving the patient of the "responsibility" (and the anxiety). Henceforth, assignments of this nature were carried out with the patient in view, but with the therapist far enough away so that he could not be held "responsible" for the action that "endangered" others. Gradually, as the patient became less anxious about the task, sessions incorporated items that were higher in the hierarchy so that he eventually was able to cross the street without difficulty, refrain from picking up rocks and paper in the street while on walks, toss rocks in the street, leave coins in chairs, ride in a car without double-checking behind him, and so forth.

In general, Mr. A.'s motivation for treatment was good. Nonetheless, a daily checklist was initiated to ensure compliance both by acting as a prompt and by allowing staff to reinforce homework completion during a daily review of the checklist. As one might suspect, a patient with the severe dysfunction of Mr. A. is likely to have multiple problem areas. Indeed, complete inpatient treatment included marital and family therapy, individual psychotherapy, antidepressant pharmacotherapy, vocational rehabilitation, and group psychotherapy. The patient and his wife also elected to participate in a psychoeducational group for patients and their relatives or close friends in order to foster a better understanding of OCD and better communication regarding the disorder. After 37 sessions of treatment in the hospital, this patient was rated much improved but required some further assistance in driving alone without checking and in transferring gains to his home environment.

Summary

The conceptualization of obsessions as anxiety-increasing thoughts, images, impulses, or actions, and of compulsions as anxiety-reducing behaviors or cognitions, has led to very successful treatments for OCD. Prolonged exposure to feared situations, accompanied by blocking of ritualistic responses, has proven to be a highly successful treatment for 65% to 75% of those who elect it. Research studies indicate that exposure should be lengthy rather than brief to allow anxiety to decline, and that imaginal exposure to images that include the patient's feared disastrous consequence is a helpful adjunct to exposure in practice for those who have such fears. Both exposure and ritual prevention are needed to effectively reduce OCD symptoms. The addition of cognitive therapy as it currently exists or of drug treatment has not significantly improved the benefits of this behavioral treatment. In general, the more rigorous the program, the better the success achieved.

References

American Psychiatric Association: Diagnostic and Statistical Manual of Mental Disorders, 3rd Edition, Revised. Washington, DC, American Psychiatric Association, 1987

Beech HR, Liddell A: Decision making, mood states, and ritualistic behavior among obsessional patients, in Obsessional States. Edited by Beech HR. London, Methuen, 1974, pp 143–160

Beech HR, Vaughn M: Behavioral Treatment of Obsessional States. New York, John Wiley, 1978

Black A: The natural history of obsessional neurosis, in Obsessional States. Edited by Beech HR. London, Methuen, 1974, pp 19–54

Boersma K, Den Hengst S, Dekker J, et al: Exposure and response prevention: a comparison with obsessive-compulsive patients. Behav Res Ther 14:19–24, 1976

Boulougouris JC: Variables affecting the behavior modification of obsessive-compulsive patients treated by flooding, in The Treatment of Phobic and Obsessive-Compulsive Disorders. Edited by Boulougouris JC, Rabavilas AD. Oxford, UK, Pergamon, 1977, pp 73–84

Boulougouris JC, Bassiakos L: Prolonged flooding in cases with obsessive-compulsive neurosis. Behav Res Ther 11:227–231, 1973

Boulougouris JC, Rabavilas AD, Stefanic S: Psychophysiological responses in obsessive compulsive patients. Behav Res Ther 15:221–230, 1977

Carr AI: Compulsive neurosis: a review of the literature. Psychol Bull 8: 311–318, 1974

Catts S, McConaghy M: Ritual prevention in the treatment of obsessive-compulsive neurosis. Aust N Z J Psychiatry 9:37–41, 1975

Christensen H, Hadzi-Pavlovic D, Andrews G, et al: Behavior therapy and tricyclic medication in the treatment of obsessive-compulsive disorder: a quantitative review. J Consult Clin Psychol 55:701–711, 1987

Cobb J, McDonald R, Marks IM, et al: Marital versus exposure therapy: psychological treatments of co-existing marital and phobic obsessive problems. Behavioural Analysis and Modification 4:3–16, 1980

Cooper J: The Leyton obsessional inventory. Psychol Med 1:48–64, 1970

Cooper JE, Gelder MG, Marks IM: The results of behavior therapy in 77 psychiatric patients. Br Med J 1:1222–1225, 1965

Cottraux G, Bouvard M, Defayolle M, et al: Validity and factorial structure study of the compulsive activity checklist. Behavior Therapy 19:45–53, 1988

Cottraux J, Mollard E, Bouvard M, et al: A controlled study of fluvoxamine and exposure in obsessive-compulsive disorder. Int Clin Psychopharmacol Vol 5, 1989

Dollard J, Miller NE: Personality and Psychotherapy: An Analysis in Terms of Learning, Thinking and Culture. New York, McGraw-Hill, 1950

Emmelkamp PMG: Phobic and Obsessive Compulsive Disorders: Theory, Research, and Practice. New York, Plenum, 1982

Emmelkamp PMG, DeLange I: Spouse involvement in the treatment of obsessive-compulsive patients. Behav Res Ther 21:341–346, 1983

Emmelkamp PMG, Kwee KG: Obsessional ruminations: a comparison between thought stopping and prolonged exposure in imagination. Behav Res Ther 15:441–444, 1977

Emmelkamp PMG, van der Heyden H: The treatment of harming obsessions. Behavioural Analysis and Modification 4:28–35, 1980

Emmelkamp PMG, van Kraanen J: Therapist-controlled exposure in vivo: a comparison with obsessive-compulsive patients. Behav Res Ther 15: 491–495, 1977

Emmelkamp PMG, van der Helm M, van Zanten BL, et al: Contributions of self-instructional training to the effectiveness of exposure in vivo: a comparison with obsessive-compulsive patients. Behav Res Ther 18:61–66, 1980

Emmelkamp PMG, Viser S, Hoekstra RJ: Cognitive therapy vs exposure in vivo in the treatment of obsessive-compulsives. Cognitive Therapy and Research 12:103–114, 1988

Foa EB, Goldstein A: Continuous exposure and complete response prevention of obsessive-compulsive disorder. Behavior Therapy 9:821–829, 1978

Foa EB, Kozak MJ: Emotional processing of fear: exposure to corrective information. Psychol Bull 99:20–35, 1986

Foa EB, Tillmanns A: The treatment of obsessive-compulsive neurosis, in Handbook of Behavioral Interventions: A Clinical Guide. Edited by Goldstein A, Foa EB. New York, John Wiley, 1980, pp 416–500

Foa EB, Steketee GS, Milby JB: Differential effects of exposure and response prevention in obsessive-compulsive washers. J Consult Clin Psychol 48: 71–79, 1980a

Foa EB, Steketee G, Turner RM, et al: Effects of imaginal exposure to feared disasters in obsessive-compulsive checkers. Behav Res Ther 18:449–455, 1980b

Foa EB, Grayson JB, Steketee GS, et al: Success and failure in the behavioral treatment of obsessive-compulsives. J Consult Clin Psychol 51:287–297, 1983

Foa EB, Steketee GS, Grayson J, et al: Deliberate exposure and blocking of obsessive-compulsive rituals: immediate and long-term effects. Behavior Therapy 15:450–472, 1984

Foa EB, Steketee GS, Kozak MJ, et al: Treatment of depressive and obsessive-compulsive symptoms in OCD by imipramine and behavior therapy. Arch Gen Psychiatry (submitted for publication)

Freund B, Steketee GS, Foa EB: Compulsive activity checklist (CAC): psychometric analysis with obsessive-compulsive disorder. Behavioral Assessment 9:67–79, 1987

Goodman WK, Price LH, Rasmussen SA, et al: The Yale-Brown Obsessive Compulsive Scale, I: development, use, and reliability. Arch Gen Psychiatry 46:1006–1011, 1989a

Goodman WK, Price LH, Rasmussen SA, et al: The Yale-Brown Obsessive Compulsive Scale, II: validity. Arch Gen Psychiatry 46:1012–1016, 1989b

Guidano VL, Liotti G: Cognitive Processes and Emotional Disorders. New York, Guilford, 1983

Hafner RJ: Marital interaction in persisting obsessive-compulsive disorders. Aust N Z J Psychiatry 16:171–178, 1982

Hodgson RJ, Rachman S: The effect of contamination and washing in obsessional patients. Behav Res Ther 10:111–117, 1972

Hodgson RJ, Rachman S: Obsessional compulsive complaints. Behav Res Ther 15:389–395, 1977

Hoogduin CAL, Duivenvoorden HJ: A decision model in the treatment of obsessive-compulsive neuroses. Br J Psychiatry 152:516–521, 1988

Hoogduin K, DeHaan E, Schaap C, et al: Exposure and response prevention in patients with obsessions. Acta Psychiatr Belg 87:640–653, 1987

Hornsveld RHJ, Kraaimaat FW, van Dam-Baggen RMJ: Anxiety/discomfort and handwashing in obsessive compulsive and psychiatric control patients. Behav Res Ther 17:223–228, 1979

Julien RA, Riviere B, Note ID: Traitement comportenmental et cognitif des obsessions et compulsions resultats et discussion. Seance due Lundi, 27 Octobre 1980, pp 1123–1133

Kenny FT, Solyom L, Solyom C: Faradic disruption of obsessive ideation in the treatment of obsessive neurosis. Behavior Therapy 4:448–451, 1973

Kenny FT, Mowbray RM, Lalani S: Faradic disruption of obsessive ideation in the treatment of obsessive neurosis: a controlled study. Behavior Therapy 9:209–221, 1978

Mahoney MJ: The self-management of covert behavior: a case study. Behavior Therapy 2:575–578, 1971

Makhlouf-Norris F, Norris H: The obsessive-compulsive syndrome as a neurotic device for the reduction of self-uncertainty. Br J Psychiatry 121: 277–288, 1972

Makhlouf-Norris F, Jones HG, Norris H: Articulation of the conceptual structure in obsessive-neurosis. British Journal of Social and Clinical Psychology 9:264–274, 1970

Marks IM: Cure and Care of the Neuroses. New York, John Wiley, 1981

Marks IM, Hodgson R, Rachman S: Treatment of chronic obsessive-compulsive neurosis with in vivo exposure: a 2-year follow-up and issues in treatment. Br J Psychiatry 127:349–364, 1975

Marks IM, Hallam RS, Connolly J, et al: Nursing in Behavioral Psychotherapy. London, Royal College of Nursing of the United Kingdom, 1977

Marks IM, Stern RS, Mawson D, et al: Clomipramine and exposure for obsessive-compulsive rituals. Br J Psychiatry 136:1–25, 1980

Marks IM, Lelliott P, Basoglu M, et al: Clomipramine, self-exposure and therapist-aided exposure for obsessive-compulsive rituals. Br J Psychiatry 152:522–534, 1988

Mavissakalian M, Turner SM, Michelson L, et al: Tricyclic antidepressants in obsessive-compulsive disorder: antiobsessional or antidepressant agents? Am J Psychiatry 142:572–576, 1985

McFall ME, Wollersheim JP: Obsessive-compulsive neurosis: a behavioral formulation and approach to treatment. Cognitive Therapy and Research 3:333–348, 1979

McGuire RJ, Vallance M: Aversion therapy by electric shock: a simple technique. Br Med J 1:151–153, 1964

Meyer V: Modification of expectations in cases with obsessional rituals. Behav Res Ther 4:273–280, 1966

Meyer V, Levy R: Modification of behavior in obsessive-compulsive disorders, in Issues and Trends in Behavior Therapy. Edited by Adams HE, Unikel P. Springfield, IL, Charles C Thomas, 1973, pp 77–137

Meyer V, Levy R, Schnurer A: A behavioral treatment of obsessive-compulsive disorders, in Obsessional States. Edited by Beech HR. London, Methuen, 1974, pp 233–258

Mills HL, Agras WS, Barlow DH, et al: Compulsive rituals treated by response prevention. Arch Gen Psychiatry 28:524–527, 1973

Milner AD, Beech HR, Walker VJ: Decision processes and obsessional behaviour. British Journal of Social and Clinical Psychology 10:88–89, 1971

Mowrer OH: Learning Theory and Behavior. New York, John Wiley, 1960

Persons JB, Foa EB: Processing of fearful and neutral information by obsessive-compulsives. Behav Res Ther 22:259–265, 1984

Philpott R: Recent advances in the behavioral measurement of obsessional illnesses: difficulties common to these and other instruments. Scott Med J 20 (suppl):33–40, 1975

Queiroz LOS, Motta MA, Madi MBBP, et al: A functional analysis of obsessive-compulsive problems with related therapeutic procedures. Behav Res Ther 19:377–388, 1981

Rabavilas AD, Boulougouris JC: Physiological accompaniments of ruminations, flooding and thought-stopping in obsessive patients. Behav Res Ther 12:239–243, 1974

Rabavilas AD, Boulougouris JC, Stefanic S: Duration of flooding sessions in the treatment of obsessive-compulsive patients. Behav Res Ther 14: 349–355, 1976

Rabavilas AD, Boulougouris JC, Perissaki C: Therapist qualities related to outcome with exposure in vivo in neurotic patients. J Behav Ther Exp Psychiatry 10:293–299, 1979

Rachman S: Obsessional ruminations. Behav Res Ther 9:229–235, 1971

Rachman S: Obsessional-compulsive checking. Behav Res Ther 14:437–443, 1976

Rachman S, Hodgson R: Obsessions and Compulsions. Englewood Cliffs, NJ, Prentice-Hall, 1980

Rachman S, Hodgson R, Marzillier J: Treatment of an obsessional-compulsive disorder by modelling. Behav Res Ther 8:385–392, 1970

Rachman S, Marks IM, Hodgson R: The treatment of obsessive-compulsive neurotics by modelling and flooding in vivo. Behav Res Ther 11:463–471, 1973

Reed GF: Some formal qualities of obsessional thinking. Psychiatria Clinica 1:382–392, 1968

Roper G, Rachman S, Hodgson R: An experiment on obsessional checking. Behav Res Ther 11:271–277, 1973

Roper G, Rachman S, Marks IM: Passive and participant modelling in exposure treatment of obsessive-compulsive neurotics. Behav Res Ther 13: 271–279, 1975

Salkovskiis PM, Westbrook D: Behaviour therapy and obsessional ruminations: can failure be turned into success? Behav Res Ther 27:149–169, 1989

Sanavio E: Obsessions and compulsions: the Padua inventory. Behav Res Ther 26:169–177, 1988

Solyom L, Garza-Perez J, Ledwidge BL, et al: Paradoxical intention in the treatment of obsessive thoughts: a pilot study. Compr Psychiatry 13: 291–297, 1972

Stampfl TG: Implosive therapy: the theory, the subhuman analogue, the strategy and the technique, Part 1: the theory, in Behavior Modification Techniques in the Treatment of Emotional Disorders. Edited by Armitage SG. Battle Creek, MI, VA Publications, 1967

Steketee GS: Predicting relapse following behavioral treatment for obsessive-compulsive disorder: the impact of social support. Dissertation Abstracts International 1987

Steketee GS, Cleere L: Obsessive-compulsive disorders, in International Handbook of Behavior Modification and Therapy. Edited by Bellack AS, Hersen M, Kazdin AE. New York, Plenum, 1989, pp 307–332

Steketee GS, Foa EB, Kozak MJ: Predictors of outcome for obsessive-compulsives treated with exposure and response prevention. Paper presented at the 15th annual meeting of the European Association for Behaviour Therapy, Munich, FRG, August 1985

Stern RS: Treatment of a case of obsessional neurosis using thought-stopping technique. Br J Psychiatry 117:441–442, 1970

Stern RS: Obsessive thoughts: the problem of therapy. Br J Psychiatry 133: 200–205, 1978

Stern RS, Lipsedge MS, Marks IM: Obsessive ruminations: a controlled trial of thought-stopping technique. Behav Res Ther 11:659–662, 1975

Teasdale UD: Learning models of obsessional compulsive disorder, in Obsessional States. Edited by Beech HR. London, Methuen, 1974, pp 197–229

Truax CB, Carkuff RR: Toward Effective Counseling in Psychotherapy: Training and Practice. Chicago, IL, Aldine, 1967

Turner SM, Hersen M, Bellack S, et al: Behavioral and pharmacological treatment of obsessive-compulsive disorders. J Nerv Ment Dis 167:651–657, 1980

Volans PJ: Styles of decision making and probability appraised in selected obsessional and phobic patients. British Journal of Social and Clinical Psychology 15:305–317, 1976

Walton D: The relevance of learning theory to the treatment of an obsessive-compulsive state, in Behaviour Therapy and the Neuroses. Edited by Eysenck HJ. Oxford, UK, Pergamon, 1960, pp 153–163

Walton D, Mather MD: The application of learning principles to the treatment of obsessive-compulsive states in the acute and chronic phases of illness. Behav Res Ther 1:163–174, 1963

Watts EN: An investigation of imaginal desensitization as a habituation process. Unpublished doctoral dissertation, University of London, London, 1971

Yamagami T: Treatment of an obsession by thought-stopping. J Behav Ther Exp Psychiatry 2:133–135, 1971

Chapter 6

Diagnosis and Treatment of Obsessive-Compulsive Disorder in Children and Adolescents

Henrietta L. Leonard, M.D.
Susan E. Swedo, M.D.
Judith L. Rapoport, M.D.

*I*t is estimated that perhaps as many as one million children and adolescents in this country may have obsessive-compulsive disorder (OCD). (This figure is extrapolated from a weighted lifetime point prevalence of 1% [Flament et al. 1988].) In the past, psychiatrists saw few such patients, perhaps because the sufferers concealed their disorder or were not optimistic about treatment. But with both the great professional and media interest in this disorder and the greater sensitivity to diagnosis, many patients are now coming forth and/or being recognized. In this chapter we review the phenomenology, the neurobiology, and the treatment of OCD in children and adolescents. The two controlled pediatric pharmacological studies of OCD will be emphasized, as well as recommendations for other treatments.

Phenomenology

In the largest prospective study of childhood OCD to date, 70 consecutive child and adolescent patients were examined at the National Institute of Mental Health (NIMH) (Swedo et al. 1989b). These 47 boys and 23 girls who met diagnostic criteria for primary severe OCD had a mean ($\pm$ SD) age of 13.7 ($\pm$ 2.67) years and a mean age of onset of 10.1 ($\pm$ 3.52) years, with seven of the patients having had the onset of their illness prior to the age of 7 years. Boys seemed to have an earlier age of onset, around age 9, whereas girls were more likely to have theirs around age 12. Overall, the ratio of male to female cases was 2:1, but this ratio changed with age, such that the earliest ages had a high preponderance of males. Twenty percent of personally interviewed first-degree family relatives of the probands met diagnostic criteria for OCD (Lenane et al. 1988). Interestingly, the primary OCD symptom in the affected family member was usually different from that of the proband, suggesting against a modeling theory for the transmission of OCD, and against familial symptom subtypes.

Only 26% of the OCD patients had OCD as their only psychiatric diagnosis. Associated diagnoses seen most frequently were depression (39%), developmental disabilities (24%), simple phobia (17%), overanxious disorder (16%), oppositional disorder (11%), and attention-deficit disorder (10%). Tourette's syndrome was an exclusionary criterion, so there were no patients with this diagnosis, although intriguing links have been found between this illness and OCD (Pauls et al. 1986). Twenty percent of the NIMH patients had had a simple motor or vocal tic at some time in their life. In our population there was little difficulty in distinguishing a simple motor tic from a ritual (i.e., eye blinks). However, in Tourette's patients a complex motor tic preceded by a cognition is frequently difficult to distinguish from a compulsive ritual.

Eleven percent of the NIMH patients had a coexisting obsessive-compulsive personality disorder (OCPD) (Swedo et al. 1989b). Berg et al. (1989) reported that some adolescents in an epidemiologic study who initially met criteria for OCD, but not OCPD, at follow-up were found to have OCPD and not OCD. Berg and colleagues speculated that some children and adolescents with early-onset OCD might develop OCPD as a means of coping with the disorder. Thus, the relation between OCPD and OCD remains unsettled for children as well as for adults.

Parents of a group of OCD children ($N = 38$) reported that their children had had significantly more early ritualized developmental behaviors than did parents of matched healthy controls (Leonard et al. 1989). It is tempting to speculate that these behaviors might represent early subclinical "bouts" of OCD, but the reported differences may merely be the result of biased recall. A prospective study of exaggerated early developmental rituals is warranted, for it might identify a group at risk for OCD.

Childhood OCD presents in a form essentially identical to that seen in adults (Rapoport 1986), and one-third of adult cases have had their onset in childhood (Black 1974). Indeed, the major presenting ritual symptoms (starting with the most frequently seen) include washing, repeating, checking, touching, counting, arranging, hoarding, and scrupulosity (Swedo et al. 1989b). Washing rituals occurred at some time in the illness of 85% of the NIMH population, with hand washing and showering being the principal manifestations. (Case studies at the end of this chapter describe the specific presentations and course of treatment of patients in more detail.)

Most children, like their adult counterparts, report a combination of both obsessive thoughts and compulsive rituals (Swedo et al. 1989b). In the NIMH series there were only 3 cases (4%) of "pure obsessives" who felt painfully possessed by their thoughts but had no specific ritual in response to them. Several of the younger children were quick to describe their ritualistic behaviors but were unable to attribute them to any obsessive thought. We are impressed with the size of this "pure compulsive" subgroup. For the most part, the obsessions and compulsions were egodystonic, but some of the very young children did deny any anxiety or distress in association with their symptoms. Almost all patients reported a change in their principal symptom over time, that is, one might wash for 2 years and then begin to have checking rituals. Patients reported that the intensity of their illness ranged from episodic bouts to almost continuous symptomatology.

Initially, most children disguise their rituals (Swedo et al. 1989b). For example, "hand washers" would not tell their family what they were doing, and only when the disorder progressed to the point that the child had raw, chapped, and bleeding hands, would the family "discover" the extent of illness. One 16-year-old girl's hand washing became detected when she used two bottles of liquid hand-washing soap every day and started carrying around a carton of hand wipes. In another family the extensive showering became apparent when the utility bills for hot water skyrocketed, dozens of towels would "appear" in the laundry every day, and all the soap in the house would be gone. An 8-year-old boy was able to hide his elaborate 2-hour bedtime ritual of arranging until it turned into a contamination fear of his bed. When he began sleeping on the floor of his bedroom, his OCD was recognized.

Obviously, severely incapacitated children and adolescents with classic symptoms will be easily diagnosed. However, the less severely ill patients—those with unusual symptoms (such as "a tune in the head") and those in which the patient hides his or her symptoms—are more difficult to recognize. "Red flags" for OCD include the unproductive hours spent on homework, holes erased into test papers and homework, retracing over letters or words, unexplained high utility bills, a dramatic increase in laundry, toilets being stopped up from too much paper, exaggerated requests for reassurance, requests for family members to repeat phrases, a preoccupying fear of harm coming to self or others, a persistent fear that he or she has an illness, long bedtime rituals, difficulty with leaving the house, hoarding of useless objects, or peculiar patterns for walking or sitting.

The differential diagnosis of OCD includes the depression and anxiety disorders (separation anxiety, overanxious, and generalized anxiety) with obsessional features; phobias; stereotypies seen in mental retardation, pervasive developmental disorders, autism, and brain damage syndromes; anorexia and bulimia; Tourette's syndrome; and, more rarely, in childhood schizophrenia. (The differential diagnosis with Tourette's syndrome has been discussed earlier in this chapter.) Although the OCD rituals may superficially resemble the stereotypies seen in autism (and other pervasive developmental disorders), OCD rituals are well organized, complex, and ego-dystonic. The anorexic or bulimic patient's consuming interest in calories, exercise, and food certainly bears resemblance to an obsession. Indeed, adult women with OCD have an increased incidence (15%) of a history of anorexia (Y.G. Kasvikis et al., submitted for publication). Although the two can coexist, usually the distinction can be made between OCD and a primary eating disorder. Since DSM-III-R recognizes that these disorders may coexist with OCD, the primary symptoms may be difficult to distinguish in mild cases and in those cases with coexisting disorders.

Neurobiology of Childhood-Onset Obsessive-Compulsive Disorder

Research has focused on brain imaging and neuropharmacological studies. The "serotonin hypothesis of OCD" is based on the results of treatment and challenge studies, which demonstrate the serotonin (5-hydroxytryptamine [5-HT]) reuptake inhibitors to be specifically efficacious for the treatment of OCD (see review by Zohar and Insel 1987). The two controlled pediatric trials of clomipramine (a 5-HT reuptake inhibitor) indicated that clomipramine is safe and effective in children as well (Flament et al. 1985; Leonard et al. 1989).

Evidence supporting a theory of frontal lobe–basal ganglia dysfunction (Wise and Rapoport 1989) includes both neuroanatomic and metabolic abnormalities. Adult OCD patients with a history of childhood on-set of their illness have been reported to have a decreased left caudate size on computed tomography (CT) (Luxenberg et al. 1988) and increased ra-tios of regional activity to mean cortical gray matter metabolism in the right prefrontal and left anterior cingulate regions on positron-emission tomography (PET) scans when compared to healthy control subjects (Swedo et al. 1989c). The basal ganglia are also implicated by the associa-tion of OCD and Sydenham's chorea in pediatric patients (Swedo et al. 1989a); by the presence of obsessive-compulsive symptoms in Tourette's syndrome, with the possible genetic link between the two illnesses (Pauls et al. 1986); and by the association of OCD with postencephalitic Parkin-son's disease (von Economo 1931).

Behavioral Treatment

Behavioral treatment has not been systematically studied in children and adolescents. What data there are suggest that the techniques employed with adults (Marks 1987) will also be appropriate for children (for reviews see Berg et al. 1989; Wolff and Rapoport 1988).

Only 20 studies of the use of behavioral treatment of OCD in chil-dren could be found since 1967 (Berg et al. 1989). All were clinical reports consisting of only one or two patients, except for Apter et al.'s (1984) and Bolton et al.'s (1983) report of 8 and 15 patients, respectively. Because the majority of reports were not designed to specifically test the effect of a single behavioral procedure, it was difficult to draw conclusions. The methodological concerns specifically include the lack of standardized di-agnostic definitions; the use of concurrent treatments; the absence of baseline observations or established treatment time course; and the use of mixed objective rating scales for obsessions, anxiety, and fear where most outcomes were self-reported. Additionally, in most of these studies the behavioral treatment was only one part of the multimodal approach and sometimes had only a secondary role.

Response prevention was the predominant treatment in nine studies but was usually utilized in addition to other treatment techniques. Bolton et al. (1983), in the largest pediatric behavioral study, used response pre-vention in 11 of 15 obsessive adolescents. This was a retrospective record analysis of children admitted to the hospital over a 4-year period. Re-sponse prevention with in vivo exposure, the most successful approach with adults, was used in only two studies (Apter et al. 1984; Zikis 1983).

Thought stopping for obsessive ruminations has been applied with positive results in three reports (Campbell 1973; Friedman and Silvers 1977; Ownby 1983).

The involvement of family members is an important consideration in the behavioral treatment. Family dynamics and psychopathology in relationship to the OCD patient's treatment and recovery has been addressed in adults (Hoover and Insel 1984) and children (Hafner et al. 1981). Familial overinvolvement, marital stress, and psychopathology can interfere with the success of behavior modification, so involving the family in a positive way is necessary. (See Lenane 1989; Lenane, Chapter 7, this volume, for discussion of these issues in greater detail.)

As long as the child is motivated and able to understand directions, he or she is suitable for behavior treatment. Not surprisingly, cooperation of hospitalized adolescents is often a problem, as is the secretiveness of many of these patients.

A major void in the literature involves large studies comparing drug and behavorial treatments with unselected groups of OCD children. There are few guidelines suggesting which children will respond to which treatment, and the decision remains a complex clinical balance between the availability of behavioral treatment, cooperation on the part of the child, and the child's symptom pattern.

Pharmacological Treatment of Childhood Obsessive-Compulsive Disorder

Obsessive-compulsive disorder has been remarkably resistant to traditional psychotherapeutic interventions. Numerous controlled trials in adults have shown the efficacy of drug treatment with 5-HT reuptake inhibitors (clomipramine, fluoxetine, and fluvoxamine) for OCD (Zohar and Insel 1987; Pato and Zohar, Chapter 2; Pigott, Chapter 3; Goodman and Price, Chapter 4, this volume). Two recent trials (Flament et al. 1985; Leonard et al. 1989) have extended the findings seen with adults to a pediatric population (also see case histories at the end of this chapter).

In the first controlled pharmacological treatment trial for OCD in children and adolescents, 19 pediatric patients (mean age $=14.5 \pm 2.3$ years) participated in a 20-week double-blind, placebo-controlled crossover study (5 weeks of active medication) (Flament et al. 1985, 1987). Dosages of clomipramine targeting 3 mg/kg/day were used with a mean dose ($\pm$ SD) of 141 ($\pm$ 30) mg/day. In the 14 OCD patients who completed the trial, clomipramine was significantly better than placebo in decreasing obsessive-compulsive symptomatology at week 5 (P = .02 on the NIMH-OC Scale [Insel et al. 1983]). An improvement in symptoms could usually be seen as early as week 3, and 75% of the patients had a moderate to marked improvement. Drug response could not be predicted from baseline measures of age, intelligence, mode or age of onset, or duration of severity of illness. As with adults, the obsessive-compulsive symptom response was independent of initial depression (although primarily depressed subjects had been excluded). Clomipramine was well tolerated, and there were only two patients who dropped out, both secondary to side effects. There were no untoward effects from the clomipramine; tremor, dry mouth, dizziness, and constipation were the most frequently reported side effects.

In a double-blind crossover comparison of clomipramine and desipramine (a selective noradrenergic reuptake inhibitor) in 48 children and adolescents with OCD, the comparison drug (desipramine) was used because of its similar side-effects profile and antidepressant efficacy. Thirty-one boys and 18 girls with a mean ($\pm$ SD) age of 13.9 ($\pm$ 2.8) years (range 7–19 years) and a mean age of onset of 10.2 ($\pm$ 5.8) years (range 5–16 years) were studied. After an initial 2-week single-blind placebo phase, the active treatment phase consisted of a double-blind crossover of two consecutive 5-week treatments of clomipramine and desipramine (randomized for drug order). The average clomipramine dosage was 157 ($\pm$ 53) mg/day, and the dosage of desipramine was 153 ($\pm$ 55) mg/day, with a range of 50 to 250 mg for each drug.

Clomipramine was significantly better than desipramine in ameliorating the OCD symptoms at week 5 (e.g., P = .00001 on the NIMH-OC Scale), and on some ratings a significant difference could be seen as early as week 3. Desipramine was no more effective in improving obsessive-compulsive symptoms than placebo had been in the Flament et al. (1985) study. In fact, when desipramine was given as the second active medication, 64% of the patients had some degree of relapse. Depression scores also increased during the second active phase if the patient was on desipramine. This increase in depression was felt to be due to the demoralization experienced by the patients as their obsessive-compulsive symptoms returned, although it is possible that desipramine may not be as effective an antidepressant in OCD patients as clomipramine is.

Both clomipramine and desipramine were well tolerated, and the side-effects profiles between the two drugs were very similar. Clomipramine had a slightly higher incidence of tremor and "other" (e.g., sweating, flushing, middle insomnia) side effects than did desipramine. Clinical observations suggested that clomipramine was not helpful in treating the attention-deficit disorder symptoms in these patients with that coexisting diagnosis. Several adolescents who unilaterally discontinued clomipramine abruptly (during long-term maintenance) experienced withdrawal symptoms of nausea and vomiting, which appeared to be more pronounced than those seen with desipramine withdrawal.

Fluoxetine, a bicyclic 5-HT reuptake inhibitor, has been reported to be effective for OCD in adults in open studies (Fontaine and Chouinard 1986; Jenike et al. 1989) and in single-blind and double-blind trails (Pigott et al. 1990; Turner et al. 1985). A multicenter controlled trial is ongoing for OCD. Fluoxetine is currently available by prescription, but its indicated use is that of an antidepressant for adults. Its safety and efficacy in the pediatric age group have not yet been established, although there are numerous ancecdotal reports of such in this age group. Riddle et al. (1989) concluded that fluoxetine appeared to be safe and well tolerated in dosages of 10 to 40 mg per day in a group of 10 children and adolescents with primary OCD or Tourette's syndrome and OCD. Fifteen adolescents who completed the NIMH trial and did not respond to clomipramine, or could not tolerate its side effects, have been administered fluoxetine without any untoward side effects, and most showed a clinical response. This adolescent group has been maintained on 20 to 80 mg of fluoxetine, with some patients obtaining improvement at 20 mg and others requiring up to 80 mg to achieve the equivalent response. Frequently, the younger age group is started on one-half tab of 20 mg of fluoxetine in the A.M., as opposed to the full tab frequently used for adults. These anecdotal reports suggest that fluoxetine is usually well tolerated and may prove useful in younger patients with OCD.

In summary, the superiority of clomipramine to desipramine has been demonstrated for the treatment of childhood OCD. Clomipramine is the current psychopharmacological treatment of choice. Fluoxetine, which is available on the market, may prove to be safe and effective in the pediatric population after more systemic studies have been done.

Maintenance and Follow-up

The patients in the NIMH trial who responded to clomipramine were maintained on that medication at dosages averaging 3 mg/kg/day as required and as tolerated. Electrocardiograms and general laboratory studies (i.e., complete blood count and chemistries) were repeated every 3 months. Four patients have been maintained on clomipramine for over 4 years and 26 patients for more than a year without difficulties. It is recommended that the medication be periodically tapered to establish whether it is necessary. Currently, a maintenance-discontinuation study to assess the safety of long-term clomipramine maintenance and the length of therapy required is being conducted. Our initial impression is that many patients appear to relapse when clomipramine is decreased or discontinued (desipramine is substituted in a double-blind fashion). This finding is consistent with that reported by Pato et al. (1988) in which the majority of adult patients relapsed when taken off maintenance clomipramine. However, until the controlled study is completed, it is inappropriate to speculate.

Augmentation of clomipramine with L-tryptophan and/or lithium to maximize a "partial response" has been reported to be beneficial (Rasmussen 1984).[1] Our experience with augmentation of clomipramine has been mixed at best. In eight children who added L-tryptophan to clomipramine maintenance (dosages ranging from 500 to 3,000 mg/day), three children reported improvement, two became worse, and three had no change in their symptoms. The two adolescents who tried lithium augmentation reported minimal improvement and did not continue on that medication. Clearly, a more systematic study of the use of augmentation medications in children and adolescents is indicated.

Follow-up studies indicate that at least half of pediatric OCD cases are still symptomatic as adults (Berman 1942; Hollingsworth et al. 1980; Warren 1965). Flament et al. (in press) contacted 27 OCD children and adolescents from the original clomipramine treatment trial at a point 2 to 5 years later (Flament et al. 1985). Twenty-five (93%) of those patients were reevaluated. Only 7 (28%) met no DSM-III diagnostic criteria. Seventeen patients (68%) still met criteria for OCD, and 12 (48%) of these had an additional diagnosis (most often, depression or anxiety). Surprisingly, neither baseline measures nor a positive response to clomipramine treatment was able to predict long-term outcome. However, this group had not been actively followed during the 2- to 5-year interim period, and

---

[1]Because the use of L-tryptophan has recently (Fall 1989) been implicated in an increased incidence of eosinophilia, the authors advise against the prescribing and use of this agent, as discussed in this book, until the issue is resolved.

only 12 subjects had been on clomipramine for more than a few months after the initial study. The poor outcome of this group spurred the ongoing prospective follow-up study utilizing intensive intervention with staff encouragement of psychopharmacological, behavioral modification, and other psychotherapeutic treatments. It is hoped that these increased interventions will improve the poor follow-up outcome seen with the initial group of patients.

Case Histories

Case 1: Contamination Fears and Washing

K.W., age 8, was brought to NIMH by his parents after 2 years of excessive hand washing. He would spend 4 hours or more per day washing and rewashing his hands, which caused him to be late to school and to stay up late at night. K.W.'s hands were chapped and bleeding from the washing, and he would not allow any lotion to be put on his hands for fear of "contamination." He walked around with his hands up in the air in a "surgeon's position" for fear of contacting anything dirty. He was no longer able to touch doorknobs, flush toilets, touch anyone else, or play with his dog or in any contact sports. K.W. responded to clomipramine (at 3 mg/kg) and not desipramine during the NIMH double-blind study with a dramatic decrease (85%) in his washing and avoidance rituals. K.W. was maintained on clomipramine for 1½ years and spent only 20 minutes per day washing his hands. Although traces of the rituals remained, they did not interfere in his life (e.g., he could play with his dog). When the patient's clomipramine was blindly substituted with desipramine, he relapsed within 3 weeks and was returned to his maintenance clomipramine dosage.

Case 2: Repetition

J.R., age 17, would have to retrace his steps from the car into the house in a very elaborate and specific manner (two steps forward, look to the sky, three steps backward, glance to the left and think a good thought). It took 20 minutes to go a distance that normally should have taken seconds. His complex rituals made him the object of neighborhood curiosity. If interrupted or prevented from completing his elaborate walking ritual, he became enraged and inconsolable. J.R. had a good response (70%) to clomipramine, but not desipramine, during the NIMH double-blind study. He completely stopped his repeating rituals, although he acknowledged still having the thought to do so, but was able without much effort to resist acting on them. J.R. was maintained on clomipramine (at 3 mg/kg/day) and developed tachycardia and orthostatic hypotension without any electrocardiogram changes. When his dosage was dropped (to 2 mg/kg/day) and 1,000 mg/day of L-tryptophan was added to augment the clomipramine, the tachycardia resolved, but he was unable to maintain his clinical response. J.R. was switched to fluoxetine, 60 mg/day, and had an excellent response without side effects.

Case 3: Checking

L.S. is a 16-year-old girl who had checking rituals as the predominant symptom. Approximately 1 year prior to presentation, she rather suddenly had begun to spend an hour at night checking whether the doors and windows were locked and all electrical plugs were pulled out. She could not trust her parents' efforts. Her elaborate pattern of checking the house included many repetitions until she felt "it had been done right." When her symptoms increased and she began to wake her parents up at 3 A.M. to recheck the house, help was sought. L.S. showed a dramatic response to clomipramine (80% reduction in time spent doing her rituals), but not to desipramine, during the NIMH double-blind study. L.S. was maintained on clomipramine at 3 mg/kg/day with minimal side effects (dry mouth, mild tiredness). After 1 year of maintenance, she was tapered off the clomipramine to assess whether it was necessary, and her symptoms returned 3 weeks after discontinuing the medication. L.S. resumed her previous dosage of clomipramine, and she regained her clinical response within 3 weeks.

Case 4: Touching

Touching rituals are slightly less common than the washing and checking ones. D.D. is a 13-year-old girl who felt incapacitated by having to touch the corners of chairs, refrigerators, doors, and walls. She developed callouses on her hands from touching the walls so many times. She felt compelled to touch them "just the right way" for as long as 2 hours per day. If the ritual was interrupted, she had to start all over again. This behavior was extremely distressing to her, yet she was unable to stop. D.D. had a moderate response (50% reduction in time spent in rituals) to clomipramine at 3 mg/kg/day, but not to desipramine, in the NIMH double-blind comparison. D.D. felt moderately troubled by the side effects of excessive sweating and daytime tiredness, and she elected not to continue clomipramine maintenance. Currently, the family reports that she is "doing well," but she has not been seen for reevaluation.

Case 5: Arranging

S.E. is an 11-year-old girl who was brought for evaluation for having to "have everything in her room just so." She would spend about 3 hours every day straightening every item in each drawer in her bedroom and every article of clothing in her closet. The rituals increased in time and became so subjectively incapacitating that she refused to go into her room anymore, and she had to sleep on the floor outside her room to make sure that no one went in to mess anything up. S.E. had a favorable response to clomipramine (75% reduction in time spent in rituals) during the NIMH study. Clomipramine maintenance at 3 mg/kg/day was adequate for continuing the response; however, with an increase of medication to 3.5 mg/kg/day and the addition of behavior therapy, her rituals were decreased 95%, to where she would spend about 5 minutes per day "making things right."

Case 6: Hoarding

B.W. is a 6-year-old boy who had to pick up anything that he might walk over. He began to bring home old pieces of paper, rocks, twigs, and trash that he found on the way home from school. The problem progressed to where he was late to school because of having to pick everything up, and he would not allow anything that he had collected to be thrown away. He would go through the house trash and save old coffee envelopes, empty toothpaste tubes, ads, and newspapers. The problem progressed to such a point that his room was full of trash, and his parents felt that it was a health hazard. Whenever they tried to clean his room, B.W. would become agitated and have to be restrained. B.W. had an excellent response to clomipramine (at 3 mg/kg/day) but was unable to tolerate desipramine (caused agitation). Unfortunately, B.W.'s coexisting severe attention-deficit disorder with hyperactivity was unchanged by the clomipramine and remained a continuous problem. When fluoxetine was substituted, the patient experienced agitation and was unable to tolerate the medication for this reason. During a trial of methylphenidate, the patient developed tics, and the medication was discontinued. Trials of imipramine, desipramine, and clonidine to target the attention-deficit disorder symptomatology were unsuccessful. Other psychopharmacological interventions are being considered.

Case 7: Scrupulosity

W.S. is a 17-year-old boy who prayed about 4 hours per day. Although he came from a very religious family, they became quite concerned about what they perceived as excessive prayer. W.S. would ruminate over past deeds for hours, tortuously reviewing them and wondering if he had done something wrong. He began to go to confession three times per day seeking forgiveness for imagined misdeeds, and would repeatedly ask his parents if he had done anything wrong and if he were going to Hell. Although W.S. experienced a decrease in symptomatology on clomipramine, he chose not to continue on the medication, for he was not distressed enough by his praying to want it treated.

Case 8: Somatic Preoccupation

A recent presentation of OCD is the preoccupying fear that one might have AIDS. K.T., a 17-year-old girl, believed that she had contracted AIDS from having touched a sterile, packaged syringe on the ground at a carnival. This conviction that she had AIDS later transformed into fearing that she had herpes and rabies. K.T. was able to totally lose her obsession about AIDS on clomipramine (3 mg/kg/day) after 4 weeks of treatment. She remained on clomipramine maintenance for 6 months. When the medication was discontinued, her symptoms did not return. She has been symptom-free for 2 years now.

Summary

It is estimated that perhaps as many as one million children and adolescents in this country may have OCD. Childhood OCD presents in a form essentially identical to that seen in adults, and one-third of adult cases have had their onset in childhood. Boys seem to have an earlier age of onset of OCD (pre-puberty), whereas girls are more likely to have theirs around puberty. Washing, repeating, checking, touching, counting, arranging, hoarding, and scrupulosity are the most commonly seen rituals. Almost all patients reported a change in their principal symptom over time. Increasing evidence supports a neurobiological theory for the etiology of OCD, specifically a frontal lobe–basal ganglia dysfunction.

Childhood OCD appears to have a similar treatment response to that seen in adults with the illness. Behavioral treatment has not been systemically studied in children and adolescents, but reports suggest that response prevention techniques are useful. Flament et al. (1985) found clomipramine superior to placebo at week 5 in a double-blind crossover design. Leonard et al. (1989) reported that clomipramine was significantly better than desipramine at week 5 in a double-blind crossover comparison. Fluoxetine, which is available on the market, has been reported in anecdotal cases to be safe and well tolerated in the pediatric population, although systemic studies are needed. Follow-up studies indicate that at least 50% of pediatric OCD cases are still symptomatic as adults; however, it is hoped that the new treatment modalities available will improve the long-term follow-up outcome.

References

Apter A, Bernhout E, Tyano S: Severe obsessive compulsive disorder in adolescence: a report of eight cases. J Adolesc 7:349–358, 1984

Berg CZ, Rapoport JL, Wolff RP: Behavioral treatment for obsessive-compulsive disorder in childhood, in Obsessive-Compulsive Disorder in Children and Adolescents. Edited by Rapoport JL. Washington, DC, American Psychiatric Press, 1989, pp 169–185

Berman L: Obsessive-compulsive neurosis in children. J Nerv Ment Dis 95: 26–39, 1942

Black A: The natural history of obsessional neurosis, in Obsessional States. Edited by Beech HR. London, Methuen, 1974, pp 19–54

Bolton D, Collins S, Steinberg D: The treatment of obsessive-compulsive disorder in adolescence: a report of fifteen cases. Br J Psychiatry 142:456–464, 1983

Campbell LM: A variation of thought-stopping in a twelve-year-old boy: a case report. J Behav Ther Exp Psychiatry 4:69–70, 1973

Flament MF, Rapoport JL, Berg CJ, et al: Clomipramine treatment of childhood compulsive disorder. Arch Gen Psychiatry 42:977–983, 1985

Flament MF, Rapoport JL, Murphy DL: Biochemical changes during clomipramine treatment of childhood obsessive compulsive disorder. Arch Gen Psychiatry 44:219–225, 1987

Flament MF, Whitaker A, Rapoport JL: Obsessive compulsive disorder in adolescence: an epidemiological study. J Am Acad Child Adolesc Psychiatry 27:764–771, 1988

Flament MF, Koby E, Rapoport JL, et al: Childhood obsessive compulsive disorder: a prospective follow-up study. J Child Psychol Psychiatry (in press)

Fontaine R, Chouinard G: An open clinical trial of fluoxetine in the treatment of obsessive compulsive disorder. J Clin Psychopharmacol 6:98–101, 1986

Friedman CTH, Silvers FM: A multimodality approach to inpatient treatment of obsessive compulsive disorder. Am J Psychother 31:456–465, 1977

Hafner RJ, Gilchrist P, Bowling J, et al: The treatment of obsessional neurosis in a family setting. Aust N Z J Psychiatry 15:145–151, 1981

Hollingsworth C, Tanguey P, Grossman L, et al: Longterm outcome of obsessive compulsive disorder in children. J Am Acad Child Psychiatry 19: 134–144, 1980

Hoover C, Insel TR: Families of origin in obsessive compulsive disorder. J Nerv Ment Dis 172:207–215, 1984

Insel TR, Murphy DL, Cohen RM, et al: Obsessive-compulsive disorder: a double-blind trial of clomipramine and clorgyline. Arch Gen Psychiatry 40:605–612, 1983

Jenike MA, Buttolph L, Baer L, et al: Open trial of fluoxetine in obsessive-compulsive disorder. Am J Psychiatry 146:909–911, 1989

Lenane M: Families and obsessive-compulsive disorder, in Obsessive-Compulsive Disorder in Children and Adolescents. Edited by Rapoport JL. Washington, DC, American Psychiatric Press, 1989, pp 237–252

Lenane M, Swedo S, Leonard H, et al: Obsessive compulsive disorder in first degree relatives of obsessive compulsive disorder children. Paper presented at the annual meeting of the American Psychiatric Association, Montreal, Canada, May 1988

Leonard HL, Swedo S, Rapoport JL: Treatment of obsessive compulsive disorder with clomipramine and desipramine in children and adolescents: a double-blind crossover comparison. Arch Gen Psychiatry 46:1088–1092, 1989

Luxenburg JS, Swedo SE, Flament MF, et al: Neuroanatomic abnormalities in obsessive-compulsive disorder detected with quantitative X-ray computed tomography. Am J Psychiatry 145:1089–1093, 1988

Marks IM: Fears, Phobias and Rituals, Panic Anxiety and Their Disorders. Oxford, Oxford University Press, 1987

Ownby RL: A cognitive behavorial intervention for compulsive handwashing with a thirteen-year old boy. Psychology in the Schools 20:219–222, 1983

Pato MT, Zohar-Kadouch R, Zohar J, et al: Return of symptoms after discontinuation of clomipramine in patients with obsessive compulsive disorder. Am J Psychiatry 145:1521–1525, 1988

Pauls DL, Towbin K, Leckman J, et al: Gilles de la Tourette syndrome and obsessive compulsive disorder: evidence supporting a genetic relationship. Arch Gen Psychiatry 43:1180–1182, 1986

Rapoport JL: Annotation, child obsessive-compulsive disorder. J Child Psychol Psychiatry 27:285–289, 1986

Rasmussen SA: Lithium and tryptophan augmentation in clomipramine-resistant obsessive compulsive disorder. Am J Psychiatry 141:1283–1285, 1984

Riddle M, Hardin M, King R, et al: Fluoxetine treatment of children and adolescents with Tourette's and obsessive compulsive disorders. Paper presented at the annual meeting of the American Academy of Child and Adolescent Psychiatry, New York, October 1989

Swedo SE, Rapoport JL, Cheslow DL, et al: High prevalence of obsessive compulsive symptoms in patients with Sydenham's chorea. Am J Psychiatry 146:246–249, 1989a

Swedo SE, Rapoport JL, Leonard HL, et al: Obsessive compulsive disorder in children and adolescents: clinical phenomenology of 70 consecutive cases. Arch Gen Psychiatry 46:335–341, 1989b

Swedo SE, Shapiro MB, Grady CL, et al: Cerebral glucose metabolism in childhood onset obsessive compulsive disorder. Arch Gen Psychiatry 46:518–523, 1989c

Turner SM, Jacob RG, Beidel DC, et al: Fluoxetine treatment of obsessive compulsive disorder. J Clin Psychopharmacol 5:207–212, 1985

von Economo C: Encephalitis Lethargica: Its Sequelae and Treatment. Translated by Newman KO. New York, Oxford University Press, 1931

Warren W: A study of adolescent psychiatric inpatients and the outcome six or more years later. J Child Psychol Psychiatry 6:141–160, 1965

Wise SP, Rapoport JL: Obsessive compulsive disorder: is it basal ganglia dysfunction? in Obsessive-Compulsive Disorder in Children and Adolescents. Edited by Rapoport JL. Washington, DC, American Psychiatric Press, 1989, pp 327–344

Wolff R, Rapoport JL: Behavioral treatment of childhood obsessive compulsive disorder. Behav Modif 12:252–266, 1988

Zikis P: Treatment of an 11-year old obsessive compulsive ritualizer and Tiqueur girl with in vivo exposure and response prevention. Behavior Psychotherapy 11:75–81, 1983

Zohar J, Insel TR: Obsessive compulsive disorder: psychobiological approaches to diagnosis, treatment and pathophysiology. Biol Psychiatry 22:667–687, 1987

Chapter 7

Family Therapy for Children With Obsessive-Compulsive Disorder

Marge C. Lenane, M.S.W.

*P*sychiatric treatment of children with obsessive-compulsive disorder (OCD) is more likely to be successful when the therapist's interactions with the families of these children are successful. Hafner (1982), in his treatment of five cases of persisting OCD in married women, used "spouse-aided therapy" wherein the spouse acted as cotherapist or coagent of change. (The use of family therapy in the treatment of OCD is also addressed in Leonard et al., Chapter 6, and Livingston Van Noppen et al., Chapter 8, this volume.) OCD is not unique in benefiting from family treatment. Frey (1984), Goodyer (1986), and Weidman (1985) found that engaging families of ill adolescents in family therapy increased the adolescents' compliance with treatment.

In this chapter the treatment of families of children with OCD will be defined and reviewed. The treatment uses four objectives: 1) involving the whole family in treatment; 2) identifying all behaviors, especially all OCD behaviors; 3) obtaining a full and accurate understanding of how everyone participates in the OCD behavior; and 4) positively reframing less-than-positive behavior. All these objectives are important in the initial visit, and positive reframing has an important role throughout the treatment in helping to stimulate change in OCD behavior.

Family Therapy Versus Family Intervention

Family therapy is defined as regular sessions with various family members over an extended period of time, focused on improving the functioning of the whole family. In the case of OCD, infrequent contact is probably sufficient if the family appears to function relatively well, colludes minimally with the child's OCD behavior, and is receptive to suggestions regarding minor changes that may need to be made in how they relate to their child. It would be more accurate to call this "family intervention" rather than family therapy (see the first case history at the end of this chapter). Family therapy is indicated when one or both parents are extensively involved in the child's OCD behavior and resistant to decreasing that involvement; when the parents are in considerable conflict over how to treat the OCD child or over how to treat each other (see the second case history at the end of this chapter); or when previous individual treatment of the child by competent mental health professionals has failed.

Certain circumstances can inhibit the success of family therapy or intervention. Such instances can include when the parent's individual pathology is severe (e.g., spousal abuse, chronic addiction, paranoia) and when parental pathology is severe (e.g., extensive overinvolvement with the child's disorder and absolute refusal to modify behavior). Obstacles can also occur when the parents have a long history of withdrawing the child from treatment prematurely and when the parents intrude into the therapist's individual work with the child to such an extent as to render it ineffective.

Family therapy with OCD children can be conducted by the person treating the patient in individual therapy or by a colleague. Feldman (1988) suggests the following benefits to a one-therapist structure:

- The therapist has direct access to the information and observations derived from the child, parent, and family interview.
- The therapist has the opportunity to form therapeutic alliances with the child, parents, and family.
- There is maximum coordination of the individual and family therapy components.
- There is maximum flexibility in regard to structure change (i.e., increasing or decreasing the frequency of child, parent, or family interview).
- There is minimum conflict between the individual and family therapies.

Family therapy can be especially beneficial in the treatment of OCD because of the frequency of involvement by other family members in the OCD child's rituals. At times, a decision is made to divide the individual and family therapies between two therapists. In those instances, Steinhauer and Tisdall (1984) suggest the following prerequisites between the two therapists: mutual respect and a compatible theoretical base; lack of competition; and freedom of communication, when required. With OCD families there needs to be frequent contact between the therapists to chart the decrease in parental involvement in the child's OCD behaviors.

Involving the Whole Family

We think it is important to involve and evaluate the whole family of the OCD patient in the assessment phase in order to decide on which intervention to make. The therapist cannot rely on one person's interpretation of the family.

The first telephone contact with the parent who calls for treatment for his or her child sets the stage for how much of an alliance we will make with the family. The therapist's goal for this contact is to connect with and involve the family so that all household and significant family members will attend the first family interview. Several techniques increase the likelihood of meeting with all the important members of a patient's family:

- Identify who lives with the child; if the parents are not living together, inquire about the nonresidential parent's contact with the child.
- Convey to the caller that it is a routine part of your evaluation of the child to see the whole family together to get everyone's input regarding the problem.
- Suggest that the whole family may only need to be seen once and that later meetings may not need to include everyone.
- Be clear with the caller that it is essential that everyone participate and that you will be happy to talk with any and all family members on the phone to explain your reasoning.

Anytime parents disagree about whether to seek treatment for the child, we recommend never agreeing to see the child without the reluctant parent (see case histories at the end of this chapter).

Often in OCD families, one parent, usually the mother, is more involved than the other parent. Occasionally, an overinvolved parent of an OCD child will purposely try to keep the underinvolved parent out of a session by not notifying that his or her presence is requested. When a parent makes the excuse that his or her spouse is too busy to attend, an appropriate response would be to acknowledge that the family is hard working, but that unfortunately there is no other way for the family to meet without the other spouse having to take leave from work. It is rare to lose a patient because of this requirement if it is explained in terms of maximizing the chances of successful treatment.

The initial interview with the whole family provides the therapist with an opportunity to gain detailed information about the patient's OCD case and family roles and relationships. It can reveal OCD behaviors, previous attempts to treat the disorder, and parental involvement in the OCD behaviors. It also allows the therapist to identify the family's characteristic patterns of communication, affect expression, relationships and roles, problem solving, and conflict resolution. In OCD families, roles and relationships tend to be very rigid, problem-solving skills are limited, and conflict resolution consists of agreeing not to discuss the issue. Family interviews enable the therapist to identify structural imbalances such as scapegoating, alliances, collusions, generation reversals, and possible concurrent marital problems. This information is used to determine what kind of contact with the family is indicated.

It is the therapist's responsibility to engage the OCD family, join with them, and encourage them to feel accepted and hopeful. The therapist can anticipate that the parents feel guilty and inadequate. They need help in feeling competent and supported in their efforts to parent their child. If possible, try to reframe in positive terms those behaviors that the parents have displayed that need to be changed. When possible, use the parents' words and style of communication when sharing with the family your perceptions and recommendations for treatment. Finally, convey to the family a real sense of hope and optimism that treatment will work.

Identifying Behaviors

During the initial interview it is important to ask all the difficult questions that need to be asked. If these questions are asked after the therapist has seen the child alone, the therapist may be putting the child at risk if the family feels that the questions are prompted by something the child has told the therapist. Families should be routinely evaluated for physical violence (including spousal abuse and sexual abuse), drug and alcohol addictions, and OCD behaviors in other family members. Furthermore, it is important to detect whether a parent has OCD (see the first case history at the end of this chapter); otherwise, the OCD parent will often either minimize the child's OCD or be excessively harsh with the child.

When the parent acknowledges having OCD, an appropriate response might be, "That's fairly common, given the genetic aspects to the disorder. You're in a good position to understand what your child is going through."

This first session is the time to get very detailed information about all of the patient's OCD behaviors and the ways in which the various family members assist in the OCD behavior. The therapist and the family need to be able to gauge their progress from week to week; one way to do this is to chart decrease in the undesirable behavior. If there is time, an open-ended question works best to expose the full range of behaviors. If time is too limited for the open-ended question, the therapist can go through a checklist covering the most common OCD behavior and then ask the family if there are any OCD behaviors that were not mentioned.

Documenting the Family's Participation in the Obsessive-Compulsive Disorder Behavior

It is important to document the ways other family members assist in the OCD behaviors because these interventions will continue unless confronted directly as being loving but unhelpful behavior. A checklist works best here. Using the patient's list of OCD behaviors as a guide, ask the family if they assist with the behavior in any way. For example, do they do extra laundry, use special dishes, stay out of the child's room, sleep with the child, buy extra soap, or initiate any other acts intended to help the child? Most families participate to some extent in a child's OCD behavior. That participation can range from waiting an extra 5 minutes while the child washes his or her hands for the 10th time, to revolving the family's whole life around the child's OCD behavior. Although in seriously pathological families it is often necessary to uncover the reasons why family members thoroughly involve themselves in a child's OCD behavior, it is usually not required in the average family in order to stop their participation in the behavior. However, it is essential that the participation stop.

Positive Reframing

Positive reframing of family patterns and attitudes is important for several reasons. Focusing on the well-intentioned and caring aspects of the behaviors reorients the therapist toward the positive, enabling the therapist to retain control of the therapy. The family members feel appreciated for their efforts and are less inclined to feel attacked if their behavior is seen as originating out of love and not out of pathology. This increases the family's ability to join with the therapist in considering whether some behaviors should be changed. Minuchin and Fishman (1981) and Satir (1964) provide many examples of positive reframing. (See the second case history below for a demonstration of positive reframing.)

Case Histories

Case 1

Fifteen-year-old Priscilla required that her father, Mr. Center, go around the house each night at 11:00 to check that everything was locked. After awhile, when that was not sufficient, Mr. Center made a checklist that both father and daughter signed and dated each night. Eventually, the patient felt she needed to do this routine at 2:00 A.M., and she would wake her father, who would accompany her on her rounds. Often, they would retrace their steps because Priscilla was not sure that the door, for example, was indeed locked. Another symptom was her excessive fear that her father would die in a car accident on his way home from work. Mr. Center agreed to call home before he left work and, at some point, agreed to stop and telephone on the way home to reassure Priscilla that he was okay. His 15-minute drive home grew into a 30-minute drive.

Before the first session with the Centers, I requested that 12-year-old Colleen Center join the session. Priscilla was upset at this request and threatened to not attend. I said to Priscilla that it would be a shame if we had a meeting about her without her being there but that we would meet anyway. It was important to have everyone who lived in the family present during the screening session, as the presence of other family members keeps the divulging of information more honest. It also sends a message to the family that OCD is nothing to be ashamed of or to be talked about in whispers.

When the Centers first came to the session, I asked them their understanding of why they were asked to come together. Because it is important to set up an atmosphere where the family feels accepted and knowledgeable, I agree with their responses unless the reasons given are so wrong as to be harmful to the patient or family. Building on what the family has said, I then review my reasons for inviting everyone, namely, that when people in a family join together they have more power to overcome difficulties than they do individually. I imply to the family that I see them as powerful and united.

When I give the family feedback on how I see them, I describe them as how I think they can become. Families will work to improve themselves if they feel they are in an accepting environment. Mr. Center was overinvolved with his daughter, and Mrs. Center was somewhat distant. Rather than pointing this out and making the parents defensive, I told them I felt that they were very concerned parents who had consistently worked together to help their daughter. I indicated that those strengths would be necessary as we worked together to help Priscilla deal with her OCD and prepare for a more independent life in a couple of years, when she will go to college or work full-time. It was essential that the parents see Priscilla's growing independence as reflecting positively on their parenting. Many OCD parents have difficulty letting go, and some even interpret their children's maturation as a rejection. The Centers responded well to my praise of them and agreed that Priscilla would need their help in dealing with her OCD. They said that they were willing to do anything they could to help her.

No one in the Center family acknowledged any concerns about alcohol or drug use, physical violence, or money; however, Mr. Center looked sheepish when I asked about OCD behaviors. When he did not volunteer any information, I told him that it was my sense that he was a little uncomfortable when I asked that question. He still did not say anything, but Colleen said, "Dad and Priscilla do the same kinds of stupid things," to which Mr. Center agreed. I commented about it not being unusual for a parent to have OCD too.

All parents of OCD children usually feel guilty that their child has OCD; parents who themselves have OCD feel doubly guilty for having passed on the disorder to their child. At this point in the session with the Centers, I asked Mrs. Center how she felt about Mr. Center's disorder having been passed on to their daughter. She said that she had known that Mr. Center had the disorder and that she felt the family could deal with a second member having OCD.

During the first interview with the Centers, I learned that Mr. Center would accompany Priscilla's checking rounds and that he would telephone her before leaving work and on his way home. It was also revealed that Mrs. Center frequently slept with Priscilla so that she could reassure her daughter if she awoke and was worried about whether doors and windows were locked. Keeping in mind the goal of having the parents feel supported and not criticized, I remarked that it appeared that they had tried a variety of ways to help Priscilla, and asked them what had and had not been effective. My goal is for the parents to say that what they had tried had not been effective; then I can ask if they would like to try something different.

The directives that I give are often difficult, so I review for the family the large numbers of families successfully treated using the methods I propose we use. Because Priscilla would be on medicine, I recommended that the family discuss the dosages and side effects with the treating physician. The Centers were directed to let Priscilla manage her OCD on her own. They were not to accompany her on her checking rounds; the father was not to call Priscilla before he left work, nor was he to call her on his way home; and the mother was not to sleep in Priscilla's room. They were advised to continue to be warm and caring with Priscilla but not assist or hinder her rituals in any way. I explained to the Centers that, in my experience, a child interprets a parent's compliance with an unreasonable request as an indication that the child's fear is reasonable. I explained that if Priscilla did not respond to the medicine, she would need their encouragement to live as normal a life as possible despite the OCD and that they could begin now by letting her assume responsibility for managing her OCD on her own. The Centers said they could understand this plan, and they agreed to do their part.

I contracted to meet once a month with the parents to review with them how they were carrying out their assignment. Priscilla and I met weekly, and fortunately Priscilla responded to the medicine. Mr. and Mrs. Center came in monthly for 3 months; they had followed my directions completely, and the family was doing very well. At our final session a year later, we all agreed that our treatment plan had been successful.

Case 2

Eight-year-old Brian Clark had been displaying symptoms of OCD for about 2 years. His parents had a long history of marital conflict and did not agree on how to deal with Brian's OCD. Mrs. Clark was 12 when her OCD began, so she started worrying immediately when Brian began retracing his steps and excessively washing his hands at 6 years of age. She did not share her concerns with her husband because she feared he would use this information to criticize her. Mr. Clark did not become aware of Brian's OCD until Brian was washing his hands up to 100 times a day, erasing his school papers so much that they were regularly torn, and taking up to 1 hour to walk to his bedroom from the living room because of his need to retrace his steps. Unfortunately, as Mrs. Clark had feared, Mr. Clark blamed her for Brian's OCD.

The first session started with each parent saying he or she understood the situation better than the other and accusing the other of not loving Brian enough to have prevented him from getting OCD. Attempts at reframing were only marginally successful. Each parent wanted me to castigate the other parent; anything short of that was unsatisfactory to them. Brian's attempts to distract the parents from their fighting worked only briefly.

It was clear that this was a family who needed regular family sessions in addition to sessions for Brian alone. I told the parents that I was impressed by how strongly each of them felt about issues related to Brian and that I realized that this was a painful time for them. Using my OCD checklist, I learned that Brian's OCD behaviors included excessive hand washing, retracing steps, excessive concern about homework, frequent overflowing of the toilet, and a 15-minute ritualized goodnight to his parents. Mr. and Mrs. Clark assisted in these OCD behaviors by purchasing five containers a week of the special liquid soap Brian requested, routinely waiting for him while he retraced his steps, helping him with his homework to excess, plunging the toilet when needed, and engaging in the 15-minute ritual goodnight.

I recommended that we meet weekly in family sessions and that Brian and I meet every other week, to which the Clarks agreed. They were agreeable to my suggestion that the first four sessions be held without Brian. The focus of these four sessions was on changes the parents might want to make regarding the ways they responded to Brian's requests for help with his OCD behaviors. I sympathized with how difficult it was for them to resist their child's requests when he would cry and beg them for help, promising to not wash his hands again if they would just let him wash one more time, or when he would accuse them of not loving him if they would not drive him to school after he had missed the bus for the third time that week because of retracing his steps. The Clarks acknowledged that what they were doing to help Brian was not helping him; yet they were afraid to modify their behavior for fear that Brian's OCD behavior would worsen. I told them their fear was accurate; I predicted a temporary increase and promised to help them deal with it when it happened.

Together we devised specific strategies to change their assistance

with Brian's OCD behavior. Mr. and Mrs. Clark would no longer pur-
chase special soap; each family member would keep his or her bar of soap
in a container outside the bathroom. To address the issue of the family
waiting for Brian while he traced his steps, the family arranged for a
babysitter for Brian if he were not ready at the time the parents had
agreed upon to leave; Brian would be warned in advance and there would
be no "second chances." Neither parent would help Brian with his homework except in the normal way. They would not copy his work for him
nor would they allow him to stay up past his usual bedtime to do homework. The parents told Brian they would no longer engage in the 15-
minute goodnight rituals. Brian was warned that toilet paper might be
rationed in the future if he did not come up with a solution for clogging
the toilet.

When the parents had improved their ability to talk with each other
about Brian and were in agreement about what changes they wanted in
Brian's behavior, I had Brian join the weekly sessions. The parents were
taught specific strategies for dealing with problem behaviors, such as
communicating clear expectations and limits; responding to inappropriate
behavior with consistent, reasonable consequences; and responding to appropriate behavior with attention. The Clarks slowly learned to present a
united front to Brian when he requested assistance with OCD behaviors.
As predicted, his OCD behavior increased when the Clarks changed their
assistance. For several weeks I needed to be available to the parents for
emergency telephone calls. I reassured the parents that the OCD behavior
would eventually decrease if they remained firm.

As the therapist I interrupted dysfunctional interactions, suggested
more functional alternatives, and reinforced positive changes when they
occurred. Although Mr. and Mrs. Clark's marriage still has significant
difficulties and they both continue to be fairly unhappy people, they did
learn how to deal with Brian's OCD behavior despite his limited response
to medicine. We met weekly for a year; I met less often with Brian. Therapy was ended when the family moved out of the state. A 1-year telephone
follow-up suggested that the parents have remained in agreement on how
to deal with Brian. Brian's OCD waxes and wanes but usually does not
seriously interfere with his functioning.

Summary

Family therapy or family interventions can be an integral part of successful treatment of OCD in children, adolescents, and adults. We think that

important steps in the family treatment of OCD children are involving the whole family, identifying all OCD behaviors and family participation in those behaviors, and positively reframing unhelpful parental behavior. Ultimately, this treatment should decrease and help to eliminate these behaviors.

References

Feldman LB: Integrating individual and family therapy in the treatment of symptomatic children and adolescents. Am J Psychother 42:272–280, 1988

Frey J: A family/systems approach to illness-maintaining behaviors in chronically ill adolescents. Family Processes 23:251–260, 1984

Goodyer IM: Family therapy and the handicapped child. Dev Med Child Neurol 28:244–250, 1986

Hafner RJ: Marital interaction in persisting obsessive-compulsive disorders. Aust N Z J Psychiatry 16:171–178, 1982

Minuchin S, Fishman HC: Family Therapy Techniques. Cambridge, MA, Harvard University Press, 1981

Satir V: Conjoint Family Therapy. Palo Alto, CA, Science and Behavior Books, 1964

Steinhauer PD, Tisdall GW: The integrated use of individual and family psychotherapy. Can J Psychiatry 29:89–97, 1984

Weidman AA: Engaging the families of substance abusing adolescents in family therapy. Journal of Substance Abuse Treatment 2:97–105, 1985

Chapter 8

A Multifamily Group Approach as an Adjunct to Treatment of Obsessive-Compulsive Disorder

Barbara Livingston Van Noppen, M.S.W.
Steven A. Rasmussen, M.D.
Jane Eisen, M.D.
Lois McCartney, M.S.W.

*T*he role of psychosocial factors in the pathogenesis and treatment of obsessive-compulsive disorder (OCD) has been overshadowed by recent advances in our understanding of the neurobiology of the disorder as well as by newly developed pharmacological and behavioral treatment strategies. In spite of this progress, 30% to 40% of the patients who initially present to our clinic refuse behavioral treatment, while 15% to 20% do not wish to take medication. Approximately 30% of those patients who are willing to engage in pharmacotherapy or behavior therapy are "non-responders." Finally, although we significantly improve the symptoms of the remaining 70%, the majority are still left with chronic symptoms that significantly interfere with their work and family function. Our clinical experience suggests that the family support system often plays a critical role in the prognosis and outcome of treatment. This may be particularly true for those patients who fail to respond to behavioral and pharmacological interventions. It is consistent with numerous studies that have demonstrated the importance of family treatment and education in the outcome of schizophrenia and affective disorders (Brown et al. 1972; Falloon et al. 1984; Miller et al. 1986).

The devastating impact that severe OCD can have on family function is illustrated in the following condensation of a letter sent to us by the sister of a patient who is enrolled in our clinic:

Dear Dr. Rasmussen:

The person afflicted with obsessive compulsive disorder is my sister Jane who is now twenty three years old.

Jane's obsessive compulsive disorder became most severely disruptive to both her and our family's daily existence about two years ago. Both she and the family realize that the OCD began long ago. . . . its visible manifestations, however, have grown more and more extreme. She lives in my parent's home, and has barricaded herself in the living room of the house. No one else is allowed to enter these "quarantined" areas. The entire upstairs floor and the living room are filled with empty cans that have created an unbelievably vile odor. Life is unbearable not only for Jane but for my mother, who is now living alone with Jane since the death of my father.

Since the death of my father I have in some way assumed the role of "keeping the peace" between Jane and my mother, and I realize as she did, that this is no solution, that it will eventually erupt into violence.

The issue of power and control has always been an overriding one with both Jane and the family, and for the past twelve years everyone and everything has been controlled by her and her problems. The situation has deteriorated to such a point that I feel definitive action is desperately needed, and would be grateful for any advice you may have.

This family had become victims of a disorder that by the very force of its symptoms causes its sufferers to practice emotional blackmail in an attempt to maintain control of their increasingly irrational world. Ironically, in their very wish to keep the peace, this family continued to reinforce the ever-increasing spiral of symptoms. The parents had not been in their daughter's bedroom for over 4 years when we received this letter. When the sister finally understood that giving in was only going to make the symptoms worse, she managed to get up the courage to go into her sister's room. To her astonishment she found the room was stacked from floor to ceiling with thousands of tin cans, all filled with urine and feces. Unbeknown to the family, Jane had not been able to use the toilet because of a fear of contamination. In addition, her fears had prevented her from throwing away the cans. While this case represents the extreme, OCD rarely leaves the family system unaffected. Perhaps in no other psychiatric disorder is the family so inexorably brought into the patient's pathology.

Marital discord, divorce and separation, alcohol abuse, and poor school performance are common results of the stress that OCD puts on both patient and family members. In addition, guilt, blame, and social stigma affect both patient and relatives. It is not unusual for family members to blame themselves for their child or spouse's illness. Relatives fear that early childhood traumas or child-rearing practices are causative.

Advice from friends and relatives may further reinforce the family's sense of guilt and shame. They are often told that the patient is "not ill, just going through a phase" or are given suggestions that more discipline or more attention is the solution to the patient's problem. The family is uncertain whether the prolonged rituals and constant need for reassurance are really part of an illness or willful rebelliousness and demands for attention and control. OCD patients may try to hide their rituals and not divulge their thoughts out of shame. Preoccupied with the needs of the patient, and feeling blamed and burdened, family members may pull away from their usual social contacts and become increasingly socially isolated themselves.

In spite of the clear importance of the family in treatment outcome, the literature on the role the family plays in the course of OCD has been limited to either case reports or descriptive papers. Hafner (1986) sites the paucity of literature on "spouse-aided behavioral therapy." Hand (1988) also notes that most therapists neglect the role of families and systems and tend to treat the OCD patient individually. The few examples in the literature on family treatment of OCD are inconsistent in their results. Hoover and Insel (1984) describe a study of 10 patients with severe OCD in whom psychosocial factors influenced treatment outcome. Fine (1973) described a combined family approach to treatment in two cases of childhood OCD neurosis and noted the supportive benefit that the two families seemed to derive from being together. However, Foa and Steketee (1980) suggest that reduction in interpersonal problems does not affect OCD symptoms. Similarly, Cobb et al. (1980) reported that while it helped the marital relationships, conjoint marital therapy did not reduce OCD symptoms.

Family Response

Our clinical experience has shown that family response to obsessive-compulsive symptoms falls on a continuum of behavioral transactional patterns. This continuum can be visualized as having two polar opposites of either totally giving in to, and even assisting in, the symptomatic behavior or unequivocally opposing the behavior. The two most extreme positions are depicted in Figure 8-1.

A third type of response pattern that is commonly seen is a *split fam-*

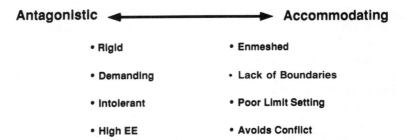

Figure 8-1. The spectrum of family response patterns in OCD.

ily. In this case the family members (usually parents) are divided in their response to the symptomatology, with one parent at the antagonistic end and one at the enmeshed end of the continuum of responses. In what follows, we give clinical examples of each of these family patterns. It should be kept in mind that these examples represent the extremes of the spectrum and that the majority of families lie somewhere in the middle of the continuum.

The Accommodating Family

Accommodating families are usually overinvolved, permissive, and intrusive in relating to the identified patient. The family members who are consistent in joining in and helping with the rituals do so in an effort to keep the peace and reduce the patient's anxiety. This not only is counterproductive for the patient but also creates tension and stress throughout the family. Mrs. A. and her family fit into this model and illustrate how the whole family life-style can be affected:

Mrs. A. is a 30-year-old woman who presented with a 10-year history of contamination obsessions and cleaning compulsions. Married for 15 years, she lives with her husband, a successful businessman, and her 11-year-old son. It was only at her husband's insistence that she sought treatment. He felt that the family could no longer tolerate the "desperate situation" that his wife's illness had inflicted upon them. During the past 2 years she had become increasingly fearful that someone would track germs into the house. She never allowed anyone into her house except her husband and son. This dictum included relatives, friends, and neighbors, as well as her son's friends. She would often spend up to 16 hours per day with cleaning and washing rituals. Her son was not allowed to touch the clothes in his closet because of possible contamination with germs. Because Mrs. A. felt she could not keep the house clean enough, various areas became off limits to the family. As is often the case, the physical space in which Mrs. A. and her family could exist gradually became more and more limited. For the 2 years prior to evaluation, no one had been allowed to sleep on the second floor. Her husband was only "allowed" to go into his bedroom upstairs after he had showered downstairs. His study on the second floor was completely off limits at all times. Naturally, these various restrictions on the family's activities in the house caused a great deal of friction between husband and wife. However, in order to avoid what he described as an intolerable conflict, Mr. A. would consistently give in to his wife's requests and demands.

As Mr. A. gave up more and more territory in the household, he began to realize that Mrs. A. was only getting worse in her preoccupation with germs and cleaning. He was also increasingly concerned about the impact of the family's behavior on their son. In desperation, Mr. A. finally threatened divorce unless his wife agreed to seek treatment.

The Antagonistic Family

At the other end of the continuum is the family whose members consistently refuse to condone or involve themselves with the patient's symptomatic behavior. These antagonistic families tend to be rigid, detached, hostile, critical, and punitive. The stress that ensues may lead to open conflict and anger, and at times physical violence, as is seen in the following example:

L. is a 15-year-old white male living with his parents and two siblings, ages 11 and 2½. L. was referred to the OCD clinic after his family read of the disorder and the existence of our clinic in a newspaper article. L. had been suffering from OCD symptoms for at least 2½ to 3 years. The family described him as hypervigilant and perfectionistic from an early age. They reported that since the age of 6 he had exhibited an overly strict conscience, apologizing to his parents for "anything I may have done wrong" when saying goodnight.

L.'s symptoms included obsessions over feelings of responsibility for potential harm or danger to others and severe contamination obsessions.

Checking and washing rituals interfered with family routines and caused increasing conflict within the family. His contamination obsessions and resulting fear of multiple body fluids led not only to the washing of his hands hundreds of times daily, but also to the avoidance of all garbage or trash, the refusal to touch things in the yard, and eventually the avoidance of physical contact with any family members. He no longer did any of his usual household chores such as taking out garbage, doing yard work, baby-sitting, assisting in the care of his youngest sibling, or helping with kitchen and food responsibilities.

Tension and conflict erupted between L. and his parents, who could not understand what they perceived as rebellious behavior on the part of their heretofore dutiful, conscientious, helpful child. The family sought counseling. The behavior was seen as a family problem—an "adolescent rebellion" resulting from overly controlling, overly demanding parents— while the OCD went unrecognized as a distinct syndrome. The parents resented the implication that they were the cause of their son's strange behaviors. They did follow through on some recommendations such as giving L. his own bedroom, but they took the stance of refusing to go along with his obsessions and compulsions. They attempted to put tight limits on his symptomatic behavior. Their tight limits led to a feeling of being out of control on L.'s part. Physical violence arose between father and son, and eventually L. was restricted to living only in his bedroom. It was there he ate his meals, did his homework, and spent his time. Parents reported additional stress in the form of criticism and advice from their extended family. They withdrew from this previously supportive social network and as a result felt even more isolated and more at odds with one another. The parents expressed rejection, confusion, and anger.

The Split Family

In the split family, parental responses are inconsistent and divided at opposite ends of the continuum of joining (accommodating) or opposing (antagonizing) the patient's symptomatic behaviors. One parent may feel it is characterological and take an angry punitive stance. The other believes the behavior is beyond the patient's control, and takes a totally permissive, indulgent approach, often to the point of assisting in rituals. In families where there is a divided response, there is certain to be dissension and conflict. The lack of agreement between parents can destroy the marital relationship or result in a truly chaotic family system. As the more harsh parent comes down hard, the "softer" parent feels sorry for the patient and either attempts to undo the action of his or her spouse, or indulges and assists the patient whom he or she feels is being treated unfairly. This dynamic is commonly found to a mild degree in relatively normal families. When the family is faced with the stress of OCD symptomatology, the pattern escalates easily, as illustrated below:

P. is a 20-year-old with contamination obsessions and washing compulsions. He is also troubled by a need for reassurance and checking. When the obsessive-compulsive symptoms began to disrupt his social and occupational functioning and severe family conflict erupted, his mother insisted he seek treatment.

From the onset of his illness, P.'s mother had been more sympathetic to his problem. She gently coached him along to get out of bed, into the shower, and dressed in a timely manner before his father wanted to use the bathroom.

P. began treatment with fluoxetine and was encouraged to attend the monthly multifamily psychoeducational support group with his parents and his 18-year-old sister. The family's participation in the group was illustrative of the common split between parents. In response to hearing numerous patients talk about the sense of imperative urgency that accompanies the compulsions, his father commented: "Well, I have habits too. I take my shoes off before coming in the house, but if I had to stop I would. It's like quitting any bad habit, why can't you people just change your ways?!" The mother replied, "I think my husband just can't accept that his son has anything wrong with him beyond his control. I have finally come to terms with this, and I want our family to join together to help him. My husband thinks it's an excuse for laziness or weak moral character. I give in more, then I resent John [her husband] for his harsh aloofness. My daughter, Ann, understands her brother. She sees him struggling with this unwanted OCD, so she gets upset by her father's cruelty. We don't even eat dinner together anymore."

In addition to being the identified patient, P. felt guilty for causing family conflict, and emasculated because he had lost his father's respect. His sister, who identified with the mother, was supportive of him on the one hand, but further aligned him with "womanly overprotection." The sister, like the mother, eschewed her father's disdain and emotional "insensitivity." The patient and sister became triangulated in the parental dyad's issues. These conflicts that were present even before P.'s symptoms developed became magnified as the OC symptoms worsened.

Boundary Issues in Family Response Patterns

Like most families, those with at least one member with OCD tend to resist any change in the previously established equilibrium or norms. This phenomenon of homeostasis, or "family homeostasis," is seen in our case examples. Thus, in A.'s family (see above) the father and son were willing to go to great extremes to maintain the previous peace at all costs, while in L.'s family the members were willing to go to great extremes to maintain their pattern of firm parental control of family behavior.

The boundary concept, a key concept in structural family theory, focuses on the distance or closeness of family members with one another, the alignment or coalitions between various family members, and the permeability and appropriateness of boundaries. Dysfunction is understood in terms of appropriations and adaptiveness of the family pattern of coalitions and the rigidity or permeability of its boundaries. In A.'s family (see above) the boundaries between family members became blurred as father and son became a part of the mother's rituals. While Mrs. A. felt supported, all three members of the family became overinvolved and isolated from others, and were stunted in their ability to have a full life. In P.'s family (see above) boundary issues were also important. In this case the mother became aligned across generational boundaries with her son, and a corresponding strain was placed on the marital relationship.

The concept of expressed emotion, based on the British studies of schizophrenia published in the 1970s (see Brown et al. 1972; Falloon et al. 1984), appears to be particularly applicable to our treatment approach with OCD patients and their families. Expressed emotion is a measure of relatives' critical, hostile, or overinvolved attitudes toward the patient. In the course of schizophrenia it appears to have predictive validity in that patients in families with low expressed emotion have lower relapse rates. Anderson et al. (1986) and Falloon et al. (1984) integrated the expressed emotion concept into their overall treatment strategy for schizophrenia. Intervention approaches that included family involvement through psychoeducation, supportive psychotherapy, and task-oriented psychotherapy were utilized in order to lower expressed emotion in the family setting. Our clinical observations demonstrate an unfavorable impact from high expressed emotion in OCD families. This finding raises the possibility of intervening in these families in a way similar to that of the schizophrenic families to improve outcome.

Regardless of which combination of the three response patterns emerges, patient and family are often left feeling confused, angry, and anxious. In actual clinical practice most families fall somewhere in the middle of the spectrum. It is quite common to see families oscillating from one end of the spectrum to the other, alternately begging (accommodating) and demanding (antagonizing) as the frustration and anger toward the patient and his or her symptoms escalate.

Treatment: The Multifamily Group Approach

Multifamily groups permit greater freedom of participant self-expression and therapist intervention under less restrictive conditions than in traditional family therapy (Detre et al. 1962; Lacqueur et al. 1964.) These advantages may be attributed to the diluted power and role structure when families are in a group. Anderson et al. (1986) pioneered the use of multifamily groups that utilizes psychoeducation and support as a therapeutic modality in the treatment of schizophrenia and depression.

We have found that a structured multifamily psychoeducational support group has been particularly effective for enhancing each family's knowledge and acceptance of the disorder. (The important therapeutic elements of behavioral contracting are presented in Table 8-1.) It has also served as a useful introduction to subsequent behavior therapy. The support group is a professionally led group for family members and patients. The purpose of the group is to provide education on OCD, offer a structure for support, and enhance coping skills. In our experience it has been best to limit the size of the group to about five families. The group runs for eight consecutive weekly sessions of 1½ hours. We outline a weekly agenda, yet build in flexibility to allow for spontaneous interaction, cohesiveness, and trust. In the first 4 weeks we focus on disseminating information and education, and in the last 4 weeks we address the issue of how to cope with OCD.

Some multifamily psychoeducational support groups exclude the patient. We have found that including the patient allows each family unit to take advantage of the cross-parenting phenomenon seen in these multi-

Table 8-1.   Important elements of behavioral contracting

Realistic expectations on the part of patient and family are clearly defined.

The family learns how to be supportive in ways that are therapeutic to the patient.

The patient is given responsibility for therapy that enhances his or her sense of control, motivation, and confidence.

Limits of responsibility are clarified and family members are redirected to get involved in their own lives again.

A third party (or group) moderating the negotiations decreases emotional tension between family members, encourages objective feedback during the behavioral task negotiation, and teaches families how to engage in clear and direct communication.

family groups. The family member–patient format neutralizes powerful interpersonal issues so that they can be addressed in a nonthreatening way. Furthermore, it decreases the "us" and "them" struggle that often develops in families because of a lack of understanding of the pain felt on both sides. Family members have a better chance of helping the patient if they participate in the treatment by first becoming as knowledgeable as they can about OCD, and then learning how they can most effectively respond to the symptoms.

Preliminary data from 85 patients treated in these groups reveal that the most helpful experiences in the group are 1) consensual validation of the impact of OCD on the family, and 2) learning practical techniques for how to cope with their symptoms.

The Intake Process

Not all families will benefit from this particular type of intervention. We interview patients and family members to obtain information about their expectations of the group, their biopsychosocial history, their course of treatment, the consent to contact psychiatrist or therapist, primary OCD symptoms, the family response to illness, and so forth. A description of the group is given to clarify its goals and objectives.

Families and patients bring up predictable questions regarding the group. "I don't know if I'll be able to talk in the group" and "Are the other patients really disturbed? Do they look sick?" are among the most common concerns. Pointing out just how out of control their situation has become, as well as how they can take an active role in changing, can help to overcome initial resistance. For many families this is the first time a professional has included them in the patient's treatment. It is essential for the therapist to communicate to the family that they are a valuable resource and important factor in the patient's eventual recovery. This awareness also validates what the family members have known all along: that they as well as the patient are imprisoned by the OCD. However, families with severe interpersonal conflict, severe cognitive deficits, character pathology, unrealistic expectations, major depression, and/or psychosis are not appropriate for this type of intervention.

The intake process plays a large part in determining the overall success of the group. Whenever the mistake of not screening someone carefully is made in the initial phase, it is regretted subsequently.

Session 1

Anxiety runs high. The beginning is always awkward. Some families arrive very early to be certain they are not late, while others, arriving late, rush through the door with apologies. Often a family will report that the patient has trouble getting to places on time because of obsessions and compulsions. The initial anxiety about the group can be alleviated by providing structure, especially at the first session. However, it is also important to allow room for individual expression that collectively determines the "climate" of the group. The climate can reflect where the group is in terms of issues and emotion—anger at OCD, blame, responsibility, overprotection, overinvolvement, distance, impotence, denial. Our experience has been that once people get started talking, they feel so relieved to be with others "who know," that it is difficult to redirect the informal conversation to begin the session. We pay attention to the level of interaction and content while people find their seat. In a multifamily group the clusterings can be very revealing of alliances, conflicts, and the level of trust within the group.

Humor eases anxiety in the group and illuminates the cathartic benefits of laughter. Humor is a pleasant and productive way for families and patients to share the emotional pain as a result of coping with OCD. When family members learn how to join with the patient to poke fun at the irrational aspects of the obsessive-compulsive symptoms, feelings of isolation, guilt, and fear are reduced. Furthermore, this helps patients distance themselves from their symptoms. Humor, however, must be presented in an empathic context to be effective.

We ask each person to introduce himself or herself and say what he or she hopes to get out of the group. This facilitates participation and lays the foundation for the cohesiveness and trust that leads to group bonding. The themes are the same even though the particulars may vary: "What should I do when my daughter is in the shower for 3 hours? Can that really be OCD?" "How do other families deal with the rituals?" "What is OCD?" "How can each of us cope with it effectively?"

A quick review of the "ground rules" clarifies group expectations about the time frame of the group, the meeting place, confidentiality, and notification of absence from the group. Group members are encouraged to contact the leader(s) to discuss any feelings or issues that arise as a result of their group experience. At this point, the proposed agenda for the eight sessions is outlined and the climate of the group becomes apparent. In one case the group was so intent on continuing interacting with each other, occasionally posing a question to the leader(s), that we did not get beyond discussing the second session. When the process was identified—"It seems like people would rather get to know one another than continue the agenda"—one mother, whose 16-year-old son had OCD, responded: "I came here to talk with other families living with OCD... hear about the symptoms, other treatments, what families do and gain some hope that my son can get better. We don't want to spend any more time with that stuff." This is the climate of many groups: finally families and patients are no longer isolated, because others have validated their experiences and feelings. It is safe to disclose (what are perceived to be) embarrassing thoughts and actions.

It is a powerful experience when family members hear someone else, a stranger, describe the identical symptoms and feelings they have suffered from for many years. They listen. This plants the seed that perhaps OCD is a real disorder, beyond the patient's control. When five people from five families all describe the same phenomena, family members begin to give credence to the existence of the disorder. They start to attend to what patients say with a little more objectivity. The notion that all of this is displaced aggression ("They're just trying to spite me") or a result of faulty parenting ("Was I too strict?") is challenged in the multifamily group.

Especially in the early stages of the group, medication often becomes the focus of conversation: "What are you on? What dosage? Any side effects? How does the doctor choose which medication is best?" Despite reminders to save these concerns for the session with the physician, the families often repeat these questions. At times it is easier to talk about medicine instead of having to deal with the OCD. Tension between the wish for an instant cure and the reality of living with a chronic and at times disabling illness is ubiquitous.

One indicator that the group is not ready to move to issues with direct emotional content is if they continue to discuss medications or switch to questions about another possible "cure," for example, nutrition ("I heard bananas are high in serotonin. Will OCD go away if I change my diet?"). One can acknowledge the universal search for a cure and introduce the reality that the obsessive-compulsive symptoms did not begin yesterday. While it is important to state that most people with OCD do get better with the treatments available, it is unrealistic to expect that OCD will go away completely because of its chronic course and waxing and waning nature.

Another common thread running through these beginning sessions is, "We have suffered long enough, we don't deserve this, take it away!" Often there is denial and disbelief that advanced medical technology cannot perform miracles. As therapists it is crucial to instill hope, yet not guarantee cure.

In time, families enthusiastically compare experiences because they are no longer alone. They can talk about the bizarre symptoms in an atmosphere with little social stigma. The anxiety and fear that maybe their loved one is going crazy is quieted by meeting others with OCD who, outside of their irrational fears, are also "normal people." To their surprise family members begin to realize that in most ways they often cannot distinguish patients from family members.

It is often difficult to end the session because families want to stay and talk more. This is acknowledged. The leader(s) formally finishes, and those who would like to are allowed to stay. This informal networking enhances the group cohesiveness at the risk of the development of subgroups who may go on to control or monopolize the group. The benefits usually outweigh the risks. However, the therapist must be prepared to deal with subgrouping that may slow down group bonding and progress.

Sessions 2, 3, and 4

During these sessions we cover information on our "What is OCD?" handout. Definitions of obsessions and compulsions, theories of etiology, course of illness, common coexisting disorders, and treatment are covered during these sessions.

We reinforce a stress diathesis model of OCD's pathogenesis. In addition to genetic factors, the following familial and cultural factors are important in the development and expression of OCD: 1) child development and parent-child interaction, 2) family functioning, and 3) overall levels of stress. Patients and their families often attempt to understand the patients' symptoms in psychodynamic terms. Attempts to explain causation by analyzing the content of the obsessions are speculative at best and further confuse the issue of how to effectively manage the symptoms. For example, a 38-year-old married female developed repugnant sexual and aggressive obsessions toward her infant shortly after his birth. She was relieved to find out that this may be a biochemically based problem that she could do something about. She could not stop it from happening but she could better control the symptoms by learning about OCD and how to cope with the fears: "You mean I don't have those thoughts because of repressed anger?"

Patients express anger and frustration. They feel cheated because they have to contend with these ridiculous yet inescapable, compelling fears. They feel misunderstood: "My family didn't believe me, who could I turn to. . . . I felt like I couldn't let anyone know." At times there are moments of silence in the group, and the excitement of comparing stories dies down. The emotional experience of collectively coming to terms with the illness often takes place in these silences.

The course of illness is described as "waxing and waning," which many people readily identify with. Families and patients tend to have unrealistic expectations of the recovery phase. Just because patients are able to resist some of their compulsions today does not mean that tomorrow they should expect to exert even more control. People with OCD have good days and bad days. After a set back it is common for families and patients to report feeling very discouraged because "we are afraid of slipping back to the start."

A psychiatrist is present at one of the sessions to discuss biological theories of etiology and issues related to the effectiveness of medication in treatment. This discussion provides group members with an opportunity to ask questions about medications and side effects. The importance of a multimodel treatment approach that encourages family involvement is stressed.

Sessions 5, 6, and 7

The first four sessions provided patients and families with a clearer understanding of OCD. The next step is for them to learn how to cope more productively with the symptoms as a family. This process involves both cognitive and behavioral techniques. The content of sessions 5 and 6 prepares families for the family behavior therapy contracting in session 7 that brings to life the essence of family collaboration in the treatment of OCD.

In sessions 5 and 6 a psychoeducational pamphlet based on our group experience, *Learning to Live With OCD*, is distributed to group members, read aloud, and discussed.

During these sessions, individual responses to OCD are discussed in greater detail. Group interaction becomes highly personalized as families describe the interpersonal conflict that emerges in their attempt to manage the obsessive-compulsive symptoms.

Families are supported in their efforts "to help." Usually they are unaware of how to negotiate a family approach with patient consent. For example, a husband whose wife has had obsessive-compulsive symptoms for 20 years heard in the group that family members should try to discourage the compulsions and avoid participation in the rituals. He came back the next week angry and told the group how bad the advice was: "Last week I made up my mind to put a stop to this nonsense. Within hours, I went back to my other approach because the arguing that erupted was unbearable. J. [his wife] misconstrued my intentions. 'You must not love me anymore; why do you want to hurt me?' This broke my heart. What did I do wrong?" He had grasped the general concept of exposure and response prevention, yet employing a new approach without discussing it with the patient resulted in the patient feeling powerless and out of control.

As familial conflict increases, patients feel even more isolated and stressed, which makes it even more difficult for them to exert control over their symptoms. Family members observing the increase in OCD following interpersonal conflict often attribute it to affective issues that are unrelated to the symptoms—"See, Craig is trying to manipulate me!" "I can't help but believe that this is Lisa's way of getting back at me!" After receiving education on OCD and validation from so many other families, most family members are able to cognitively interpret this sequence of events in a different way, as depicted in Figure 8-2 (see also Table 8-1).

Session 7 arrives. Often group members who complained about not enough guidance or who have tried to rush the group ahead to the contracting are the ones who avoid committing to a task when given the opportunity. It is paramount for the group leader(s) to be very active during the family negotiation. Groups that are comfortable with direct interaction will assist the leader(s) to help each family member with clarification of the group's initial tasks. Those patients who are not ready to choose a therapy goal can consume group time; they must be confronted about their behavior and given permission to pass or to work on a behavior therapy plan of their own without family involvement. The decision to change is placed upon the patient. The group coaches the family to accept that they cannot make the patient participate in a treatment that the family chooses. It has to be the patient's choice. At the same time, if the task chosen by the patient is not sufficiently challenging in the thera-

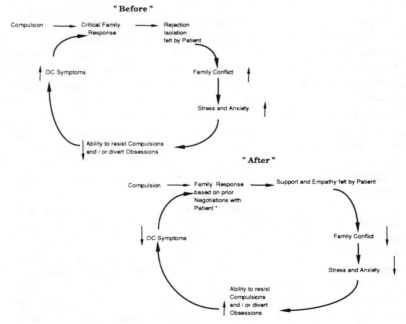

Figure 8-2. Effects of behavioral contracting in the treatment of OCD.

pist's mind, the therapist can use the group process to encourage a more meaningful task. Other patients and family members can be instrumental in helping a particular patient come to terms with this reality. Often adolescents have the most difficulty in accepting family limits as reasonable.

We ask which family would like to initiate the contracting first. The patient is asked to define a specific obsessive-compulsive symptom that he or she would like to reduce. It usually takes a while to identify the symptom clearly within realistic behavioral parameters. For example, J., the woman with a 20-year obsessive-compulsive symptom history whose husband tried to initiate limit setting on his own, stated that she would make a conscious effort to reduce unnecessary hand washing (e.g., anytime she entered the house or anytime she touched anything in the house she suspected of being "contaminated"). J. explained to her husband that she was aware of the OCD and would try to resist when she could. She asked him to go about his business without extra effort to accommodate her. J. also asked her husband not to "hover" around her, specifically, "Don't ask me how I do everyday; I put enough pressure on myself. When you notice I've done well or that I've really tried, give me praise, a simple 'You're doing well. Keep it up,' etc." Family members can get hooked on lengthy discussions centered on reassurance or rationalization that are unproductive. Behavioral contracting gives the patient permission to resume responsibility for his or her treatment and enhances an internal locus of control to promote change. When family members impose the task or goal, yet another struggle ensues over control issues.

The question "How much should I push?" reflects a pervasive concern. Using force or ultimatums in the midst of rituals usually leads to escalating conflict, even possibly physical violence or destructive acts out of frustration and anger. We tell families as a general rule to encourage resistance and discourage avoidance as much as possible. Mounting tension, often manifested as an increase in obsessive-compulsive symptoms, is a warning signal to "back off." If a situation arises that could clearly result in physical harm to the patient and/or family members, someone must directly intervene. Families with a suicidal patient or with violent interactions should seek more intensive professional guidance. Any acute crisis is addressed and resolved before behavioral family contracting can resume.

Each family in the group is guided through the behavioral contracting by the leader(s) and the group. Each successive family incorporates what they observed from the family before. For example, an astute mother whose 18-year-old son had washing and checking rituals identified a conflict between her husband and herself that came out in the son: "It's not a matter of where S. leaves his 'contaminated' towels. The problem of where to leave used towels in general is between my husband and me." This came out while the three negotiated the son's reducing the number of towels he uses after showering and where the towels are to be placed. Apparently, the mother also objected to where the father put his used towels! This provided the family with an opportunity to separate preexisting interpersonal issues that are often magnified by the impact of the obsessive-compulsive symptoms. In this case, the parents were asked to resolve their conflict about the towels before they could clearly communicate expectations to their son. Other parent-patient families identified with this dilemma and shared their situations with the group in an effort to consider problem-solving alternatives.

Session 8

Each family is asked to report to the group on their "homework assignment" from the previous week. Often a group member initiates this spontaneously. Group members listen to one another with a keen sense of empathy. Some families identify obstacles and redefine their goals and behavioral expectations. A sense of collective accomplishment and purpose emanates from the group.

Families ask: "What will we do now?" "Does this group have to end?" "Can't we extend it? We just got to know each other." The leader(s) addresses feelings of sadness and loss as part of ending the group. At one group the leader reminded the group of the eight-session contract. An 11-year-old patient responded: "Well, can't we renegotiate the contract?!" The leader responded that the patient grasped the idea of family behavior therapy, but that unfortunately the group had to end.

Anger is often expressed along with sadness. Group members are encouraged to pursue any of the follow-up options that are reviewed prior to termination: 1) individual therapy, 2) individual family therapy, 3) a monthly multifamily psychoeducational support group for OCD, 4) a biweekly multifamily self-help group for OCD, 5) a multifamily behavior therapy group, 6) an individual behavior therapy group, and 7) no further intervention. Time is spent discussing the various choices, and then patients and families begin to thank one another and prepare for termination.

Last-minute questions about whom to tell about OCD and how, medication (again!), follow-up, etc., are asked. Evaluation forms are distributed. As soon as the last "just one more thing" is answered, the leader(s) departs, leaving group members to informally and personally wish each other well.

The Family-Professional Alliance

Identification of stress factors and a shift away from causal theories, as well as the growth of family organized self-help groups and advocacy groups for the mentally ill and their families, have resulted in a shift in the attitude of professionals away from blaming families to one of collaborating with families. OCD is a disorder that lends itself well to a strong alliance between families and professionals. The rapid growth of a national OCD foundation over the past 2 years and the establishment of local advocacy groups testify to the power and importance of this alliance.

Summary

We have only begun to touch the surface of understanding the role of psychosocial factors in the pathogenesis and treatment of OCD. Our clinical experience in treating over 100 OCD patients over the past 5 years has shown that family treatment is an essential component of any integrated therapeutic approach. On the whole, although OCD families are more disturbed in all areas of family function than are control families, they are not as pathological as families of schizophrenic or depressive patients. The majority of conflict centers on the patient's symptoms and their effect on family function. If family strengths can be mobilized to form an effective alliance among patient, family, and therapist, then outcome can be significantly improved. We have utilized a multifamily psychoeducational and behavioral group approach to take maximum advantage of limited therapist resources. These groups are time-limited and highly structured, emphasizing increased understanding of the symptoms as a disorder and behavioral contracting between family members and patients.

References

Anderson CM, Russ DJ, Hogarty GE: Schizophrenia and the Family: A Practitioner's Guide to Psychoeducation and Management. New York, Guilford, 1986

Brown GW, Berley JLT, Wing JK: Influence of family life on the course of schizophrenic disorders: a replication. Br J Psychol 121:241–258, 1972

Cobb JP, McDonald R, Marks IM, et al: Psychological treatments of coexisting marital and phobic-obsessive problems. Behavioral Ana Mod 4:3–16, 1980

Detre T, Sayers J, Norton N, et al: An experimental approach to the treatment of the acutely ill psychiatric patient. Conn Med 25:613–619, 1962

Falloon IRH, Boyd JL, McGill CW: Family Care of Schizophrenia: A Problem-Solving Approach to the Treatment of Mental Illness. New York, Guilford, 1984

Fine S: Family therapy and a behavioral approach to childhood obsessive-compulsive neurosis. Arch Gen Psychiatry 28:695–697, 1973

Foa E, Steketee G: Obsessive compulsives: conceptual issues and treatment interventions, in Progress in Behavior Modification. Edited by Hersen RM, Eisler RM, Miller P. New York, Academic, 1980, pp 1–53

Hafner RJ: Marriage and Mental Illness: A Sex-Roles Perspective. New York, Guilford, 1986

Hand I: Families and anxiety disorders, in Handbook of Behavioral Family Therapy. Edited by Falloon I. New York, Guilford, 1988

Hoover CF, Insel TR: Families of origin in obsessive-compulsive disorder. J Nerv Ment Dis 172:207–215, 1984

Lacqueur HP, LaBurt HA, Morong E: Multiple family therapy. Current Psychiatric Therapies 4:150–154, 1964

Miller IW, Kabacoff RI, Keitner GI, et al: Family functioning in the families of psychiatric patients. Compr Psychiatry 27:302–312, 1986

Chapter 9

Management of Patients With Treatment-Resistant Obsessive-Compulsive Disorder

Michael A. Jenike, M.D.

*U*p to the last decade almost all patients with obsessive-compulsive disorder (OCD) were thought to be refractory to treatment. Modern therapies, however, have dramatically improved the outlook for these patients, but many clinicians are not aware of what is presently available in terms of effective treatments. The first task of the clinician faced with an OCD patient who has not responded to treatment is to find out if the patient has, in fact, received adequate treatment trials; a careful, detailed history is needed (Table 9–1). For each medication trial, dosage and length of trial must be elicited. There is growing evidence that full 10-week trials of potentially effective medications, such as clomipramine or fluoxetine, are required before assuming that the drug is ineffective. Also, certain behavioral techniques—specifically exposure and response prevention—are most likely to be of help, while other approaches such as simple relaxation, hypnosis, or biofeedback are not effective treatments.

We now know that if patients receive appropriate treatment, usually consisting of behavior therapy plus psychotropic medication, the majority will improve substantially, and occasionally completely, within a few months (Jenike et al. 1986c). In the experience of our clinic, the most common reason for resistance to treatment was that ineffective treatments had been attempted. Many patients primarily received psychodynamic psychotherapy, electroconvulsive therapy, or neuroleptics without result. Despite the well-documented efficacy of behavioral therapies, it is still unusual for patients to arrive at our clinic who have been given even a cursory trial of these treatments.

Even with good treatments, certain patients continue to be refractory. Predictors of treatment failure in behavior therapy for OCD include

Table 9–1. Some common reasons for treatment failure in patients with OCD

Inadequate diagnosis (e.g., schizophrenia, obsessive-compulsive personality disorder)
Inadequate treatment Inappropriate or ineffective medication
Medication trial too short
Medication dosage too low
No behavior therapy
Poor compliance Patient willful, prefers sickness to health, cannot tolerate demands when well
Unrecognized cognitive impairment
Other concomitant psychiatric illness (e.g., schizophrenia, major depression, bipolar illness)
Poor understanding of treatment plan by patients (e.g., only takes medication when feeling "stressed")

noncompliance with treatment, concomitant severe depression (Foa 1979), absence of rituals, fixed beliefs in the necessity of rituals, presence of concomitant personality disorder (Jenike et al. 1986a, 1986b), and type of compulsive ritual. Patients with schizotypal and possibly other severe personality disorders (Axis II in DSM-III-R; American Psychiatric Association 1987) also do poorly with pharmacotherapy (Jenike et al. 1986b; Minichiello et al. 1987).

Outcome studies and anecdotal evidence indicate that poor compliance with the behavioral treatment program is the most common reason for treatment failure with behavior therapy for OCD (Marks 1981). Behavior therapy is more demanding of the patient than many other forms of psychotherapy, and the patient must comply with behavioral instructions both during treatment sessions and also during "homework" assignments. If the patient is inconsistent in doing this, treatment is unlikely to be successful.

Severe depression has also been found to be a negative predictor for improvement with behavior therapy of OCD (Foa 1979), possibly due to impaired learning. In patients with major depression, the behavioral processes of physiological habituation to the feared stimuli do not occur, regardless of the length of exposure (Lader and Wing 1969). Because most antiobsessional drugs are also powerful antidepressants, depression is not a poor predictive factor for drug outcome.

If a patient has severe obsessive thoughts without rituals, behavior therapy is unlikely to succeed. In these cases pharmacotherapy is the treatment of choice. Patients who strongly hold the belief that their compulsive rituals are necessary to forestall future catastrophes (i.e., "overvalued ideas") have a poorer outcome with behavioral treatments (Foa 1979). For example, the patient who really believes that someone in his family will die if he does not wash his entire house every day is unlikely to give up the rituals with behavior therapy alone.

As noted above, patients meeting DSM-III-R criteria for both OCD and schizotypal personality disorder do not respond well to either behavior therapy or pharmacotherapy. The idea of concomitant schizotypal personality disorder as a poor prognostic indicator in OCD appears to have validity in light of the literature on treatment failure. This personality disorder encompasses several of the poor predictive factors reviewed above. Most noticeably, these patients may have strongly held beliefs that their rituals are necessary to prevent some terrible event. Also, they have a difficult time complying with proscribed treatment and assigned record keeping. Rachman and Hodgson (1980) have similarly found that the presence of an "abnormal personality" is a negative predictor of outcome in behavior therapy for OCD; and more recently, Solyom et al. (1985) have reported on a subcategory of patients with "obsessional psychosis" similar (perhaps identical) to the schizotypal subgroup, who also respond poorly to both behavior therapy and pharmacotherapy.

For a patient who meets criteria for schizotypal personality disorder, placement in a structured environment such as a day treatment center or halfway house during and after behavioral treatment produces small decreases in patients' obsessive-compulsive symptoms, along with moderate improvements in overall functioning.

Patients with contamination fears and cleaning rituals appear to respond best to behavioral treatment (Rachman and Hodgson 1980), while patients with checking compulsions may not do as well. Even when responsive to behavioral techniques, patients with checking rituals appear to improve more slowly than those with cleaning rituals (Foa and Goldstein 1978). A possible explanation for this difference is that many patients with checking rituals are unable to engage in the prescribed response prevention, especially those who check excessively at home

(Rachman and Hodgson 1980). In addition, patients with primary obsessional slowness respond more slowly to behavior therapy than do patients with either cleaning or checking rituals (Baer and Minichiello 1986).

Importance of Correct Diagnosis: Diagnostic Criteria and Distinction From Obsessive-Compulsive Personality Disorder

Another reason for poor treatment outcome is inaccurate diagnosis. If a patient meets criteria for schizophrenia or suffers from obsessive-compulsive personality disorder (OCPD), the standard treatments for OCD are not likely to be of help. The currently accepted definition of OCD is given in the *Diagnostic and Statistical Manual of Mental Disorders*, Third Edition, Revised (DSM-III-R; 1987) and is described elsewhere in this book.

Although patients diagnosed with OCPD may have some obsessions and minor compulsions associated with their perfectionism, indecisiveness, or procrastination, these rituals do not interfere with the patient's life to the extent of OCD. However, some patients with OCD also have compulsive personality traits (Rasmussen and Tsuang 1986), and roughly 6% (Baer et al. 1990) meet DSM-III (American Psychiatric Association 1980) criteria for OCPD. With the change in diagnostic criteria in DSM-III-R, preliminary data indicate that as many as 20% of OCD patients meet criteria for OCPD (Baer et al. 1990).

The differential diagnosis of these two disorders has important implications for treatment. For example, although traditional psychotherapy produces little change in obsessions and compulsions in the context of OCD, it may be of some value in the treatment of patients with OCPD (Jenike et al. 1986c; Salzman 1969). Conversely, although behavior therapy and psychopharmacological treatments have been found in controlled trials to be very effective for OCD, there is no evidence that these approaches are helpful for patients with OCPD.

Drug Treatments: What Is Reported to Work?

Much has been learned about somatic treatments for OCD in the last few years. New medications, unfortunately some only available in the United States for experimental purposes, reliably help more than half of the OCD patients. The number of controlled clinical trials is increasing rapidly as specialty OCD clinics are seeing larger numbers of patients. The standard randomized, prospective, placebo-controlled trial, so useful to depression research, had until recently been almost impossible to conduct because of the small numbers of OCD patients available to any one researcher. As the pharmaceutical industry realizes the potential market for effective antiobsessional agents, they are putting millions of dollars into research on agents such as fluvoxamine and sertraline that are not yet on the United States market.

Electroconvulsive Therapy

Many severe OCD patients who have been referred by clinicians to the OCD clinic at the Massachusetts General Hospital over the past few years have had at least one course of electroconvulsive therapy (ECT). Most did not suffer from a major mood disorder, and the main reason for administering ECT was for treatment of OCD.

ECT is generally regarded as ineffective for the OCD patient who is not endogenously depressed (American Psychiatric Association 1978; Gruber 1971), although scant literature exists concerning the effects of ECT alone on OCD. In a review of this subject, Mellman and Gorman (1984) found a few studies reporting that ECT in combination with other treatment modalities was associated with clinical improvement in some OCD patients. They also reported one atypical patient (having only obsessions that developed after his wife's death) who had a good response to ECT after not responding to a number of treatments including a 12-week trial of clomipramine. Walter et al. (1972) assessed the combined effects of ECT, modified narcosis, and antidepressants on obsessional neurotic patients (unclear diagnostic criteria) and found that 40% of the patients improved. The relative effect of each form of treatment separately was obscure. Grimshaw (1965) studied 100 patients with obsessional symptoms (also poorly defined) and concluded that ECT had little effect on obsessional states.

Psychosurgery

Because most OCD patients who undergo psychosurgery have a very severe illness that has not responded to multiple therapeutic approaches, the results of surgical intervention are impressive (Bailey et al. 1975; Ballantine et al. 1987; Bernstein et al. 1975; Birley 1964; Bridges et al.

1973; Jenike et al. 1986c; Kelly et al. 1972; Le Beau 1952; Mitchell-Heggs et al. 1976; Smith et al. 1976; Ström-Olsen and Carlisle 1971; Sykes and Tredgold 1964; Tan et al. 1971; Tippin and Henn 1982; Whitty and Duffield 1952).

Tippin and Henn (1982) reviewed the results of six studies of modified leukotomy that included 110 patients with obsessional disease. Nearly 81% ($n = 89$) were at least "improved," while more than half of those improved were in complete remission. The long-term outcome of these patients remains unreported.

Bilateral stereotactic, anterior, internal capsulotomy appears to be the most effective of the surgical procedures (Fodstad et al. 1982; Mindus 1986; Modell et al. 1989). A review of this procedure in over 325 cases by Mindus (1986) revealed that 70% of patients experienced a significant reduction in target symptoms of anxiety or obsessions and compulsions, and the risk of serious surgical complications was very low. The portion of the internal capsule through which the surgical lesions of the anterior capsulotomy are placed contains the sole pathway for the reciprocal fiber bundles interconnecting the orbitofrontal cortex with the dorsomedial and related thalamic nuclei; adequacy in size and placement of the operative lesions in the anterior limb of the internal capsule, as verified by magnetic resonance imaging (MRI), has been shown to correlate strongly with postoperative reduction in obsessive-compulsive symptoms (Mindus et al. 1987). Of interest, most studies show either no adverse effects on personality and cognition from highly localized lesions (using modern techniques) of the anterior capsule, cingulum, or frontal lobes, or slight improvement in these functions presumably owing to a reduction in obsessive-compulsive symptoms (Ballantine et al. 1987; Herner 1961; Mindus 1986; Modell et al. 1989).

Side effects of modern site-specific lesion techniques are rare. The data on the efficacy of surgical treatment for OCD should be interpreted with some caution, however, because negative results are rarely reported.

Behavior Therapy

Behavior therapy is a directive psychotherapeutic approach, based on proven learning principles, that teaches the patient how to directly alter his or her compulsive rituals. The techniques most consistently effective in reducing compulsive behaviors (and along with them, obsessive thoughts) are exposure to the feared situation or object and response prevention, in which the patient is helped to resist the urge to perform the compulsion after this exposure.

Behavior therapy produces the largest changes in rituals, such as compulsive cleaning or checking, whereas changes in obsessive thoughts are less predictable (Marks 1981). This is in contrast to traditional psychotherapy, where any changes that might be produced are mainly in obsessional thoughts, while little effect is seen in rituals (Sturgis and Meyer 1980). (See Steketee and Tynes, Chapter 5, this volume, for a more detailed discussion of behavior therapy.)

Managing the Patient With Obsessive-Compulsive Disorder Who Has Not Responded to Treatment

Initial Evaluation

The majority of OCD patients who present as treatment-resistant have, in fact, not received appropriate treatments for the disorder. The majority of clinician-referred OCD patients presenting to our clinic have never had trials of behavior therapy and almost half of them have not undergone antidepressant trials. A flow sheet of possible treatment options is listed in Table 9–2.

In order to outline a treatment plan for an OCD patient, it is necessary to have a clear idea of the problem, what exacerbates and what improves it, how it has evolved over the life of the patient, and what other symptoms and difficulties exist concomitantly. The clinical history and interview must reflect behavioral, psychodynamic, and family systems principles. To determine the appropriate treatment approach and understand the individual's potential for compliance, a thorough mental status examination is required. A depressed, manic, cognitively impaired, or psychotic patient will require a special treatment strategy. Behavioral treatments are unlikely to be effective until associated functional illnesses are well controlled. Also, alcoholic patients require treatment for alcoholism before they can comply with treatment aimed specifically at their obsessive-compulsive symptoms.

The importance of treating other concomitant psychiatric disorders, such as psychosis or depression, cannot be overemphasized. For example, as mentioned earlier, obsessive-compulsive behaviors are sometimes found in patients suffering from bipolar affective disorder (Baer et al. 1985; Black 1974). Although behavior therapy techniques of in vivo ex-

Table 9–2.   Possible treatment options for patients with OCD

As soon as the patient has at least a partial response to medication, and if the patient has rituals, begin behavior therapy of exposure and response prevention.

1. Begin fluoxetine trial (up to 80 mg daily).
2. Try augmenting fluoxetine for one month (see Table 9–3).
3. Begin clomipramine trial (up to 250 mg daily).
4. Try augmenting clomipramine for 1 month (see Table 9–3).
5. Stop fluoxetine or clomipramine for 5 weeks.
6. Then begin MAOI trial.
7. Try augmenting MAOI for 1 month (see Table 9–3).
8. Begin trials of experimental agents when available.
9. Begin other medication trials (e.g., trazodone, imipramine).
10. If severe personality disorder is present, consider halfway-house placement or day treatment program.
11. If patient is severely disabled, despite adequate treatment trials, consider psychosurgical procedure.
12. If poor compliance is a persistent problem, or patient prefers symptoms to being rid of them, or if patient also has obsessive-compulsive personality disorder, consider concomitant psychodynamic psychotherapy.

posure and response prevention are highly effective in treating these behaviors, until recently there were no reports of their use in patients with bipolar disorder and concomitant OCD. A recent report of two patients meeting criteria for both disorders who were treated with a combination of therapist-aided and self-administered exposure and response prevention, demonstrated that behavior therapy was effective only after their major mood disorder was effectively controlled with lithium and neuroleptics (Baer et al. 1985).

Medical Evaluation

It is extremely unusual for a medical or neurological illness to be the cause of classical OCD. If onset of the illness is over age 50, the likelihood of associated disease probably increases. Possible neurological etiologies are reviewed elsewhere (Jenike 1984; Jenike et al. 1986c).

Treatment

Patients with only obsessive thoughts.   In OCD patients who suffer only from severe obsessive thoughts and do not have rituals, a trial of antidepressant medication is a reasonable first choice. Adequate trials of clomipramine may require as much as 250 mg/day for as long as 10 weeks. Even though dosage above 250 mg/day has been associated with a higher incidence of seizure, the manufacturer has allowed doses of up to 300 mg as part of a multicenter trial for treatment-resistant patients. Fluoxetine may also be effective, but the optimal dose is as yet undetermined. Until more data are available, dosages may slowly be increased to 80 mg/day (Jenike et al. 1989). Other antidepressants may work, but they seem to be effective in a smaller percentage of patients. Experimental agents, such as fluvoxamine and sertraline, may be effective and lack some of clomipramine's troubling side effects; a number of studies are in progress to evaluate the effectiveness of these newer agents (see Goodman and Price, Chapter 4, and Hollander, Chapter 11, this volume).

Occasionally obsessions improve within a few days with pharmacotherapy. Anecdotal experience suggests that monoamine oxidase inhibitors (MAOIs) may be particularly rapid in onset of effect.

Behavior therapy has little to offer the patient with severe obsessions who does not have rituals. In those patients who do not respond to drugs, thought stopping, assertiveness training, systematic desensitization, imaginal flooding, and cognitive restructuring may be of assistance in diminishing symptoms (Jenike et al. 1986c).

Patients with rituals. A few patients with compulsive rituals will respond completely to either drugs or behavior therapy alone, but the majority require a combination of the two approaches for optimal clinical improvement. The techniques of exposure and response prevention as outlined earlier are the mainstay of behavioral treatment. In patients with concomitant major depression, psychosis, or mania, it is unlikely that behavior therapy will be of help until these symptoms are well controlled pharmacologically. In such cases initial treatment should be drug-oriented and behavior therapy should begin only after these affective or psychotic symptoms are optimally controlled.

In patients who only perform rituals at home, behavioral treatment will have to take place in the home. Family members will need to function as surrogate therapists and supervise the exposure plus response prevention. Many patients can be treated in an office setting with homework given at the end of each session. The aid of a family member or friend in carrying out homework assignments is often critical to ensure compliance. In addition, the concurrent use of antidepressants with behavior therapy often increases patients' compliance with exposure treatments

(Marks et al. 1980). New methods of improving compliance with behavioral treatment are under investigation, including use of portable computers that assist the patient in carrying out homework assignments (Baer et al. 1987).

Patients with severe depression often respond well to behavior therapy procedures after depression is controlled with medication (Baer and Minichiello 1986).

Patients with personality disorders. Assessment of personality disorders in OCD patients is important for predicting outcome and selecting the preferred treatment approach. As noted, patients with severe personality disorder are often refractory to usual therapeutic strategies. These patients respond atypically to previously validated behavioral techniques of exposure plus response prevention and do not usually respond to drugs. Preliminary anecdotal data, however, indicate that fluoxetine is more helpful in these difficult patients than clomipramine and that occasional schizotypal patients have quite dramatic improvement with this serotonergic agent (Jenike et al. 1990). In particular, schizotypal personality disorder significantly impairs treatment outcome and should be considered along with other predictors of poor outcomes such as severe depression, overvalued ideas, and noncompliance. So powerful is this effect that treatment-outcome studies should probably analyze data separately for patients with and without this personality disorder.

In some cases treatment with antidepressant medication will produce changes in a patient's fixed beliefs, and behavior therapy may then be successful in eliminating rituals. For the majority of cases we manage these patients by reducing stress and conflict in their environments, which is best done with behavioral family or couples counseling. In addition, we attempt to arrange for day treatment, halfway-house placement, or other alternative living arrangements away from the usually stressful environment where obsessive-compulsive symptoms often are exacerbated and reinforced. Once out of a stressful environment, supportive therapy of these patients, with encouragement for exposure and response prevention and enthusiastic reinforcement of the slightest gains, has been helpful in producing modest improvements in obsessions and compulsions. The long-term outcome of these patients requires further study.

Medication trials

Either fluoxetine or clomipramine can be tried as the drug of first choice. Because clomipramine has prominent anticholinergic effects, it is best not to use it initially in elderly patients or in those patients sensitive to anticholinergic side effects of drugs.

Research centers may have access to other agents that might possibly be as effective as clomipramine and fluoxetine. If none of these drugs are available, any of the standard heterocyclic agents can be tried. Dosages should be in the antidepressant range, and blood levels may be helpful for imipramine, nortriptyline, and desipramine (Task Force 1985). Response to any of the antidepressants may take up to 10 weeks, and patients should be advised that medication trials cannot be evaluated if discontinued for lack of efficacy until at least 2 months have passed at therapeutic levels. Occasionally patients respond early, but this will be the exception.

If two antidepressant trials plus the use of augmenting agents (see below) fail or if the patient suffers concomitant panic attacks or very severe anxiety, we will generally proceed with an MAOI trial. Tranylcypromine, up to 60 mg daily, or phenelzine, up to 90 mg daily, are the two drugs most commonly used. *Patients should discontinue clomipramine or fluoxetine for a full 5 weeks prior to starting an MAOI*, because fatal reactions have been reported when these agents have been given in close proximity.

Augmenting antidepressants with other drugs

As in patients with treatment-resistant depression, augmentation strategies are worth trying. Augmentation involves adding another drug to the treatment regimen when the patient has had no improvement or only a partial response to an antidepressant. Some potential augmenting agents are outlined in Table 9–3. Some of our preliminary open data on augmenting agents are presented in Table 9–4. Even though the overall percentage of patients that responded is quite small, occasionally patients had quite dramatic improvement that justified such trials before switching to another drug. Certain limitations are inherent in such open trials, not the least of which is the possibility that some of the enhanced improvement may, in fact, be secondary to the patient being on fluoxetine for a longer duration of time. In each of the patients presented in Table 9–4, fluoxetine had been continued alone for a minimum of 10 weeks before

Table 9–3.　Potential augmenting agents for treatment-resistant OCD patients

Augmenting agent	Suggested dosage range[a]
Lithium	300–600 mg/day[b]
Clonazepam	1–3 mg/day
Tryptophan	2–10 g/day[c]
Trazodone	100–200 mg/day
Buspirone	15–60 mg/day
Alprazolam	0.5–2 mg/day
Methylphenidate	10–30 mg/day
Haloperidol	2–10 mg/day
Pimozide	2–10 mg/day
Nifedipine	10 mg tid
Liothyronine sodium	10–25 μg/day
Clonidine	0.1–0.6 mg/day
Fenfluramine	Up to 60 mg/day

[a] Add these to an ongoing trial of antidepressant medication. It should be noted that most of these dosages have not been tested with rigorous clinical trials but simply represent some of the reported doses tried in the current literature.
[b] *Use with caution*—there have been some reports of elevated lithium levels with ongoing fluoxetine treatment (Noveske et al. 1989; Salama and Shafey 1989).
[c] Because the use of L-tryptophan has recently (Fall 1989) been implicated in an increased incidence of eosinophilia, the authors advise against the prescribing and use of this agent, as discussed in this book, until the issue is resolved.

Table 9–4.　Massachusetts General Hospital open trials of fluoxetine plus augmenting agents

Drug	Daily dosage range (mg)	Number of patients	Percentage points over 20% improvement[a]	Percentage of patients stopped for side effects
Clonidine	0.1–0.6	17	19%	56%
Trazodone	100–200	13	31%	31%
Lithium	300–600	7	14%	29%
Clonazepam	1.0–3.0	7	14%	0%

Note. All trials were roughly 1 month in duration.
[a] As assessed by the Yale-Brown Obsessive Compulsive Scale (Goodman et al. 1989b, 1989c).

the augmenting agent was added. In addition to the seven patients who were augmented with clonazepam, another nine patients received clonazepam and fluoxetine almost simultaneously; of these, seven (78%) improved at least 20% during the next 10 weeks. Clonazepam was sometimes added early in the course of a fluoxetine trial to counter drug-induced anxiety and restlessness. In two other patients, fluoxetine was augmented with alprazolam (0.5 and 2.0 mg/day, respectively) without improvement. Similarly, two others who had received buspirone (15 and 60 mg/day, respectively) after failing to improve with fluoxetine had no added response to their symptoms.

Despite reports of improvement with intravenous clonidine (Hollander et al. 1988), our results with orally administered clonidine were not impressive. Side effects with clonidine, consisting mainly of excessive sedation and unsteadiness, necessitated stopping the drug before completing a 1-month trial in over half of the patients. Similarly, almost one-third of the patients who were augmented with trazodone had to discontinue the medication because of excessive daily sedation, even though the drug was given at bedtime.

Rasmussen (1984) reported a 22-year-old woman with classical OCD who did not respond to clomipramine alone, but who improved greatly a few days after lithium carbonate was added with a lithium level of 0.9 meq/l. Whether lithium augmentation of other antidepressants or MAOIs for obsessive-compulsive symptoms is helpful remains to be tested. Improvement in depressed patients has been demonstrated in tricyclic "nonresponders" after addition of lithium to the antidepressant (Dé Montigny et al. 1981). In addition, Rasmussen (1984) reported a male OCD patient who had a partial response to clomipramine that was dramatically boosted when 6 g/day of L-tryptophan was added.[1] This patient relapsed when the tryptophan was stopped and improved again when it was restarted. Whether tryptophan boosts the antiobsessional effects of other tricyclic antidepressants or MAOIs remains to be determined. Of interest, Walinder and associates (1976) have demonstrated that L-tryptophan may potentiate tricyclic antidepressant effects in endogenously depressed patients.

There are conflicting reports on buspirone as an antiobsessional agent. In two recent trials with buspirone up to 60 mg, one trial (Jenike and Baer 1988) found buspirone to be ineffective, and the other trial (Pato et al., in press) found it to be effective. In addition, there has been a recent report which found that adding buspirone to an ongoing antide-

---

[1]Because the use of L-tryptophan has recently (Fall 1989) been implicated in an increased incidence of eosinophilia, the authors advise against the prescribing and use of this agent, as discussed in this book, until the issue is resolved.

pressant trial augmented the efficacy of the initial medication (Markovitz et al. 1989).

Prior to changing any antidepressant medication, it is worth trying to augment the response by adding each augmenting agent used, for a 2- to 4-week period. Based on case reports with clomipramine and on our anecdotal experience (see Table 9–4), this strategy will occasionally yield positive results.

Although neuroleptic agents are not generally useful for patients with OCD, of interest is a recent report by Goodman et al. (1989a) of an open case series of 13 OCD patients where 8 were much improved after pimozide was added to ongoing fluvoxamine. McDougle et al. (1990) presented data on the addition of a neuroleptic (haloperidol or pimozide) to ongoing fluvoxamine treatment in 17 OCD patients (probably included the same 13 patients as in the Goodman et al. series above). Nine of the patients improved to a clinically significant degree. Some of the patients were also taking lithium in combination with fluoxetine during this augmentation trial; the contribution of lithium to overall improvement is not clear, but none of the patients had significant improvement prior to neuroleptic augmentation. If neuroleptic augmentation is used, specific target symptoms should be identified, and if there is no improvement within a few months, the neuroleptic should be stopped because of the dangers of irreversible neurological sequelae with these agents.

Anxiolytic agents are often used as adjuncts to other medications and may be helpful in facilitating behavior therapy in patients who are unable to tolerate the anxiety produced by exposure and response prevention techniques. It is unlikely that these agents will have significant effect on OCD symptoms when used alone.

ECT or psychosurgery

ECT is generally not helpful in OCD patients. In those cases, however, where there is a depressive illness that preceded obsessive-compulsive symptoms, ECT may prove beneficial (American Psychiatric Association 1978; Grimshaw 1965; Gruber 1971; Mellman and Gorman 1984; Walter et al. 1972).

From the collective data on psychosurgery, over half of the severe OCD patients improve. Postoperative personality changes are not evident with modern restricted operations, and surgical complications are few. A patient who has suffered for years with disabling OCD that has responded poorly to more conventional therapies has a reasonable chance of favorable outcome with relatively few risks. When more conservative treatments fail, psychosurgery is a viable option. Whether it will improve the clinical situation of the very severe OCD patients with concomitant personality disorder is unknown (Bailey et al. 1975; Ballantine et al. 1987; Bernstein et al. 1975; Birley 1964; Bridges et al. 1973; Jenike et al. 1986b, 1986c; Kelly et al. 1972; Le Beau 1952; Mitchell-Heggs et al. 1976; Smith et al. 1976; Ström-Olsen and Carlisle 1971; Sykes and Tredgold 1964; Tan et al. 1971; Tippin and Henn 1982; Whitty and Duffield 1952).

Case Histories

Case 1

Mrs. A. reported an 11-year history of hand washing and excessive showering that took up to 5 hours per day. She described vague fears that there was some sort of substance associated with air pollution, and she felt "dirty and contaminated" unless she washed excessively every day. She was distressed that she had started to force her 7-year-old son to wash his hands repetitively and to shower three to four times a day.

About 3 years prior to coming to our clinic, Mrs. A. had sought treatment from a local psychiatrist who told her that much of her fear came from her relationship with her father, who had been quite aggressive and hostile but who had never abused her physically or sexually, and from difficulties involving her toilet training. He recommended twice-weekly psychotherapy, which she underwent for 5 months without improvement in her obsessive fears or compulsive rituals despite her being able to confront her father. Family relationships were definitely improved, but, frustrated by no change in symptoms, she abruptly stopped therapy. A year later she saw a psychopharmacologist who recommended imipramine that was increased to 200 mg/day. Her obsessional symptoms improved slightly over the next 4 months. She decided that the side effects of dry mouth, constipation, and increased anxiety were not worth putting up with for such a small improvement, and she stopped imipramine and never called the physician again.

After hearing about a specialty OCD clinic on a local television program, she made an appointment for an evaluation. The psychiatrist recommended a trial of fluoxetine that was gradually increased to 40 mg twice daily. At 2-month follow-up, obsessional symptoms were 20% better as assessed by the Yale-Brown Obsessive Compulsive Scale (Y-BOCS) (Goodman et al. 1989b, 1989c). After 3 months of well-tolerated fluoxetine, clonazepam was added and titrated to 0.5 mg three times daily. When seen 1 month later her Y-BOCS score had dropped to 13, which was half her initial score. Behavior therapy consisting of exposure and response prevention was begun; 3 months later her Y-BOCS score had decreased to 3, and she reported feeling "completely well." Behavior therapy was stopped and she remained on fluoxetine, 40 mg daily, and clonazepam, 0.5 mg three times a day. Her symptoms remained well controlled on the lower dose of fluoxetine.

Case 2

Mr. B., an accountant, was evaluated at an OCD clinic at a large hospital and reported a 6-year history of severe checking rituals. He often retraced the route by which he had driven to work to be sure that he had not caused an accident or caused "debris" to get into the road which might injure someone driving by. On a bad day, he spent over 3 hours a day driving his car over the same route; he averaged about 45 minutes of excess driving per day. He also spent about 30 minutes each evening before going to bed checking windows, doors, and the stove. Occasionally, he would be up all night with checking rituals. Because he aggressively persisted in attempts to get his wife to perform rituals as well, she was about to leave him and take their two children. She loved him but could not "put up with his nonsense anymore." Also, the children were embarrassed by his rituals and his pleas for them to check items around the house. He felt a complete loss of control and was even performing checking rituals when clients were in his office; he felt that his whole life was about to collapse.

After a complete evaluation, he was begun on fluoxetine, which was increased to 80 mg daily in two divided doses. Because he could not sleep on 80 mg, the dosage was decreased to 60 mg daily, and sleep improved. Over the next 3 months, his depression improved (Beck Depression Inventory score fell from 24 to 6), but his obsessional symptoms did not change. His wife agreed not to take any action for a few months to give him time to get treatment. He was continued on fluoxetine at the same dose, and trazodone, 100 mg at bedtime, was added. Two weeks later, with symptoms unchanged, trazodone was increased to 200 mg at bedtime. Again, no improvement was noted over the next month.

Two- to four-week trials of augmenting agents were conducted over the next several months including clonidine (0.2 mg tid), clonazepam (0.5 mg qid), buspirone (15 mg qid), haloperidol (0.5 mg tid), and lithium carbonate (300 mg tid). There was no improvement on fluoxetine plus any of these agents. All medications were stopped and clomipramine was started and titrated eventually to 250 mg daily, again without response despite 4 months of treatment. Again, all medications were stopped except for low doses of clonazepam, which helped his anxiety. Five weeks later he was given a trial of phenelzine to 90 mg daily, but there was no response.

During the above trials Mr. B. kept behavior therapy appointments but generally refused exposure that produced significant anxiety and was unable to perform homework exposure despite his family members' heroic efforts. He quit his job and his savings were dwindling when neurosurgical consultation recommended bilateral stereotactic cingulotomy. He underwent the operation and recovered without complications. Fluoxetine was begun again, and over the next 2 months he became much more cooperative with behavior therapy. At 6-month follow-up his obsessional symptoms were 80% better, he had returned to work, and his family was delighted and reported that "his personality had returned to normal" and that he was again able to think of his wife and children and was not entirely focused on his symptoms.

Summary

The majority of OCD patients labeled as treatment-resistant have, in fact, not received adequate trials of appropriate medications and/or behavior therapy; thus careful assessment of previous treatments, including medication type, dosage, and duration of treatment, should be part of the initial assessment. It is also important to distinguish between OCD and obsessive-compulsive personality disorder, since the treatments are quite different—that is, drugs and behavior therapy for OCD and more traditional psychotherapy focusing on current issues for patients suffering mainly from the personality disorder. Predictors of treatment failure such as presence of untreated mood disorder or severe personality disorders are covered.

The effectiveness of electroconvulsive therapy and the possible efficacy of psychosurgical procedures are reviewed. Prior to consideration of surgical procedures, patients should undergo trials of augmenting agents and should also have failed trials of antiobsessional medications. Options for augmentation are listed.

The case histories presented illustrate positive responses to treatment; obviously case 2 required a more aggressive approach than did case 1. Over 90% of OCD patients have a good outcome (i.e., moderately better to completely cured) with aggressive and appropriate therapy. Some patients, however, fail to improve, even with the best of treatments, and future research endeavors will be focused on this still treatment-refractory group of patients. Hopefully, as researchers focus on these patients, answers will be forthcoming.

References

American Psychiatric Association: Electroconvulsive Therapy. Task Force Report 14. Washington, DC, American Psychiatric Association, 1978

American Psychiatric Association: Diagnostic and Statistical Manual of Mental Disorders, 3rd Edition. Washington, DC, American Psychiatric Association, 1980

American Psychiatric Association: Diagnostic and Statistical Manual of Mental Disorders, 3rd Edition, Revised. Washington, DC, American Psychiatric Association, 1987

Baer L, Minichiello WE: Behavior therapy for obsessive-compulsive disorder, in Obsessive-Compulsive Disorders: Theory and Management. Edited by Jenike MA, Baer L, Minichiello WE. Littleton, MA, PSG Publishing Company, 1986, pp 45–76

Baer L, Minichiello WE, Jenike MA: Behavioral treatment in two cases of obsessive-compulsive disorder with concomitant bipolar affective disorder. Am J Psychiatry 142:358–360, 1985

Baer L, Minichiello WE, Jenike MA: Use of a portable-computer program in behavioral treatment of obsessive-compulsive disorder (letter). Am J Psychiatry 144:1101, 1987

Baer L, Jenike MA, Ricciardi JN, et al: Standardized assessment of personality disorders in obsessive-compulsive disorder. Arch Gen Psychiatry 47: 826–830, 1990

Bailey HR, Dowling JL, Davies E: Cingulotomy and related procedures for severe depressive illness studies in depression, IV, in Neurosurgical Treatment in Pain and Epilepsy. Edited by Sweet WH, Obrador S, Martin-Rodriguez JG. Baltimore, MD, University Park Press, 1975

Ballantine HT, Bouckoms AJ, Thomas EK, et al: Treatment of psychiatric illness by stereotactic cingulotomy. Biol Psychiatry 22:807–819, 1987

Bernstein IC, Callahan WA, Jaranson JM: Lobotomy in private practice. Arch Gen Psychiatry 32:1041–1047, 1975

Birley JLT: Modified frontal leucotomy: a review of 106 cases. Br J Psychiatry 110:211–221, 1964

Black A: The natural history of obsessional neurosis, in Obsessional States. Edited by Beech HR. London, Methuen, 1974, pp 16–54

Bridges PK, Goktepe EO, Maratos J: A comparative review of patients with obsessional neurosis and with depression treated by psychosurgery. Br J Psychiatry 123:663–674, 1973

Dé Montigny C, Grunberg F, Mayer A, et al: Lithium induces rapid relief of depression in tricyclic antidepressant drug non-responders. Br J Psychiatry 138:252–256, 1981

Foa EB: Failure in treating obsessive-compulsives. Behav Res Ther 17:169–176, 1979

Foa EDB, Goldstein A: Continuous exposure and complete response prevention of obsessive-compulsive disorder. Behavior Therapy 9:821–829, 1978

Fodstad H, Strandman E, Karlsson B, et al: Treatment of chronic obsessive-compulsive states with stereotactic anterior capsulotomy or cingulotomy. Acta Neurochir (Wien) 62:1–23, 1982

Goodman WK, Price LH, Anderson GM, et al: Drug response and obsessive-compulsive disorder subtypes. Paper presented at the annual meeting of the American Psychiatric Association, San Francisco, CA, May 1989a

Goodman WK, Price LH, Rasmussen SA, et al: The Yale-Brown Obsessive Compulsive Scale, I: development, use, and reliability. Arch Gen Psychiatry 46:1006–1011, 1989b

Goodman WK, Price LH, Rasmussen SA, et al: The Yale-Brown Obsessive Compulsive Scale, II: validity. Arch Gen Psychiatry 46:1012–1016, 1989c

Grimshaw L: The outcome of obsessional disorder: a follow-up study of 100 cases. Br J Psychiatry 111:1051–1056, 1965

Gruber RP: ECT for obsessive-compulsive symptoms. Diseases of the Nervous System 32:180–182, 1971

Herner T: Treatment of mental disorders with frontal stereotactic thermolesions: a follow-up study of 116 cases. Acta Psychiatrica et Neurologica Scandinavica 158 (suppl):36, 1961

Hollander E, Fay M, Liebowitz MR: Clonidine and clomipramine in obsessive-compulsive disorder (letter). Am J Psychiatry 145:388–389, 1988

Jenike MA: Obsessive-compulsive disorder: a question of a neurologic lesion. Compr Psychiatry 25:298–304, 1984

Jenike MA, Baer L: An open trial of buspirone in obsessive-compulsive disorder. Am J Psychiatry 145:1285–1286, 1988

Jenike MA, Baer L, Minichiello WE, et al: Concomitant obsessive-compulsive disorder and schizotypal personality disorder. Am J Psychiatry 143:530–532, 1986a

Jenike MA, Baer L, Minichiello WE, et al: Concomitant obsessive-compulsive disorder and schizotypal personality disorder: a poor prognostic indicator. Arch Gen Psychiatry 43:296, 1986b

Jenike MA, Baer L, Minichiello WE: Obsessive-Compulsive Disorders: Theory and Management. Littleton, MA, PSG Publishing Company, 1986c

Jenike MA, Buttolph L, Baer L, et al: Open trial of fluoxetine in obsessive-compulsive disorder. Am J Psychiatry 146:909–911, 1989

Jenike MA, Baer L, Minichiello WE: Obsessive-Compulsive Disorders: Theory and Management, 2nd Edition. Littleton, MA, Year Book Medical Publishers, 1990

Kelly DHW, Walter C, Mitchell-Heggs N, et al: Modified leucotomy assessed clinically, physiologically and psychologically at six weeks and eighteen months. Br J Psychiatry 120:19–29, 1972

Lader M, Wing L: Physiological measures in agitated and retarded depressed patients. J Psychiatr Res 7:89–100, 1969

Le Beau J: The cingular and precingular areas in psychosurgery (agitated behavior, obsessive compulsive states, epilepsy). Acta Psychiatrica et Neurologica Scandinavica 27:305–316, 1952

Markovitz PJ, Stagno SJ, Calabrese JR: Buspirone augmentation of fluoxetine in obsessive-compulsive disorder. Biol Psychiatry 25:186A, 1989

Marks IM: Review of behavioral psychotherapy, I: obsessive-compulsive disorders. Am J Psychiatry 138:584–592, 1981

Marks IM, Stern RS, Mawson D, et al: Clomipramine and exposure for obsessive-compulsive rituals: I. Br J Psychiatry 136:1–25, 1980

McDougle CJ, Goodman WK, Price LH, et al: Neuroleptic addition in fluvoxamine-refractory obsessive-compulsive disorder. Am J Psychiatry 147:652–654, 1990

Mellman LA, Gorman JM: Successful treatment of obsessive-compulsive disorder with ECT. Am J Psychiatry 141:596–597, 1984

Minichiello WE, Baer L, Jenike MA: Schizotypal personality disorder: a poor prognostic indicator for behavior therapy in the treatment of obsessive-compulsive disorder. Journal of Anxiety Disorders 1:273–276, 1987

Mindus P: Capsulotomy, a psychosurgical intervention considered in cases of anxiety disorders unresponsive to conventional therapy, in Workshop on Anxiety Disorders. Stockholm, The Swedish National Board of Health and Welfare, Committee for Drug Information, 1986

Mindus P, Bergstrom K, Levander SE, et al: Magnetic resonance images related to clinical outcome after psychosurgical intervention in severe anxiety disorder. J Neurol Neurosurg Psychiatry 50:1288–1293, 1987

Mitchell-Heggs N, Kelly D, Richardson A: Stereotactic limbic leucotomy—follow-up at 16 months. Br J Psychiatry 128:226–240, 1976

Modell JG, Mountz JM, Curtis GC, et al: Neurophysiologic dysfunction in basal ganglia/limbic striatal and thalamocortical circuits as a pathogenetic mechanism of obsessive-compulsive disorders. Journal of Neuropsychiatry 1:27–36, 1989

Noveske FG, Hahn KR, Flynn RJ: Possible toxicity of combined fluoxetine and lithium (letter). Am J Psychiatry 146:1515, 1989

Pato MT, Pigott TA, Hill JL, et al: Clomipramine versus buspirone in OCD: a controlled trial. Am J Psychiatry (in press)

Rachman SJ, Hodgson RJ: Obsessions and Compulsions. Englewood Cliffs, NJ, Prentice-Hall, 1980

Rasmussen SA: Lithium and tryptophan augmentation in clomipramine-resistant obsessive-compulsive disorder. Am J Psychiatry 141:1283–1285, 1984

Rasmussen SA, Tsuang MT: Epidemiology and clinical features of obsessive-compulsive disorder, in Obsessive-Compulsive Disorders: Theory and Management. Edited by Jenike MA, Baer L, Minichiello WE. Littleton, MA, PSG Publishing Company, 1986, pp 23–44

Salama AA, Shafey M: A case of severe lithium toxicity induced by combined fluoxetine and lithium carbonate (letter). Am J Psychiatry 146:278, 1989

Salzman L: Obsessional Personality. New York, Science House, 1969

Smith B, Kilom LF, Cochrane N, et al: A prospective-evaluation of open prefrontal leucotomy. Med J Aust 1:731–735, 1976

Solyom L, DiNicola VF, Phil M, et al: Is there an obsessive psychosis? Aetiological and prognostic factors of an atypical form of obsessive-compulsive neurosis. Can J Psychiatry 30:372–380, 1985

Ström-Olsen R, Carlisle S: Bi-frontal stereotactic tractotomy: a follow-up study of its effects in 210 patients. Br J Psychiatry 118:141–154, 1971

Sturgis ET, Meyer V: Obsessive-compulsive disorders, in Handbook of Clinical Behavior Therapy. Edited by Turner SM, Calhoun KC, Adams HE. New York, John Wiley, 1980, pp 68–102

Sykes MK, Tredgold RF: Restricted orbital undercutting: a study of its effects on 350 patients over the ten years 1951–1960. Br J Psychiatry 110:609–640, 1964

Tan E, Marks IM, Marset P: Bimedial leucotomy in obsessive-compulsive neurosis: a controlled serial enquiry. Br J Psychiatry 118:155–164, 1971

Task Force on the Use of Laboratory Tests in Psychiatry: Tricyclic antidepressants—blood level measurements and clinical outcome. Am J Psychiatry 142:155–162, 1985

Tippin J, Henn FA: Modified leukotomy in the treatment of intractable obsessional neurosis. Am J Psychiatry 139:1601–1603, 1982

Walinder J, Skott A, Carlsson A, et al: Potentiation of the antidepressant action of clomipramine by tryptophan. Arch Gen Psychiatry 33:1384–1389, 1976

Walter CJS, Mitchell-Heggs N, Sargant W: Modified narcosis, ECT and antidepressant drugs: a review of technique and immediate outcome. Br J Psychiatry 120:651–662, 1972

Whitty CWM, Duffield JE: Anterior cingulectomy in the treatment of mental disease. Lancet 262:475–481, 1952

The Treatment of Obsessive-Compulsive Disorder in Strictly Religious Patients

David Greenberg, M.D.
Eliezer Witztum, M.D.

I advise all . . . to take heed of placing Religion too much in Fears, and Tears, and Scruples.

Richard Baxter *Reliquiae Baxterianae* (1696)

*T*reatment of obsessive-compulsive disorder (OCD) in strictly religious patients requires therapists to be sensitive to a plethora of issues not always encountered when treating other OCD patients. Therapists should be aware of the inseparable, historical influence of religious culture on psychiatric symptomatology and the areas of religious practice that lend themselves to obsessive-compulsive behavior. With this understanding, therapists need to discriminate between normal and pathological religiosity. In addition, strict religiosity can introduce unique challenges to the therapeutic relationship itself, for which therapists must be prepared. Finally, therapists should possess a set of guidelines and a repertoire of treatment approaches specialized to managing OCD in strictly religious patients. We address these topics and present a case history that illustrates treatment of OCD manifested in the matrix of this deeply rooted influence.

Historical Religious Influence and Obsessive-Compulsive Disorder

Obsessions were a feature of religious life before they achieved psychiatric status. The original meaning of obsessions was "actuation by the devil or an evil spirit from without" (*Shorter OED*). John Moore, Bishop of Norwich, in 1692 wrote of good moral worshippers who are assailed by " 'naughty, and sometimes Blasphemous Thoughts' which 'start in their Minds, while they are exercised in the Worship of God' despite 'all their endeavours to stifle and suppress them' " (Hunter and Macalpine 1963, p. 252).

Detailed accounts of obsessions with religious content are provided by two of the most significant figures in 16th-century Christendom. Ignatius of Loyola (1548/1978), father of the Jesuit order, described obsessive thoughts: "After I have trodden upon a cross formed by two straws, or after I have thought, said or done some other thing, there comes to me from without a thought that I have sinned; I feel some uneasiness on the subject inasmuch as I doubt and do not doubt." He noted that devout people need to be sure that they have pleased God and that they have not sinned. If unable to convince themselves of this, they may perform acts of penance. If these, too, fail to allay their anxiety, then they will be tormented by doubts and preoccupied by rituals. Martin Luther, prior to his revolt against Catholicism and to the founding of Protestant Christianity, was a devout monk. Bainton (1950, p. 41) reported that "Luther would repeat a confession and, to be sure of including everything, would review his entire life until the confessor grew weary and exclaimed: 'Man, God is not angry with you, you are angry with God; don't you know that God commands you to hope.' "

In this century, although religion has been listed as one of the four main topics of obsession along with dirt, harm, and sex (Lewis 1936), systematic research of OCD patients gives scant attention to religious concerns (Akhtar et al. 1975; Stern and Cobb 1978). However, the role of religion in determining the topics in OCD is demonstrated in a study comparing the content of obsessions in the ultraorthodox and nonultraorthodox Jewish population in Jerusalem. Religious concerns and rituals dominate the lives of ultraorthodox Jews, and their secular education is minimal. In 13 out of 19 ultraorthodox Jewish cases of OCD, there were symptoms of religious content, in contrast with 1 out of 15 nonultraorthodox cases of OCD. Most of the ultraorthodox patients with obsessions of a nonreligious nature (such as illness, dirt, violence, and sex) were born in nonreligious homes and had been exposed to cultural influences different from those of individuals who were born ultraorthodox. The topics in OCD, therefore, appear to mirror the prevalent habits and values of a culture.

The Presentation of Obsessive-Compulsive Disorder Within Religious Practice

The presentation of OCD in a religious context is less typically religious than it is classically obsessive-compulsive. The psychiatrist acquainted with OCD cannot fail to recognize in religious OCD patients familiar obsessions (dirt and contamination, aggression, sex, and meticulousness) and compulsive behaviors (washing, checking, repeating, and slowness) that present in any other sample of OCD cases (Rachman and Hodgson 1980). However, therapists treating strictly religious OCD patients may benefit from recognizing religious practice areas that seem especially prone to obsessive-compulsive symptoms. A survey of the sparse literature on cultural factors in OCD reveals two main areas: 1) cleanliness and purity, and 2) liturgy.

Cleanliness and Purity

A recurrent practice area across many religions is cleanliness and purity in daily life. Dietary, menstrual, and prayer laws are facets of this area. Some examples arise out of our clinical experience with Jewish patients. Meat can only come from certain animals (known as *kosher*), which must be slaughtered and prepared in a particular way; milk and meat foods must be kept separate; and all bread must be removed from every Jewish home before the festival of Passover. For weeks prior to this festival, homemakers meticulously clean their homes. An awareness of the possibility of excessive concern is to be found in the earliest rabbinic guide to Jewish law, the *Mishna*, which addressed this point 1,800 years ago:

> One is not to be concerned that, having completed the pre-Passover cleaning in one room of the house, a rat from another (as yet uncleaned) room may drag a crumb into the cleaned room. Why not?—because if such a thought could be entertained, then why not the additional possibility that the crumb may be brought from one house to another, or from one town to another—and there would be no end to the matter! (*Mishna Succa*, 1:2)

For women, menstrual purity is another potential focus for obsessive-compulsive symptoms. Maimonides, the 12th-century physician, philosopher, and codifier of Jewish law, wrote in *Mishna Tora*: "No woman can divert herself of her ritual impurity or cease being forbidden from having relations unless and until she immerses herself in ritual bath. Nor may anything interpose between herself and the water . . . if she does not, she is liable to excision" ("Laws of Forbidden Relations," 11:16). The importance of this topic is stressed by the mystical text, the *Zohar* (on Exod. 1:1): "There is no stronger ritual impurity in the world than that of the menstrually unclean woman." Men are expected to be clean before prayer, and a common presenting symptom among them is repeated wiping and washing of the perianal region prior to prayers, sometimes taking so long that the patient arrives too late in the day to pray.

Within Islamic law, similar issues are stressed. Specific parts of the body are washed three times before the five-times-daily prayers, with particular emphasis on cleanliness of the anal region. Menstrual impurity is very significant; a woman is forbidden to fast or pray at such times, and her underwear is washed separately. Clothes must be changed if they have been in contact with urine or feces, and for this reason, underwear must be changed before prayer.

Berkeley-Hill (1921) has described the Hindus of India as suffering from a "pollution complex," exemplified by the existence of the class of the "untouchables," and has stressed the anal-erotic factors in their philosophy, religion, and character. A prominent part of Hindu festivals is bathing in a certain place at a certain time; the human body is considered to be basically dirty, and repeated washing of the body is encouraged (Akhtar et al. 1975). Nevertheless, Akhtar et al. (1975) only found nine cases of religious symptoms in 82 cases of OCD in India. The topics in these cases were religious practices and festivals or matters of religious belief. Thirty-eight of the cases were concerned with dirt and contamination, such as semen, menstrual blood, and excreta, and one of the authors (N. N. Wig, personal communication, November 1984) suggested that many of these cases had a religious basis. A study of 42 cases of OCD in India (Dutta Ray 1964) found ideas of impurity and uncleanliness in 11 cases, although the author did not comment on how many were of a religious basis nor on the form they took. The author, however, did note that in three strongly religious cases, there was a dramatic improvement following a religious pilgrimage.

Liturgy

The second main area within religious life that is commonly the focus of obsessive-compulsive symptoms is liturgy, encompassing prayer and confession. Consistent with the preeminent role of prayer in Western religions, we have found that the religious topics encountered among Protestant Christians with OCD have been thoughts of blasphemy or of illness and harm coming to other people arising during prayer. In addition, obsessive-compulsive symptoms can be associated with confession, one of two sacraments that must be repeated frequently by Roman Catholics.

Vergote (1988), a Catholic philosopher and psychoanalyst, describes this phenomenon as the "religious neurosis of culpability." He states that "obsession can take a religious form. In these cases it is guilt that obsesses the individual. Its doubts and ruminations are of an immediately moral order; his fears relate to the defiances hurled against God . . . filthy words that interrupt his prayers; his means of verification or his ritualism takes the form of religious rites" (p. 51). Vergote notes that "discourse on salvation has no effect on the illness" and concludes "that this form of obsessive religiosity does not derive from a strictly religious conflict but rather that religion here serves as a means of displacing and expressing the conflict in an indirect way" (p. 51). "Religion," he adds, echoing Freud's observations, "could not divert the conflict if it did not share with the unconscious conflict certain analogies of context and structure" (p. 51). Vergote cites the example of a man tormented by the anxiety of committing "mortal sins." At certain times, the man went to confession every day, sometimes twice a day. Fortunately, his priest saw clearly into the matter and encouraged him to seek out a psychotherapist. Every incident became for him an occasion for torturous doubts of conscience, the themes of which were predominantly sexual. Vergote describes the man meeting an attractive married woman, looking at her, and desiring her, "which is, according to Christ's words, sinning in one's heart" (p. 49).

In Judaism, certain prayers are given special significance and require particular devotion. Patients with OCD may take the entire day to say their thrice-daily prayers as they have intrusive thoughts of a lewd, aggressive, or blasphemous nature, or may repeat important sections because of inadequate devotion (Greenberg 1984; Greenberg et al. 1987).

Whereas confession in Catholicism is a regular ritual involving a complete declaration of misdemeanors, in Judaism it is a minor prayer with a fixed, impersonal text: "I have sinned, I have transgressed," etc. We have noted that it becomes emphasized among Jewish patients with agitated depression and not in OCD, reconfirming our impression that it is the topics that are repetitive and are dealt with pedantically that become the focus of OCD in different cultures.

Clinical Issues in Diagnosis and Management

Equipped with an understanding of the cultural origins of the obsessions and compulsions, therapists need to be prepared to respond to challenging situations that differentiate treating OCD in strictly religious patients from treating OCD in other patients. Two of these situations are the following:

1. The symptoms are part of the regular religious practice of the individual, so the therapist needs to distinguish between normal and pathological religiosity.
2. Both therapist and patient may be suspicious of each other and have difficulty in establishing a therapeutic relationship. Specifically, the patient may find it unacceptable to allow a therapist, who might not be of his or her religion or as orthodox, to make pronouncements on his or her religious practice—usually the province of the clergy.

Discriminating Between Normal and Pathological Religiosity

A requisite of working with minorities that is stressed by all researchers is an acquaintance with the values and details of that culture (German 1987; Rogler 1989; Sue 1988). Not only does this awareness of cultural values facilitate the therapeutic relationship, but it enables the therapist to understand the language, to appreciate the meaning of a religious group's beliefs and practices, and, in the area of OCD, to be able to distinguish between obsessive-compulsive symptoms and normative religious practice.

Arising out of our clinical observations, we have found that compulsive behavior can be distinguished from religious ritual in the following ways:

- Compulsive behavior exceeds and sometimes disregards the requirements of religious law (e.g., repeating the most important line of prayer, even though Jewish law states it must not be repeated).
- Compulsive behavior usually concentrates on one specific area and does not reflect an overall concern for religious practice.
- The choice of topic is typical of OCD—cleanliness and checking—although it is trivial within religious practice.

- While the patient focuses his or her attention on this one area, other features of religious life are often neglected. Many of our ultraorthodox Jewish patients had no time for religious study, which is viewed in that culture as the most valued of behaviors. Another patient spent so much time repeating that he often had to omit large sections of the prayers.
- The patient with OCD is racked with doubts that he or she may have omitted a ritual and so repeats for this reason alone. Religious codes, however, only require a ritual to be carried out if it was definitely omitted the first time.

Therapists' Attitudes Toward Religious Patients

In general, psychiatry has demonstrated a dismissive attitude toward religion. The dissonance between the religious attitudes of psychiatrists and psychologists and the communities they treat has been noted (Marx and Spray 1969). Bergin (1983, p. 171) has observed that the training of mental health professionals "is bereft of content that would engender an appreciation of religious variables," and that while race, gender, and ethnic origin have now gained respectability, religion "is still an orphan in academia." In the early 20th century, reflecting trends in Western culture, leading psychiatrists were known for their personal rejection of religious values and for constructing psychological theories that construed religion as primitive and pathological. This attitude was reflected in such titles as *The Future of an Illusion* (Freud 1927/1971) and *Dogma and Compulsion* (Reik 1927). In Freud's (1907/1971) provocative paper on obsessive actions and religious practices, he wrote that religion might be regarded as a "universal obsessional neurosis" (p. 127).

Cohen and Smith (1976) described a case of OCD concerning a fear of illness in a Christian Scientist in order to raise the problematic issue of a condition induced, in the opinion of the authors, by religious belief. Although the therapist "neither encouraged her [the patient] to continue therapy or discouraged her from adhering to the tenets of the Christian Science philosophy" (p. 144), the authors noted that clinical improvement and disavowal of Christian Science were simultaneous. This paper precipitated a lively debate on the ethical issues of treatment of the religious patient. London (1976) stated that he considers the practice of psychotherapy that undermines the patient's belief system to be ethically justified if the therapist "believes that the client's religious convictions help sustain the disorder . . . " (p. 146). The word "believes" reflects that the therapist is responding to his or her own (professionally based) value judgments.

In Halleck's (1976) comments on the same case he candidly states that there is no value-free therapy or therapist. If the therapist thinks that therapy may challenge the patient's belief system, then at least "the consumer should be adequately forewarned of the possible consequences of treatment" (p. 147). If the patient can afford to select his or her own therapist, Halleck notes that patients tend to choose professionals who are co-religionists "as though they want to protect their belief systems while changing their behavior" (p. 147).

Religious Patients' Attitudes Toward Therapists

Likewise, therapists should be aware of their strictly religious OCD patients' perspective toward them. Within a religious group, psychology may be considered suspect and heretical, both in challenging the existence of God and in ridiculing dogma and codes of behavior. Religious patients and their families are aware that therapists might be irreligious, and may fear that the therapist will influence the patient against his or her religion, or that the content of therapy may be immoral and will relate difficulties to unconscious sexual conflicts. Furthermore, many believe that turning to a doctor is an act of weak faith, as it is God who heals all ills.

An additional powerful force preventing the seeking out of help is stigma. For ultraorthodox Jews, public psychiatric services are invidious, for the stigma of mental illness is powerful in a close community where marriages are arranged by matchmakers. Mental illness in one family member will adversely affect the matrimonial prospects of all the other children.

Guidelines for the Management of Obsessive-Compulsive Disorder in Strictly Religious Patients

Several Catholic pastoral counselors have described the presentation of religious rituals as psychiatric symptoms and have advised clergy not to cooperate with the patient's system of practice, but instead to refer him or her for psychiatric help (Autton 1963; Barbaste 1952; Ringel and Van Lun 1955). Wise (1983, p. 239) observed: "Giving assurances of a religious 'cure' must be avoided."

Before discussing some of the issues involved in the specific forms of therapy, we will suggest some general guidelines in overcoming the many barriers to establishing a therapeutic relationship that set apart strictly religious OCD patients from other OCD patients:

- It is helpful for the therapist to know basic tenets and practices of the patient's religion. As Gorkin (1987) has warned, this must not become a fascination to the extent that the patient and his or her problems disappear from view.
- The therapist should be aware of his or her own feelings about religion and the religious (Spero 1989).
- In many cases the patient is accompanied to the clinic. Allow the accompanying person to join the interview from the onset. If the patient is unsure of you, be willing to be a minority presence in the room.
- If the patient raises objections to attending and receiving treatment from irreligious people, the therapist should avoid a religious debate. If the patient wavers or refuses, he or she should be encouraged to discuss the matter with a member of his or her clergy. We invariably offer to meet with patients and clergy, clearly implying that we see no dissonance between religious affiliation and psychiatry (Greenberg 1987; Lovinger 1984; Rapoport 1989).

Therapies for OCD: Advantages and Pitfalls

Pharmacotherapy.   In general, we have found that patients are not opposed to medication. It is important to clarify what will change. The patient should be told that, for example, it will not cause him or her to stop performing regular religious ritual. Consistent with our earlier suggestions, we often write the name of the recommended medication in a letter and encourage patients to take it to their clergy for approval, adding that we would be willing to provide more information and discuss the medication further if requested. (See Pato and Zohar, Chapter 2; Pigott, Chapter 3; Goodman and Price, Chapter 4; Jenike, Chapter 9, this volume, for details and considerations of the use of medication in treating OCD.)

Behavioral psychotherapy.   The advantage of behavioral psychotherapy lies in it being symptom oriented. The patient who fears that treatment implies an assault on his or her religious beliefs will not feel threatened by a focused intervention. It is clear, nevertheless, that religious practices will be at the forefront during treatment and that the therapist can inadvertently jeopardize therapy by giving instructions that are not consistent with religious practice.

O'Flaherty (1973), a priest, has described a broad treatment package based on the principles of *agere contra* (do the opposite) originally formulated by Ignatius of Loyola for the improvement of the soul. The treatment has prominent behavioral and cognitive elements. The therapist is firmly discouraged from getting into detailed discussions over whether the patient has sinned or not, and proceeds on the assumption that no sin has occurred. O'Flaherty divides treatment into four phases:

1. *Booking the incidents.* Patients keep a diary of every event that precipitates a need to carry out the rituals.
2. *Systematically studying the incidents.* This is a form of behavioral analysis in which therapists and patients note the people, places, and events that give rise to the incidents.
3. *Rejecting by distraction.* Patients are taught to focus their mind on a neutral subject instead of thinking whether or not they have sinned.
4. *Breaking the habit.* If patients find they are preoccupied with their thoughts or with carrying out rituals, they should lay their hand upon their heart and grieve that they have fallen.

Although O'Flaherty's package contains features of behavioral treatments of proven efficacy (Marks 1987; Steketee and Tynes, Chapter 5, this volume), no outcome data are presented by the author.

Giles (1982) described an orthodox Jewish patient whose obsessive fears included possible contact with nonkosher food. A combination of exposure (holding a nonkosher sausage wrapped in plastic) and cognitive therapy resulted in a diminution of the patient's distress during sessions, although overall improvement and maintenance of gains were not described.

One example of religiously inconsistent instructions occurs if the therapist asks the patient to approach a member of his or her clergy for a "dispensation" that gives the therapist carte blanche to proceed as he or she sees fit. The therapist here demonstrates limited patience at having his or her autonomy restricted, and ignorance of the significance of the role of religion for the strictly religious. Most religions have no all-inclusive dispensations; given specific situations, clergy can permit specific solutions.

A second example of religiously inconsistent instructions occurs if the therapist asks the patient to eat nonkosher meat, to leave bread in the house on Passover, to dip in the ritual bath while still menstruating, and so forth, in order to achieve exposure. All strictly religious Jewish patients and their rabbis will decline for religious reasons. It is apposite to consider how one treats patients with OCD whose fear is that they will cause illness in their family, cause a fire at work, or kill pedestrians as they drive along the road. Clearly, therapists do not instruct patients to expose themselves to their worst fears by telling them to go out and cause these events, and expect them to participate. The disadvantage for patients with OCD is that they cannot cope with the possibility that they may have caused these events. Therapy aims to enable them to live with the risk that their behavior may or may not have caused disaster. Behavioral psychotherapy in the strictly religious aims to reduce the time spent cleaning before Passover to a sensible degree, while the patient accepts that he or she may or may not have done a thorough job.

In treating OCD patients, we first draw up a list of problems and targets (Marks 1986) that describes the patient's current concerns and ultimate goals in treatment expressed in behavioral terms. Examples of problems are the patient having difficulty at prayer times because he or she must repeat all important sections, or the patient cleaning himself or herself excessively before prayers. Targets would be having the patient pray with no repetitions, even if the patient thinks he or she does not have adequate devotion, or having the patient enter prayers without going to the toilet to clean himself or herself.

The therapist now draws up a list of "Is it permitted?" statements. Is the patient permitted to continue praying if the patient thought he or she had not been concentrating? Is this true of all prayers? What is the minimum cleaning necessary before prayer? Can it be omitted completely? The patient is now asked to nominate the clergy member of his or her choice, whom the therapist arranges to visit with the patient. At this meeting the patient introduces the problem and the therapist then presents the problems, targets, and particularly the list of "Is it permitted?" statements. Whenever the clergy member's answer is no, the therapist asks the leader to define a permissible situation that the patient cannot tolerate at present. The clergy member's replies are noted, and they define the limits of exposure treatment.

We have noted that in some cases, after leaving the meeting with the member of the clergy, the patient will refuse to follow the decisions emanating from the meeting. The reasons are usually wrapped in religious reasoning, such as, "The clergy member made particular allowances because of my problem"; "He was willing to allow anything because of the treatment"; or "I want to see a different member of the clergy." Indecision is a classical feature of OCD, and the patient's response is to be understood as emerging from that indecision. The therapist should be willing to focus briefly with the patient on this self-imposed stumbling block. Notwithstanding, behavioral psychotherapy requires a clear commitment by the patient. The therapist who is confronted by patients who disqualify their own clergy member should place the responsibility for the next step in the patients' hands and should not offer to go "clergy shopping." The patients should either return to their own clergy member or to an alternative of their choice. Therapy will proceed when the patients have found answers to the "Is it permitted?" questions from a single source.

Case History

John, a 40-year-old ultraorthodox Jew, married with four children, was excessively concerned over the religious dietary laws, particularly the concern that milk and meat may become mixed together, thereby making the food nonkosher and the food utensils unusable. As a result, he spent mealtimes anxiously watching his children, lest they touch ketchup and other bottles with greasy hands. He insisted that the children use napkins every few minutes and would get up himself to wipe them throughout the meal. If he thought a bottle or utensil might have been touched by a "milk food," he would either label it "milk" or hide it until he could decide what to do, and in this way the kitchen cupboards gathered collections of unusable items over the years. He would wipe his own hands over 30 times during the meal and would wash his mouth, teeth, face, hands, and particularly his fingernails after any meal for fear that they may have gathered food. The more crowded the mealtime, the more tense he became, and the family had not invited guests for several years. He avoided helping in the kitchen and had not washed the dishes for 10 years, for he feared that the water used to wash the milk dishes might splash onto meat dishes and foods. The onset of John's concerns was 13 years earlier when he had first become more religiously observant.

John had always been a pedantic person, with scrupulous morals. At 17, he became concerned that he had been unjustly awarded a scholarship, and the preoccupation only left him 2 years later after he had returned the money. John was slow and indecisive in many areas. He kept long, detailed lists of things to be done, and stored all the lists in case they were needed. He married at age 27, and both he and his wife became more observant, although his wife subsequently became more ambivalent over religious practice. They had been in individual and marital therapy with little change, and his wife seemed content to be practicing and ambivalent.

At interview, John was neatly dressed and carried a notebook, to which he referred throughout. He was articulate and circumstantial. John was upset by his problems, which he perceived as excessive, but there were no psychotic features.

The targets of John's treatment were to eat meals without wiping his own or his family members' hands, to invite guests regularly (especially guests with young children), to wash up with splashing water, to "rehabilitate" all stored utensils, and to leave meals without washing.

A list of "Is it permitted?" statements included the following:

- Is the patient permitted to put milk on his hands and then touch all utensils before a meat meal?
- Is the patient permitted to put milk directly onto a meat plate or vice versa?
- Is it necessary to wipe hands and utensils during a meal?
- Can the same bottle of ketchup be used for milk and meat meals despite being touched by greasy hands?
- Need one be concerned about contamination at washing-up time when water may splash from one area to another?

John's rabbi knew him well from the countless questions and requests for reassurance that were posed to him several times a week over the years. He considered that John had a psychological problem and was more than willing to help, adding with a sigh: "There are many more like him." Seeking rabbinic advice is rarely a matter of a textbook response. Within the framework of the law, the decision is tailored to the individual situation. It was clear that John's rabbi tended to make lenient decisions as much as possible in order to facilitate the therapeutic process.

Treatment consisted of 10 sessions (15 hours of therapy). As the focus of John's problems was limited to his own home—"Other people's dietary observance is their problem, not mine!"—the first sessions took place during lunchtime in the patient's home.

After modeling by the therapist, John was asked to put butter on his hands before a milk meal; set the table; actively pass bottles, food, and cutlery during the meal; and clear the table at the end of the meal. The wiping of hands was banned, as was the use of napkins. Initially, John's anxiety was high, but it reduced gradually during a 90-minute session. During homework sessions over the next 2 weeks, he became less anxious over handing out food, and reduced hand wiping to two times per meal.

At the next session, the therapist modeled hand washing without washing the face, teeth, and fingernails, and included contaminating his hands with butter immediately after washing. During the remaining sessions, residual foci were treated: John avoided using ointments and creams if it was not clear from the list of ingredients if they were kosher. In treatment, he used them and then went about the house touching door handles, chairs, and food containers. He became very anxious when he was asked to wash the dishes and splash water. Homework included washing the dishes daily, and his wife was a very encouraging cotherapist.

One year after treatment, John no longer wiped hands at the table nor stored contaminated bottles. He was relaxed at mealtime and enjoyed the company of guests. He regularly helped wash the dishes. John considered himself slightly more vigilant over the dietary laws than most people.

Summary

Although OCD in strictly religious patients presents many classical features, it also presents a series of challenges to therapists that are distinct from those faced with other OCD patients. In any therapeutic encounter between people of differing cultures, therapists are advised to be acquainted with aspects of their patients' cultures and to be aware of their own attitudes toward those cultures. The situation is more complicated in therapists' contact with religious patients, for psychiatry has a tradition of reductionist and dismissive attitudes toward religious affiliation. Furthermore, many religious groups have negative attitudes toward psychiatry and toward therapists in general. OCD in the strictly religious often has symptoms of a religious nature. Therapists assessing strictly religious OCD patients must distinguish between normal and pathological religiosity. In this task, and in the task of proposing therapy, therapists are advised to avoid all religious disputation and to work as closely as possible with the clergy of authority selected by the individual patients.

References

Akhtar S, Wig NN, Varma VK, et al: A phenomenological analysis of symptoms in obsessive-compulsive neurosis. Br J Psychiatry 127:342–348, 1975

Autton N: The Pastoral Care of the Mentally Ill. London, SPCK, 1963

Bainton RH: Here I Stand: A Life of Martin Luther. New York, New American Library, 1950

Barbaste A: Le traitement du scrupule et les données actuelles de la psychiatrie. Revue d'Ascetique et de Mystique 28:96–120, 1952

Baxter R: Reliquiae Baxterianae (1696), qtd. in Three Hundred Years of Psychiatry, 1535–1860. Edited by Hunter R, Macalpine I. London, Oxford University Press, 1963, p 240

Bergin AE: Religiosity and mental health: a critical reevaluation and meta-analysis. Professional Psychology 14:170–184, 1983

Berkeley-Hill O: The anal-erotic factor in the religion, philosophy and character of the Hindus. Int J Psychoanal 2:306–329, 1921

Cohen RJ, Smith FJ: Socially reinforced obsessing: etiology of a disorder in a Christian Scientist. J Consult Clin Psychol 44:142–144, 1976

Dutta Ray S: Obsessional states observed in New Delhi. Br J Psychiatry 110:181–182, 1964

Freud S: Obsessive actions and religious practices (1907), in The Standard Edition of the Complete Psychological Works of Sigmund Freud, Vol 9. Translated and edited by Strachey J. London, Hogarth Press, 1971, pp 115–127

Freud S: The future of an illusion (1927), in The Standard Edition of the Complete Psychological Works of Sigmund Freud, Vol 21. Translated and edited by Strachey J. London, Hogarth Press, 1971, pp 1–56

German GA: Mental health in Africa, I: the extent of mental health problems in Africa today—an update of epidemiological knowledge. Br J Psychiatry 151:435–439, 1987

Giles TR: Cognitive restructuring and exposure with a compulsive washer: a test of reciprocal inhibition. J Behav Ther Exp Psychiatry 13:221–224, 1982

Gorkin M: The Use of Countertransference. Northvale, NS, Jason Aronson, 1987

Greenberg D: The behavioral treatment of religious compulsions. Journal of Psychology and Judaism 11:41–47, 1987

Greenberg D: Are religious compulsions religious or compulsive? A phenomenological study. Am J Psychother 38:524–532, 1984

Greenberg D, Witzum E, Pisante J: Scrupulosity: religious attitudes and clinical presentations. Br J Med Psychol 60:29–37, 1987

Halleck SL: Discussion of "Socially reinforced obsessing." J Consult Clin Psychol 44:146–147, 1976

Hunter RA, Macalpine I: Three Hundred Years of Psychiatry, 1535–1860. London, Oxford University Press, 1963

Ignatius of Loyola: Spiritual Exercises of Ignatius of Loyola (1548). Boston, MA, Daughters of Saint Paul, 1978

Lewis A: Problems of obsessional illness. Proceedings of the Royal Society of Medicine 29:325–336, 1936

London P: Psychotherapy for religious neuroses? Comments on Cohen and Smith. J Consult Clin Psychol 44:145–146, 1976

Lovinger RJ: Working With Religious Issues in Therapy. New York, Jason Aronson, 1984

Marks IM: Behavioural Psychotherapy: Maudsley Pocket Book of Clinical Management. Chicago, IL, Year Book Medical Publishers, 1986

Marks IM: Fears, Phobias, and Rituals. New York, Oxford University Press, 1987

Marx JH, Spray SL: Religious bibliographies and professional characteristics of psychotherapists. J Health Soc Behav 10:275–288, 1969

Moore J: Religious melancholy (1692), in Three Hundred Years of Psychiatry, 1535–1860. Edited by Hunter R, Macalpine I. London, Oxford University Press, 1963, pp 252–253

O'Flaherty VM: Therapy for scrupulosity, in Direct Psychotherapy: Twenty-Eight American Originals. Edited by Jurjevich RM. Miami, FL, University of Miami Press, 1973, pp 221–243

Rachman SJ, Hodgson RJ: Obsessions and Compulsions. Englewood Cliffs, NJ, Prentice-Hall, 1980

Rapoport J: A thousand commitments to God, in The Boy Who Couldn't Stop Washing: The Experience and Treatment of Obsessive-Compulsive Disorder. New York, Dutton, 1989, pp 159–173

Reik T: Dogma and Compulsion. Westport, CT, Greenwood, 1927

Ringel E, Van Lun W: Psychotherapie et Direction de Conscience. Tours, France, Mame, 1955

Rogler LH: The meaning of culturally sensitive research in mental health. Am J Psychiatry 146:296–303, 1989

Spero MH: Current trends in psychotherapy, clinical social work, and religious values: a review and bibliography. Journal of Social Work and Policy in Israel 2:81–110, 1989

Stern RS, Cobb JP: Phenomenology of obsessive-compulsive neurosis. Br J Psychiatry 132:233–239, 1978

Sue S: Psychotherapeutic services for ethnic minorities. Am Psychol 43:301–308, 1988

Vergote A: Guilt and Desire: Religious Attitudes and Their Pathological Derivatives. New Haven, Yale University Press, 1988

Wise CA: Pastoral Psychotherapy. New York, Jason Aronson, 1983

Chapter 11

Serotonergic Drugs and the Treatment of Disorders Related to Obsessive-Compulsive Disorder

Eric Hollander, M.D.

Obsessive-compulsive disorder (OCD) is a common and disabling condition that has been found to be responsive to medications that are potent serotonin (5-hydroxytryptamine [5-HT]) reuptake inhibitors, as well to behavior therapy. The differential diagnosis of OCD and obsessive-compulsive personality disorder (OCPD), depression, thought disorder and psychosis, ruminations, and generalized anxiety disorder can occasionally be quite taxing (see Zohar and Pato, Chapter 1, this volume). However, there is even greater controversy among clinicians and researchers about the relationship between OCD and related disorders. This debate over the merits of disorders related to OCD is currently taking place in the Workgroup on OCD for the forthcoming edition of the *Diagnostic and Statistical Manual of Mental Disorders* (DSM-IV).

However, based on clinical presentation, symptomatology, family history, and treatment response, there appear to be a group of disorders that we might call *OCD-related disorders* (see Table 11-1). These include disorders currently classified as somatoform (i.e., body dysmorphic disorder, hypochondriasis), impulse control (i.e., trichotillomania), dissociative (i.e., depersonalization disorder), childhood or adolescent onset (i.e., Tourette's syndrome), or eating disorders (i.e., anorexia nervosa, bulimia). Patients with bowel obsessions might also be included within this group. A particularly topical issue is AIDS obsession, which might be

Supported in part by Research Scientist Development Award MH-00750 from the National Institute of Mental Health, Bethesda, Maryland.

Table 11-1. OCD-related disorders

Current diagnostic (DSM-III-R) category	Disorder
Somatoform	Body dysmorphic disorder Bowel obsessions Hypochondriasis
Impulse control	Trichotillomania
Dissociative	Depersonalization disorder
Childhood or adolescent onset	Tourette's syndrome
Eating disorders	Anorexia nervosa Bulimia

considered hypochondriacal, but is frequently a common variant of contamination fears in OCD patients.

In this chapter I will discuss diagnostic considerations and treatment approaches to this fascinating group of disorders.

Body Dysmorphic Disorder

Diagnostic Considerations

Body dysmorphic disorder is currently classified as a somatoform disorder in DSM-III-R (American Psychiatric Association 1987). (The diagnostic classification of body dysmorphic disorder and its relationship to OCD has recently been reviewed [Hollander et al. 1989c].) The essential feature is preoccupation with some imagined defect in appearance in a normal-appearing person. Common complaints involve facial flaws. If a slight physical anomaly is present, the person's concern is grossly excessive. The belief in the defect is not one of delusional intensity, as in delusional disorder, somatic type. The occurrence is not found exclusively during the course of anorexia nervosa or transexualism. While face picking may be a variant of body dysmorphic disorder, it may also occur in trichotillomania.

This disorder had been called *dysmorphophobia*, and classified in DSM-III (American Psychiatric Association 1980) as an atypical somatoform disorder. Another term for this disorder is *monosymptomatic hypochondriasis*.